MODERN SCOTTISH HISTORY
1707 TO THE PRESENT

MODERN SCOTTISH HISTORY
1707 *to the* PRESENT

VOLUME 3 : READINGS
1707 – 1850

Edited by
Anthony Cooke, Ian Donnachie,
Ann MacSween and Christopher A Whatley

TUCKWELL PRESS

In association with
THE OPEN UNIVERSITY IN SCOTLAND

and
THE UNIVERSITY OF DUNDEE

First published in 1998 by
Tuckwell Press Ltd
The Mill House
Phantassie
East Linton
East Lothian EH40 3DG
Scotland

British Library Cataloguing-in-Publication Data
A catalogue record for this book is available on request
from the British Library

Designed by James Hutcheson

Typeset by Hewertext Composition Services, Leith

Printed and bound by
Cromwell Press, Trowbridge, Wiltshire

Preface

This volume and the series of which it is part have as their central purpose the study of the history of Scotland from 1707 until the present. The series seeks to combine the products of more recent research and general findings by some of the most prominent scholars working in the subject with the enthusiasm of those who wish to study it either in a systematic way or simply by reading one or more of these volumes at leisure.

Now is a particularly appropriate moment to bring this scholarship and the wider audience together. There is enormous latent enthusiasm for Scottish history, particularly, but not exclusively, of the modern period. This springs from a variety of sources: the new political agenda in Scotland following the 1997 Referendum; the higher profile of Scottish history in school, college and university curricula; the enhanced interest in local and family history; the success of museums and heritage ventures devoted to the more recent past; and the continuous flow of books on so many aspects of Scottish history. However, explicitly academic publications, with a few honourable exceptions, have been little read by any but specialists, so new findings have frequently had little impact on general perceptions of Scotland's more recent past.

There are two main aims encapsulated in these volumes, which are overlapping and complementary. The first is to present an overview of recent scholarly work, drawing on the approaches and findings of political, economic, social, environmental and cultural historians. This should be illuminating not only for those seeking an up-to-date review of such work, but also for anyone interested in the functioning of Scotland today - the essential historical background of present-day issues and concerns. The second, equally important, aim is to help readers develop their own historical skills, using the volumes as a tool-kit containing a wide range of primary sources and more detailed readings on specific topics. This and the other volumes in the series differ from most conventional academic publications, in that the focus is on **doing** history, rather than just absorbing the facts. The volumes are full of ideas on sources and methods that can be followed up by the interested reader.

Given the vast scope of the subject, we have had to put some limits on the coverage. The timescale is the early eighteenth century to the late twentieth century, a period for which sources not only abound but can also be readily understood and critically assessed. There is no attempt to give a detailed historical narrative of the period from the Union of 1707, which can readily be found elsewhere. Rather we present a blend of topics and themes, selected with a view to providing readers with a reasonably comprehensive introduction to recent work and a context and stimulus for further reading or investigation. Although there is an organisational divide at 1850, many of the themes are explored continuously over the whole period. Hence the first volume begins with the Union of 1707 and Jacobitism, and covers topics including industrialisation, demography, politics, religion, education, class, the environment, and culture, as well as looking at the differences between Highland and Lowland society and economy. The second volume from 1850 to the present also covers a wide range of topics. Some of these, such as industrialisation, demography, urbanisation, religion, class, education, culture and Highland and Lowland society are continued while new topics include the state, Scottish identity, leisure and recreation. The third and fourth volumes contain carefully selected readings to accompany the topic / theme volumes and are likely to prove an invaluable resource for any reader wishing to pursue a particular subject in greater depth or perhaps investigate it in a local or regional project. The fifth volume in the series is a collection of primary sources for the history of modern Scotland designed to accompany the other volumes. It makes accessible between the covers of one book many of the documents of national and local importance from the eighteenth century and beyond and provides a unique and detailed insight into the period.

This book forms one part of the University of Dundee-Open University collaborative course, Modern Scottish History: 1707 to the Present. This is an honours level undergraduate course for part-time adult learners studying at a distance, and it is designed to develop the skills, methods and understanding of history and historical analysis with modern Scotland as its focus. However, these volumes are designed to be used, either singly or as a series, by anyone interested in Scottish history. The introduction to recent research findings, together with practical exercises, advice on the critical exploitation of primary sources, and suggestions for further reading, should be of wide interest and application. We hope it will encourage users to carry their enthusiasm further by investigating, for example, some aspect of their own community history based on one or more themes covered in the series.

A series of this kind depends on the efforts of many people, and accordingly there are many debts to record. Our enthusiasm was shared by the Scottish Higher Education Funding Council which provided a generous grant to fund the development of the course. Within the University of Dundee, Professor David Swinfen, Vice Principal, has played a valuable supporting role. The authors produced their contributions to agreed formats and deadlines. While they are responsible for what they have written, they have also been supported by other members of the writing team and our editorial and production specialists. The material was developed collaboratively, reflected too in the cooperation and support we have had from our publisher, Tuckwell Press. Particular thanks to Tracey Walker, the Project Secretary, for her administrative support. Thanks also to Karen Brough and Jen Petrie who transcribed some of the texts for the articles and documents volumes.

USING THIS BOOK

Activities

Volumes 1 and 2 are designed not just as a text to be read through but also as active workbooks. They are therefore punctuated by a series of activities, signalled by a different format. These include short questions, exercises, and prompts for the reader articles in Volumes 3 and 4 or documents in Volume 5. Conversely the readings and documents refer back to topics/themes discussed in detail in Volumes 1 and 2.

References

While this book is free-standing, there are cross-references to other volumes in the series. This is to aid readers using all the books. The list of books and articles that follows each chapter generally follows the scholarly convention of giving details of all works cited. They are not intended as obligatory further reading.

Series Editors

Acknowledgements

Grateful acknowledgement is made to the following sources for permission to reproduce material in this volume:

W Ferguson 1994 *Scotland's Relations with England: A Survey to 1707*, John Donald; JM Hill 1986 *Celtic Warfare 1595-1763*, John Donald; M Fry 1993 'The Disruption and the Union', *in* SJ Brown and MRG Fry (eds), *Scotland in the Age of the Disruption*, Edinburgh University Press; TC Smout 1982 'Born again at Cambuslang: New evidence on popular religion and literacy in eighteenth-century Scotland', *Past and Present* by permission of Oxford University Press; AA MacLaren 1967 'Church attendance and the Kirk Session', *Scottish Historical Review*; P Hillis 1981 'Presbyterianism and Social Class in Mid-Nineteenth Century Glasgow: a Study of Nine Churches', *Journal of Ecclesiastical History*, Cambridge University Press; G Whittington 1975 'Was there a Scottish Agricultural Revolution?', *Area*; IH Adams 1978 'The agricultural revolution in Scotland: contributions to the debate', *Area* (illustration reproduced by permission of *Imago Mundi*); ID Whyte 1978 'The agricultural revolution in Scotland: contributions to the debate', *Area*; L Leneman and R Mitchison 1987 'Scottish illegitimacy ratios in the early modern period', *Economic History Review*; A J Cooke 1979 'Richard Arkwright and the Scottish Cotton Industry', *Textile History*; I Donnachie and G Hewitt 1993 *Historic New Lanark* Edinburgh University Press; AM Smith 1982 *Jacobite Estates of the Forty-Five*, John Donald; S Nenadic 1990 'Political Reform and the 'Ordering' of Middle-Class Protest', *in* TM Devine (ed), *Conflict and Stability in Scottish Society, 1700-1850*, John Donald; AA MacLaren 1983 'Class formation and class fractions: The Aberdeen bourgeoisie, 1830-1850', *in* G Gordon and B Dicks, *Scottish Urban History*, Aberdeen University Press; S McCalman 1970 'Chartism in Aberdeen', *Scottish Labour History Society Journal*; TC Smout 1997 'Bogs and People since 1600', *in* L Parkyn, RE Stoneman and HAP Ingram (eds), *Conserving Peatlands*, Wallingford; RA Dodgshon 1994 'Budgeting for Survival: Nutrient Flow and Traditional Highland Farming', *in* S Foster and TC Smout (eds), *The History of Soils and Field Systems*, Scottish Cultural Press; RJ Morris 1976 *Cholera, 1832:*

The Social Response to an Epidemic, Croom Helm; T Kjaergaard 1994 *The Danish Revolution, 1500-1800, an Ecohistorical Interpretation,* Cambridge University Press; D Daiches 1964 *The Paradox of Scottish Culture,* Oxford University Press; H Ouston 1987 'Cultural Life from the Restoration to the Union', *in* Andrew Hook (ed), *The History of Scottish Literature II,* Aberdeen University Press; T Nairn 1977 *The Break-Up of Britain,* NLB; K Simpson 1988 *The Protean Scot,* Aberdeen University Press; C McGuirk 1987 'Scottish Hero, Scottish Victim: Myths of Robert Burns', *in* A Hook (ed), *History of Scottish Literature II,* Aberdeen University Press; A Noble 1985 'Urbane Silence: Scottish Writing and the Nineteenth-Century City', *in* G Gordon (ed), *Perspectives of the Scottish City,* Aberdeen University Press; E Muir 1936 *Scott and Scotland,* Routledge; D Gifford 1988 'Myth, Parody and Dissociation: Scottish Fiction 1814-1914', *in* D Gifford (ed), *History of Scottish Literature Vol III,* Aberdeen University Press; FR Hart 1978 *The Scottish Novel: From Smollett to Spark,* John Murray © 1978 the President and Fellows of Harvard College, reprinted by permission of Harvard University Press; R D Anderson 1983 'Education and the State in Nineteenth-Century Scotland', *Economic History Review*; D J Withrington 1962 'The S.P.C.K. and Highland Schools in Mid-Eighteenth Century', *Scottish Historical Review*.

Contents

The Attainment of Union

Extracted from W Ferguson 1994 *Scotland's Relations with England: A Survey to 1707*, Edinburgh (John Donald 1977; reprinted by Saltire Society 1994), 255–71.

The Scottish parliament opened on 3 October 1706 in an Edinburgh which, in spite of atrocious weather, was thronged with people from all parts of the kingdom.[1] Various reasons caused them to congregate in the capital, some concerned about the fate of their country, others drawn by curiosity and possibly the desire to witness what might well be the last ceremonial Riding of the Parliament – the traditional colourful pageant that preceded the formal opening of the session. But it was soon made clear that not all had come simply to spectate. Many, perhaps influenced by the recent example set by the *Worcester* affair, had obviously resorted to the capital in the hope of overawing the ministry and ensuring the rejection of the treaty. The subsequent harassing of the ministry 'out of doors' – that is, outside parliament – was not just the work of the notoriously volatile Edinburgh mob but reflected a widespread general will. There can be no avoiding the conclusion that, whether through ignorant prejudice or not, popular sympathy, and not just in the capital, lay with one segment or other of the opposition. The idea of incorporation was hated, and, in spite of differences in language, creed and politics, the Scottish nation at large was hostile to the treaty.

As much was soon demonstrated in the capital. Hamilton, who had strained his foot, was borne in a litter to and from the Parliament House, and only with difficulty could his bearers make their way through the wildly cheering crowds.[2] 'God bless his grace for defending the country against the Union!' was their battle-cry. Very different were the reception and the benisons bestowed on the commissioner and other leading unionists; as ritually as Hamilton was lionised, Queensberry and his associates were violently barracked and threatened.[3] Indeed, all sources agree that an atmosphere of menace hung over the capital[4] – as Mar wrote on 19 November to a colleague in London, only bad weather prevented a march on Edinburgh, where, as it was, 'everyday here we are in hazard of our lives'.[5] And Defoe later testified to much the same effect.

But, while giving way to the odd tremble, Queensberry's brazen fortitude proved equal to the occasion; and, taking their cue from the commissioner, the ministers for the most part kept their nerve. In holding the ministry steady the presence of Argyll was invaluable; his aloof arrogance and contempt for the mob prevented any repetition of the miserable débâcle of authority occasioned by the affair of the *Worcester*. As a result of good luck and firm management, aided in no small measure by the ineptitude of the opposition in parliament, only relatively minor disorders broke out in the capital, the worst of which occurred on 23 October when the house of a noted unionist, Sir Patrick Johnstone, was rabbled.[6] To the mob of Edinburgh Johnstone was a fallen idol, a former lord provost and sitting member for the city whose popularity failed to survive the fact that he had served as a union commissioner. The assault on his house was entirely the work of the mob, the parliamentary opposition criticising it as futile and premature and likely to give the government a good excuse to tighten up on security. The opposition read the situation correctly, and the government was indeed quick to turn the riot to advantage. The Privy Council, still rocked by the backwash of the *Worcester,* took decisive steps: not only was a strong proclamation issued against tumults but the unusual expedient was also taken of quartering troops in the city and indemnifying them against any slaughters that might occur; and as a further precaution the small standing army of 1,500 men was concentrated near Edinburgh. Even so, its commander-in-chief, the Earl of Leven, who also held Edinburgh Castle, was far from confident of the adequacy of these measures and expressed his fears to Godolphin about the weakness of the forces under his command.[7]

On the last day of October Godolphin assured Leven that strong forces would be stationed in the North of England and Ireland 'to bee in a readiness in case this ferment should continue to give any farther disturbance to the publick peace'.[8] Throughout, Godolphin acted coolly. He was convinced that there was too much talk of rebellion for there to be much substance to it; and, besides, mob riots were then commonplaces of urban existence and not to be equated with armed insurrection. On other grounds, too, the English lord treasurer did not believe that a rebellion was likely, partly because the war was draining France's strength, which would discourage any extensive commitments in Scotland, but mainly because he had come to realise that Hamilton, for all his bluster, was not cut out for desperate enterprises. The duke could not be said to lack courage, but he had much at stake and was unlikely to risk his all to please either the Pretender, Louis XIV, or the plebeian mob of Edinburgh. Whatever his precise game, Hamilton would win or lose it all in the parliament; and, in Godolphin's view, there too would the fate of the treaty be decided.

Anne's letter to the parliament again warmly recommended union, which, the queen declared, 'has long been desired by both nations and we shall esteem it as the greatest glory of our reign to have it now perfected, being fully persuaded that it must prove the greatest happiness of our people'; it would, she continued, be the surest foundation of lasting peace and increasing wealth and prosperity, enabling Britain to 'resist all its enemies, support the protestant interest everywhere and maintain the liberties of Europe'; as to religion the Scottish parliament could take whatever steps it felt were needed to secure the liberties of the established church; and in conclusion the queen guaranteed that the English parliament would be equally zealous for union.[9] These sentiments were dutifully echoed by the commissioner and the chancellor. The opening ritual over, the parliament heard the Articles of Union read, ordered them to be printed along with the record of the negotiations, and adjourned for a week.[10]

The debate on whether the union was to be or not to be really began on 12 October. From the beginning the opposition, aware that influence had been at work and fearing that the government had a majority, resorted to fabian tactics.[11] The anti-unionists, therefore, seized on every opportunity to delay matters in the hope that the ministry's nerve would break as popular clamours mounted now that the details of the treaty were known.[12] Alternatively, the opposition hoped to wreck the treaty by amendments that would make it unacceptable to the English parliament.[13] In spite of their differences and their difficulties, the anti-unionists were strong enough to prevent the ministry from rushing the treaty through the House. Although unable to defer its consideration, the opposition at least managed to secure that each article had to be voted upon and that neither the treaty, nor any part of it, could be ratified until all the Articles had been approved. This was a cumbrous and lengthy process that offered full scope for destructive tactics that could be geared up to the agitations outside parliament.

Throughout the session an appeal to the nation at large remained a basic tactic of the opposition, a point made in the important diet of 12 October when it was contended that parliament alone did not have the right to decide on such a fundamental issue as an incorporating union. Such a union, the opposition argued, would destroy the existing constitution, and this could not be done without a mandate from the country, either by a general election or by constitution at least. The request seemed reasonable but was brushed aside by the ministry on the specious plea that the parliament had been elected to consider union in 1703, which was tantamount to saying that the terms of the treaty negotiated in 1706 did not matter. Certainly, it is no coincidence that after 12 October the opposition to the ministry, inside and outside parliament, hardened. In the face of all this, the pro-unionists argued that parliament was competent to accept or reject the treaty as it saw fit. The opposition then tried to embroil the government with the church by asking parliament to sanction a national fast, which was then the traditional response to a national crisis. The ministry beat down this motion, thus strengthening the suspicions of many presbyterians that Queensberry and his impious crew were ready to betray church as well as nation. A long wrangle on these various points was ended when at last the ministry brought the House to the issue 'proceed or not'. The first important vote of the session revealed the truth of what the opposition had feared, for the motion to proceed with the consideration of the Articles of Union carried by a majority of 66, the Squadrone at last showing its hand by casting its 25 votes for the government.[14]

Strengthened by improved security measures, the ministry became more confident, and in spite of all sorts of ingenious delaying tactics by the opposition the reading of the Articles was completed by the end of October. The opposition then tried to defer detailed consideration of the Articles 'for some considerable time that the sentiments of the Parliament of England thereanent be known and the Members of Parliament may consult those whom they represent'; but these and other objections were repelled, and on 2 November the House accepted Marchmont's motion for detailed consideration of the Articles.[15] The members then began to argue about which Article should be considered first – not as odd a matter as it might appear at first blush. Defoe as usual seized the opportunity to sneer at the opposition, but in this instance his partisanship outran his good sense.[16] Everything, clearly, turned on Article I. To defer its consideration for as long as possible was the obvious tactic for the opposition; and just as obviously the ministry insisted on beginning with Article I. To defer Article I might give the anti-unionists the opportunity to undermine the treaty in the other articles, in which event Article I would either at last be rejected or go by default; but if, on the other hand, Article I were considered first and were to pass then the opposition would be put at a sore disadvantage. To accept the basic principle of incorporation and then carp about details could hardly gain the opposition kudos in its rôle of champion of the independence of the nation.

Defoe did not quite see the significance of this vital vote, but the members of the parliament did. Thus both ministry and opposition exerted themselves to the full on this issue, over which a hot debate raged until 4 November. By then petitions against the union were beginning to be presented to the House and these provided the occasion for repeating the arguments already advanced by the opposition. In answer to all this, for the government side on 2 November William Seton younger of Pitmedden, one of the commissioners for union, justified the treaty on grounds of economic and political necessity. The burden of Seton's speech was that the Union of the Crowns had proved to be unsatisfactory and that only an incorporating union with England could benefit Scotland.[17] It was an able speech, well argued, and without a trace of sentiment. Perhaps Pitmedden's very coolness annoyed the hot Belhaven who then delivered an impassioned, but probably studied, harangue to the effect that the union would destroy and impoverish the nation. It is the comical side of Belhaven's craggy rhetoric that is usually stressed nowadays; but running through his disjointed and highly emotional pleas there was a powerful substratum of sense. It was to the concept of the nation that Belhaven appealed – 'our ancient mother Caledonia'. In Belhaven's view the nation of the Scots long antedated parliaments, which in fact came into existence to safeguard the nation's rights and liberties and could not abate them. But the thought nearly drowned in the orator's lachrymose rhetoric.

Belhaven's speech, famous in its day and long thereafter, was what the Victorians described approvingly as 'a crowned masterpiece of eloquence', and as such it long figured in the repertoire of that genre; it is what our own hard-boiled generation scornfully dismisses as a 'tear jerker'. But in any given generation no uniform standards of taste can be said to apply, a considerable gulf yawning between the popular and the sophisticated. Present-day historians (all, as the Americans say, from Missouri) are evidently psychologically much nearer the 'parliament-men' of the union period than they are to the great Victorians, and, like the blasé members of the Scottish parliament, are little moved by the cloying patriotism of Belhaven's speech – except to mirth. For this the orator's histrionic style may have been largely responsible. The speech was, in fact, the work of a highly emotional political maverick and completely different from the deadly rapier thrusts of a Fletcher. But it reads much better than it must have sounded when acted, and this furious speech was indeed of considerable influence. Belhaven was carried away, but well knew where he was going. Seafield felt that the speech was 'contrived to incense the common peopel'; and here it must be remembered that large-scale political meetings were then forbidden and would have been suppressed as seditious. The press, like the pulpit, provided a bridge between parliament and people; and, when rushed into print, Belhaven's speech of 2 November 1706 made an immediate hit with the populace. It reinforced the angry anti-unionist mood outside parliament, which was doubtless a large part of the orator's intention.[18] Here its fire and fury was not held to signify nothing: its 'smeddum' had an irresistible appeal to the hoi-polloi, which, in every age, enjoys pyrotechnics, the noisier the better.

Defoe, in his *History,* printed Belhaven's speech in full but did not comment on it beyond noting that it was quashed in parliament by the laconic Marchmont, who dismissed it, in a few terse sentences, as a nightmare vision. It was unusual for Defoe not to dilate on what he took to be the follies of the opposition, and the reason for his restraint in this instance is curious. Part of the explanation is that at the time he hastily composed an anonymous skit in verse, 'The Vision', which lampooned Belhaven:

Then the Nation in Sack-cloth appear'd,
And the Visionist sadly bewail'd her;
For Mischiefs the like were ne'er heard,
Her priv'lege of Slavery fail'd her.[19]

Belhaven was stung into replying but mistook his target. He believed that 'The Vision' was from the joint pen of the Earl of Haddington and Dr. Wellwood, and his counter-production was accordingly aimed at the Squadrone. His 'A Scots Answer to a British Vision' was a witty enough piece of its kind, though, as might easily be surmised, the defects of Belhaven's prose were not wanting in his poetry. Defoe enjoyed the fun and kept it going with 'A Reply to the Scots Answer to the British Vision', in which Belhaven was apostrophised as

Supream in Thought, to Grammar unconfin'd;
Thy lofty Genius soars above the Wind.

But after the passing of the Treaty of Union, when political ardour had cooled somewhat, Defoe and Belhaven became fast friends. Defoe was forgiven for his banter and after Belhaven's death on 21 June 1708 did his best to rehabilitate his friend's memory. One way of doing this was, in the *History of the Union,* to refrain from adverse comment on Belhaven's febrile anti-union utterances, contenting himself with describing the speech as being 'much talked of in the world', and its author as 'a person of extraordinary parts and capacity'. But it is noticeable that the claims of friendship did not altogether overcome Defoe's diplomatic address or his justly renowned irony.

To return to the scene of those speeches, the debate on Article I raged on. Just before the matter was put to the vote on 4 November Hamilton made another powerful speech, which resembled Belhaven's in blending hard sense and pathos. In it he stigmatised the treaty as a base betrayal of those 'who assisted the great King Robert Bruce, to restore the constitution and revenge the falsehood of England and the usurpation of Balliol' – and much more to similar effect. But there was nothing sentimental about his peroration: 'Shall we yield up the sovereignty and independency of the nation, when we are commanded by those we represent, to preserve the same, and assured of their assistance to support us?'[20] Hamilton then made a cryptic statement about 'a peculiar concern of his family' that he would not at that moment trouble parliament with if he might be allowed to bring it forward later – a request that was readily enough granted. It is just conceivable, as Mar believed, that this may have been a veiled reference to his claim to the Scottish throne which Article I bade fair to bury forever.[21]

In the same general vein Atholl protested against the treaty as 'contrary to the honour, interests, fundamental laws and the constitution of the kingdom';[22] which complaint was to become a stock prop of opposition. The Marquis of Annandale, who had always hated the idea of incorporation, took the other tack and advocated a federal union.[23] All was to no avail. Brought to the vote at last, Article I was approved by a majority of 30, the Squadrone again supporting the ministry.[24] A crumb of victory went to the opposition, however, and for that the historian can only be grateful. This was that the votes in the House should be recorded, and henceforth voting lists were drawn up so that it was easy to see who voted for what – 'an extraordinary method' (meaning unprecedented), as the diarist Hume of Crossrigg noted.[25]

Voting on the other Articles fluctuated a good deal. The opposition again fought desperately over Article II, which required recognition of the Hanoverian succession. Hamilton was particularly exercised over this Article, which, of course, would almost certainly dispel forever his dream of a crown. Basing his pleas on the numerous anti-union petitions that were being presented to the House, the duke asked for a recess in which to acquaint 'the Queen with the general aversion of the nation'.[26] And on that same day, 15 November, Belhaven delivered another speech, briefer and more restrained than his first but still having an eccentric ring to it, though the eccentricity had, as usual, an ulterior purpose that was clearer to his contemporaries than it is today. Belhaven likened the treaty under consideration to 'the first and worst Treaty that ever was set on foot for mankind . . . when the serpent did deceive our mother Eve'. Even so, according to Belhaven, were the nation and its representatives required by the ministry to 'Eat, swallow down this incorporating union, tho it please neither eye nor taste, it must go over: You must believe your physicians, and we shall consider the reasons for it afterwards'. He continued, 'I wish, my Lord, That our loss be not in some small manner proportionable to our first parents, they thought to have been incorporate with the Gods: But in place of that, they were justly expelled Paradise, lost their sovereignty over the creatures, and were forced to earn their bread with the sweat of their brows'. Ludicrous though they appear to modern eyes, these novel commentaries on the Book of Genesis went down well with the presbyterians whose thoughts, secular as well as sacred, were saturated in Old Testament lore. But Belhaven did not dwell overlong on the theme of Paradise Lost, the rest of his speech being a reasoned plea for reform of the Scottish constitution rather than its dissolution. He concluded that 'Limitations of our own making is the best security'.[27]

Fletcher, ever on the watch for an opening, eagerly returned to his favourite theme of limitations, but, as before, his ideas on this head were of slight appeal even to his own party. Then Annandale proposed that the Hanoverian succession should be recognised and the treaty dropped. The queen had expressly warned the commissioner against such a manoeuvre, and the ministry's supporters went all out to repel it. In the end Queensberry's 'led-horses', as Lockhart called them, carried the day and Article II was put to the vote. In spite of its fierce resistance the opposition could muster only 57 votes, the ministry winning by a majority of 58.[28] Quite evidently, therefore, there was wide support for the Hanoverian succession, and some of the Countrymen parted with the Cavaliers on this issue. All the same, prior to the vote being taken, it was cannily moved, and accepted by the House, that approval of the Hanoverian succession as laid down in Article II of the Treaty of Union 'shall not be binding or have any effect unless terms and conditions of an Union of the two Kingdoms be finally adjusted and concluded'.[29]

Of all the Articles of Union, IV, conferring freedom of trade, was the most popular, which is not surprising in view of the economic resentment built up at the English Navigation Laws for nearly half a century. True, Article IV was discussed at length but mainly with a view to amending details; and when it finally came to a vote the opposition dropped to a mere 19, even Lockhart voting for the measure.[30]

In the event, the most keenly contested parts of the treaty after the first two Articles were III, XV and XXII. Article III stipulated that the United Kingdom of Great Britain should be represented by one parliament, the parliament of Great Britain; XV dealt with the Equivalent; and XXII fixed the representation of Scotland in the parliament of Great Britain.

On 18 November a bitter struggle raged over Article III in a bid to preserve the Scottish parliament in some form. At the outset of the debate the opposition argued that this article should be reserved to the end, but their motion was defeated. Annandale made the, by then, ritual protest that loss of the parliament was 'contrair to the honour, interest, fundamental laws, and constitutions of this kingdom; is a giving up of the sovereignty, the birthright of the peers, the rights and privileges of the barons and boroughs'. If all these were lost, he continued, what security did the subjects of Scotland have for their future liberties? It was a good question, and in the absence of a good answer, Annandale concluded: 'And therefore, I do protest, that this shall not prejudice the being of future Scots parliaments and conventions within the kingdom of Scotland, at no time coming'. Here it has to be recalled that Article I, which effectively disposed of the kingdoms of Scotland and England, said nothing about their respective parliaments whose fates turned on Article III. The hard fight put up over Article III, therefore, had two objectives – to preserve the Scottish parliament, and to damage the treaty. If the treaty were subjected to drastic amendment in such an important article, then it would almost certainly fail. Thus, over Article III Hamilton really exerted himself to introduce wrecking amendments, and in particular he moved that if the treaty were implemented the Scots members should have the right of veto over all measures that touched on it and that any infringement of its terms should lead to automatic dissolution of the union. Stair parried Hamilton's motion by arguing that at that stage it was not feasible to consider constitutional safeguards and that this could only be done after all the articles of the treaty had been accepted – a specious answer that showed that the opposition had no monopoly of prevarication or chicanery.[31]

In the best speech delivered in the union parliament the opposition was answered by Seton of Pitmedden the younger.[32] He had once been of the Country faction but had switched sides, either because he had changed his mind or because his personal interest lay with Seafield. Be that as it may, Seton's speech of 18 November on Article III was sensible and clearly phrased, partly, no doubt, because he had already rehearsed its leading ideas in his pamphlets. He pointed out that Scotland, a constitutional monarchy, was not 'a Polish aristocracy' (the bad example of Poland seems to have weighed heavily with the Scots unionists),[33] and that it was not lawful for the gentry, in a well-known Polish phrase, to 'explode the diet' – i.e. overturn the chamber by filibustering or even by force. Nor was the government democratic, 'whereby every subject of Scotland may claim a vote in the legislature'. According to Seton the government of Scotland had long been a limited monarchy, and sovereignty lay with the crown in parliament. He further claimed that 'there are no fundamentals of government in any nation, which are not alterable by its supreme power, where the circumstances of times requires'. Thus, in order to annihilate the Scottish parliament, the unionists were forced to stress its absolute sovereignty and omnicompetence.

Seton's arguments were cogent, but his premises were none of the soundest. His was not the normal view of the constitution, particularly since 1689 when the Claim of Right was held to have laid down fundamental law, something that even the most committed Hanoverians dared not utterly deny. There were, too, serious doubts about the omnicompetence of parliament, which was an English rather than a Scottish concept; and, clearly, the question of the *locus* of ultimate sovereignty, whether it lay with crown or parliament, was still very much *sub judice* in Scotland, as witness the session of the parliament of 1703. Seton seems to have been conscious that he was stretching his argument a bit far, for he carefully acknowledged the existence of natural rights, particularly of liberty and property, but he took care not to examine these metaphysical concepts too closely. On the other main matter of substance on which he touched, the representation granted to Scotland, Seton pointed out that it was calculated on the basis of taxable capacity and on that reckoning was more than fair. In general his arguments throughout were legalistic and drew heavily on a one-sided reading of Grotius; and his theoretical approach to politics was entirely Aristotelian. Strong echoes of Aristotle's *Politics* run all through Seton's work, and he was evidently hostile to any form of Platonism. Nonetheless, his speech was a remarkable *tour de force,* which, delivered dispassionately and persuasively, well deserved the applause it received.[34] But it suffered from a fundamental weakness. Seton could only assert as an article of faith that entrenched safeguards were unnecessary and that the British parliament would deal fairly with Scotland. Here, in a sense, he was hoist with his own petard, for his doctrine of the absolute sovereignty of parliament raised awkward questions that he could not answer. In short, in the important matter of legislation the British parliament would be free to act as it willed.

Article III finally passed with a substantial majority;[35] and a belated attempt after the vote was taken to add a clause to the effect that the parliament of Great Britain 'shall meet and sit once in three years at least in that part of Great Britain now called Scotland' was fobbed off to the Greek Kalends.[36]

The discussion on Article XV was lengthy and disjointed. Much of it was taken up with the disbursement of the Equivalent, and this mouth-watering business brought many powerful interests into conflict. The directors of the Company of Scotland felt that the Company should not be wound up as an act of state and maintained that the views of the shareholders should determine its future. In the light of what Seton had said on rights of property, this was a good point; but the real fears of the directors were lest the reimbursement of the shareholders from the Equivalent should prove illusory. Such fears were not altogether idle, as the sequel showed, and the handling of the Equivalent was to be a bitter disappointment to many besides the directors of the Company of Scotland. As to the proposed liquidation, however, the Scottish government held that the Company operated under statute and that parliament could repeal the relevant act if that was deemed necessary. After much argument on this issue the ministry had its way: the Company of Scotland was to be dissolved. The main trouble, though, concerned the distribution of the Equivalent, which the ministry was determined must be used primarily to pay government arrears of salaries, while the Company of Scotland contended that it had a prior claim. In theory, the ministry failed to win its case, but in practice carried its point, for the arrears of salary were met from the Equivalent long before the tortuous business of paying the shareholders got off the ground. Other interests tried to chisel what they could out of the situation, and the wool producers secured the lesser Equivalent of £2,000 per annum for the promotion of the wool trade. But this scheme, too, hung fire and did not even begin to be implemented until 1727, too late to provide any succour to the moribund wool trade. And throughout the debate on Article XV the anti-unionists condemned the Equivalent as a vast covert bribe, the price of their country's independence; but with politics, as with greatness, consistency has nothing to do, and, illogically, at times the opposition's argument seemed to be that the Equivalent, covert bribe and all, was not great enough. Eventually, on 30 December, Article XV was approved by 121 votes to 54. [37]

By December 1706 the Court was clearly in the ascendant, not only outvoting the opposition in parliament but also dealing firmly with disorders in the country. The opposition, aware of its weakening position, had organised a large meeting of freeholders and lairds in Edinburgh, the object of which was to draw up and forward to the queen a national address against the union – a pale carbon copy of the National Covenant of 1638. Hamilton's vacillation ruined the project.[38] Its only result was that on 27 December the ministry passed yet another proclamation against tumults, which also forbade petitioners to congregate in Edinburgh.[39] Thus, by the time Article XXII, which dealt with parliamentary representation, came to be discussed early in January 1707 the opposition was growing desperate. It had accomplished little. Only minor amendments had been made to the treaty, which were unlikely to prejudice its chances at Westminster. By that late stage, therefore, only a bold stroke could undermine the treaty; so, at Hamilton's instigation, a last-ditch stand on Article XXII was carefully planned.

The members of the opposition aimed to wreck the treaty by withdrawing from the parliament and throwing themselves upon the country. They intended to recognise the Hanoverian succession but to reject incorporation, and then to petition the queen with an elaborate justificatory address which was (shades of 1638!) actually drawn up by Lord Advocate Stewart who hated the idea of union. The object was to advertise the extent of opposition to union in Scotland in the hope that the English parliament would take alarm and drop the treaty. In 1702 Hamilton had, with no great success, employed a similar tactic; but the duke argued, somewhat speciously, that the English commissioners had been half-hearted about the negotiations in 1702 mainly because they knew that Queensberry and his friends represented neither Scottish parliament nor nation. There may have been something in all this, to some extent with reference to 1702 but even more so far as the current situation early in 1707 was concerned. Certainly, if resolutely carried out in January 1707, such a demonstration would not only have embarrassed the Court but also have caused trouble both by encouraging the Tory opposition in England and disconcerting the union's supporters. To have carried the union with little more than half a House would, at best, have been regarded as a half-hearted acceptance, and it would not have been easy to ignore or explain such a well-advertised grandstand display as the withdrawal of so many members.

But again the plan came to nothing because of Hamilton's incurable wavering. At the crucial moment, when the opposition was to state its case in parliament and then ceremoniously withdraw, he called off on the plea of toothache! The duke's health at this time does not seem to have been good, but his exasperated followers were probably correct when they diagnosed his indisposition at this point as being due to an attack of cold feet. In all likelihood the ministry had been informed of Hamilton's plan and managed to intimidate its author with veiled threats – probably a treason charge deriving from his dealings with Colonel Hooke. Hamilton's supporters, however, knew that only some dramatic move could by then damage the treaty, and they literally frog-marched their invalid leader into the Parliament House, hollow tooth and all. There he burked again, refusing to play his assigned rôle, and, to the government's intense relief, the plan flopped. Seafield later stated that if the opposition's plan had been carried out the government was resolved to 'prorogate the Parliament, and give over the prosecution of the union'.[40] Instead, as things turned out, the effect of this débâcle on the opposition was catastrophic. It deepened the general distrust of the Duke of Hamilton, and thereafter the opposition wilted.[41]

The burden of leadership then fell on the disgusted Atholl who was left to advance objections to Article XXII. He hastily put together all his old arguments and condemned the proposed representation as derogatory to the peerage of Scotland and subversive of national rights. The Scottish peers numbered 160 as against 180 in England, and yet, complained Atholl, they were to be reduced to a mere 16 in the House of Lords; the barons and burgesses were to decline in number from 155 to 45; but, Atholl held, since there was to be no reduction of English representation, surely Scotland would be left at the mercy of a predominantly English legislature. Many petitions and addresses, Atholl continued, had been presented to the House against an incorporating union, but not one for it. (In fact, the ministry, belatedly aware of this discrepancy, had tried to get up pro-union addresses but found no support, even their own vassals refusing to sign them. *Faute de mieux*, therefore, the ministry, like Argyll, had to dismiss the anti-union addresses as meaningless scraps of paper, fit only to make kites with).[42] Atholl concluded by demanding a new parliament in order 'to have the immediate sentiments of the nation since these articles have been made public'. A point worth stressing, however, is that, like the addresses to which he had referred, Atholl did not condemn union as such but pleaded for 'honourable, just, and equal terms which may unite them [the two kingdoms] in affection and interest'.[43]

Others spoke to similar purpose; but in spite of noisy opposition the ministry had its majority and Article XXII was approved. Finally, on 16 January 1707, the Treaty of Union, along with the Act of Security for the Church of Scotland, was ratified by 110 votes to 67 as the Scottish Act of Union, a majority of 43 out of 177 votes cast.[44]

Ratification of the union did not quite end the business of the last session of the Scottish parliament. The most important remaining items concerned the disbursement of the Equivalent and the mode whereby Scottish members should be returned to the parliament of the United Kingdom (a term, incidentally, that does not date from 1800 but was frequently used in the Treaty of Union of 1707). Both these matters required immediate attention and this could best be given by the Scottish parliament, which was *au fait* with the details. The intricate problems raised by representation were tackled first. The negotiators of the Treaty had agreed that Scottish electoral law and even procedure should be maintained. This was sensible, for, since the franchises in England and Scotland were completely different and rooted in deep legal as well as social differences, it would have been folly to attempt to enforce uniformity. So it was left to the Scottish parliament to work out the new constituencies and election procedures. Not without numerous protests the 45 M.P.s were allocated on the basis of 30 to the shires and 15 to the royal burghs, the latter necessitating a grouping system. When the relevant acts were passed, a further complication had to be faced. From 20 January on, it had become known that the English ministry intended to continue the existing English parliament, even if the union came into being, until the general election that was due in England in 1708. Quite apart from the revealing light that this decision cast on English attitudes to the union, it posed a practical problem.

How were the first Scottish members of the British parliament to be returned? The Scottish ministry was afraid to leave the matter to the electors, freely conceding that the mood of the country would go against the government. On 12 February the ministry solved the problem by availing itself of its safe majority to allow the parliament to nominate its representatives. The opposition naturally, and correctly, opposed the measure, which made a mockery of any known theory of representation. But the result, after furious wrangling, was a virtual nomination by the ministry. In the process the Squadrone was duped. It had been promised lavish representation in return for supporting the Court, but, with the Treaty safely through the Scottish parliament, the cynical Queensberry, to accommodate the ambitious Argyll, dismissed the Squadrone's claims, thus earning its undying hatred.[45]

The precise means of allocating the Equivalent, a matter of deep concern to many, also caused all sorts of smouldering antagonisms to flare up again. In the upshot the Squadrone were again tricked. Part of the price they had exacted for supporting the Court's measures was that they should have oversight of the disbursement of that part of the Equivalent set aside to compensate the shareholders of the Company of Scotland. This would have given them such powers of patronage that it seems unlikely that the Court ever meant to honour its pledge. However that may be, once the Treaty had been safely converted into an Act of Parliament the Court reneged on the deal and insisted, very plausibly and indeed very properly, on a Commission for the Equivalent that would be answerable to the British parliament.[46]

On 19 March the Treaty of Union and its ancillary acts, as accepted by the English parliament, received final ratification in Scotland, and on 25 March the Scottish parliament, its business completed, was adjourned to 22 April. There, on 25 March, the parliamentary record ends, from which some have concluded that there was no formal dissolution and that for over two and a half centuries the Scottish estates have been deep-frozen in the adjourned state, capable of resuscitation at need to provide 'home rule'. Apart from the patent absurdity of such anachronistic notions, the point of law is that the parliament of Scotland was formally dissolved on 28 April 1707. Private correspondence in the Mar and Kellie muniments refers to a dissolution by proclamation on 28 April;[47] and the proclamation recorded under that date in the Register of the Privy Council could not have been more specific or final: 'whereas by the treatie of Union happily concluded and approven in the parliaments of our Kingdoms of Scotland and England respectively . . . by the third Article of the said Treatie, It is stipulated that the United Kingdom of Great Brittaine be represented by one and the same parliament, to be styled the parliament of Great Brittaine . . . Therefore wee have determined to dissolve our present parliament of Scotland'.[48] The proclamation goes on to do just that.

The passing of the Act of Union in Scotland has been well summarised: 'The Union was, in fact, carried by the Parliament, with the assistance of the Church, against the country'.[49] To that we would only add that management played a large part in securing the parliament. Mar, a manager of considerable ability, well knew how and where to ply his talents to most effect. That the mood of the country, however, was hostile to incorporation is beyond dispute; and equally so is the fact that the parliamentary opposition failed to capitalise on national resentment. The failure to co-ordinate extra-parliamentary resistance to union arose partly because the opposition in parliament, from which a lead was expected, was at odds with itself and feebly led, and partly because the country too was deeply divided. In the country at large the union was clearly detested; but how to concert measures against it was the problem. Many looked for salvation in the return of the legitimist line, some clinging to the hope that James

VIII might make a reasonable constitutional monarch. The snag here was that James Edward was still a youth of 18 and an unknown political quantity. Certainly his later career showed that he was open-minded and fair, unlike his obstinate father, but that was not known in 1707. In any event, the presbyterians and constitutionalists, much as they hated the union, wanted no truck with the Pretender, especially as he remained a Roman catholic. These differences ran deep, gave rise to confused attitudes of mind, and made concerted action outside parliament difficult. Nonetheless, the principal defects stemmed from weak leadership. If Hamilton had been capable of decisive action, popular resistance to the union, in spite of divergent interests, would probably still have been feasible; but with what results it would be idle to speculate.

As it was, in November-December 1706, when the treaty still swung in the balance, though gravitating towards the Court, tentative attempts were finally made to harness up the anti-unionism of the Jacobites and that of the extreme presbyterians, the Cameronians. But the plans for a joint rebellion were feeble and ill-managed. In the end, in spite of rumours of risings on every hand, only localised disturbances occurred; and it is just possible that the chief of these, the riots in Glasgow and Dumfries, were spontaneous outbreaks.

The riots that shook Glasgow for three weeks in November and the first fortnight of December were sparked off by the refusal of the magistrates to sign an anti-union address. The local Jacobites then played upon the fears of the mob, in the process managing to demonstrate that it was possible to forge a working alliance between Jacobites and presbyterians. They cunningly whipped up Glasgow's presbyterian traditions, and appeals to patriotism and the 'good old cause' soon produced results. Indeed, it was a fiery sermon on 6 November that gave rise to the first disorders, when a Knoxian minister, James Clark of the Tron, exhorted his flock to put no trust in addresses to parliaments or princes but to follow the good old way and 'up and be valiant for the city of our God!'[50] Whether this was a reference to St. Mungo's 'Dear Green Place', or a call to build the New Jerusalem is not clear; but the day after that sermon was delivered the mob, powered as usual by the students and apprentices, rose and seized control of the city. Provost Aird, in fear of his life, fled to Edinburgh for safety. In his absence the rioters wrung an address from the council, and this address was forwarded to the capital. Glasgow's refugee provost then ventured to return home, only to run into even worse troubles. The mob was again rampant, and, not without considerable danger, the provost and some of the other dignitaries again sought refuge in the capital. By this time the rioters were led by one Finlay, who was an old soldier of Dumbarton's regiment. Finlay was evidently of Jacobite sympathies and he tried to turn rioting into armed insurrection; but, repulsed in an attack on the Tolbooth, the object of which was to obtain arms, he set out for Edinburgh. First, however, he had to increase his small band of followers by 'raising the country', and with this in mind he headed for Kilsyth where he expected to be joined by a band of supporters. They failed to materialise. Worse, at Kilsyth he got word that a force of dragoons had left Edinburgh, bound to restore order in the west. Finlay then made for Hamilton where rumour had it that a large force of anti-unionist dissidents had rallied. The Duke of Hamilton's mother, the redoubtable Duchess Anne, was indeed a strong presbyterian and a great patriot who bitterly opposed the union; but, like her son, she dreaded the thought of civil war and did not encourage musters.[51] Besides, Duchess Anne hated the Jacobites and could not bring herself to make common cause with them; so Finlay found no reinforcements at Hamilton and had to beat a hasty retreat on Glasgow, where, on the arrival of the troops, he and other ringleaders were arrested. On the premature withdrawal of the troops from Glasgow, however, fresh disorders broke out. The Privy Council, whose patience all this while had been sorely tried, then concluded that Glasgow's town council and magistrates were so inefficient as to be of suspect loyalty, and on 9 December the Council threatened to deprive Glasgow and its crafts of their rights and privileges unless order were immediately restored.[52] Coming on top of the fiasco of Finlay's rebellion the threat was effective, and the riots subsided.

Tied up with these outbreaks in Glasgow, in nebulous intention at any rate, were the disorders in the south-west that arose from Cameronian discontent with the union. On 20 November some 300 armed Cameronians entered Dumfries, ceremonially burnt the Articles of Union as 'utterly destructive of the nation's independency, crown rights, and our constitute laws, both civil and sacred', and, in their classical style, bitterly condemned and rejected the work of those in parliament who 'shall presume to carry on the said Union by a supream power, over the belly of the generality of this nation'.[53] They received much popular support, but the strong nationalism of the Westland Whigs was betrayed by their supposed leader, Cunningham of Eckat, who was in Queensberry's pay and who received £100 and a commission over a company of foot for his secret service work. The grand aim of the anti-unionists, in short, was for a concerted rising of dissidents, including Jacobite Highlanders and disgruntled presbyterians. The plan was ruined by the mercurial Duke of Hamilton who at the last moment countermanded the necessary orders.[54]

Some historians have doubted whether such an alliance, whose difficulties are obvious, was ever projected.[55] The evidence for it is considerable if not conclusive. Iain Lom, for example, in his poem on the union, states that he was present at the gathering of the clans and blames the failure on Viscount Dupplin who was supposed to bring the orders from Atholl in Edinburgh but who succumbed to the bribes offered by the ministry.[56] Most decisively of all, however, Hamilton's inactivity and Queensberry's unobtrusive preparations prevented any serious outbreak. By December the English force lying on the Border had been reinforced with 800 cavalry and was ready to move north at Queensberry's call.[57] On occasion the strain threatened to get the better of the commissioner's nerves, but Godolphin and Marlborough constantly advised determination as a better answer to Queensberry's troubles than the introduction of English troops. The event justified their cool assessment of the situation, for, though Scotland seethed with resentment and disaffection was rife, the union passed without any serious popular uprising.

The last hope of the anti-unionists lay with the English parliament; but, well aware of this, the Court took steps to ensure the treaty an easy passage. In spite of the need for supply and the claims of other pressing business, so determined was the English ministry to carry the treaty that parliament was repeatedly adjourned until 3 December 1706.[58] Not since the Revolution had there been such a long delay in dealing with public affairs; its purpose was obviously to give the Scots ministry as clear a run as possible in dealing with the treaty, for opposition to it in the English parliament could only have aggravated the problems of the Scottish ministry by stiffening the resistance of the anti-unionists in Scotland. By the end of November, however, it looked as if the treaty would succeed in the Scottish parliament; and at the opening of the English parliament on 3 December the queen again took the opportunity to recommend the union. But still the English ministry played safe and carefully managed the parliament so that it did not immediately consider the treaty. Instead the House of Commons went about its routine business, granting supply and so on, waiting really for the Scottish parliament to complete its work and, hopefully, produce an acceptable Act of Union. Not until this was done were the treaty and the Scottish Act brought up for consideration in the House of Commons on 22 January 1707.

They met with an easy reception. The English High Church Tories, who disliked the Scots and scorned the idea of union with them, had pinned their hopes on the rejection of the treaty by the Scottish parliament and were at a loss when it passed there. True, their main leaders, Nottingham and Rochester, still hoped to repeat more successfully the delaying tactics that had been tried in Edinburgh; but the English ministry, profiting from Queensberry's experiences, took care to give the opposition no openings. The Court and the Junto combined to force the necessary measures through the Commons, which on 4 February resolved itself into a Committee of the Whole House to consider the Articles of Union and the Scottish Act of Union. In vain the opposition howled 'Posthaste!' as the Articles were hurriedly read with no time allowed for debate. The government coolly countered protests that the treaty was being rushed through the Commons with the bland retort, 'That deliberation always supposes doubts and difficulties, but no material objections being offered against any of the articles, there was no room for delays'.[59] The ministry maintained its firm grip, and the opposition, soon obliged to recognise that it was powerless, put up a feeble resistance. Throughout, too, the government cleverly presented a low profile, and only a short enabling clause was left as a target for the disheartened opposition. The Court managers in fact drafted the union legislation and drove the all-important bill through the committee stage in one prolonged sitting. Shortly afterwards, on 28 February, the bill received its third reading and passed by a vote of 274–116, a majority of 158 out of 390 cast.[60] (Incidentally, the legislation that took the United Kingdom into the European Economic Community in 1972 followed remarkably similar lines.)

The Lords deliberated in the wake of the Commons, and necessarily at a slower pace that allowed some debate. In general the Tory peers were averse to the proposed union, believing that it would be harmful to the English constitution in church and state. Thus Nottingham objected to the name 'Great Britain' on the grounds that it would subvert the laws and liberties of England. The judges unanimously repelled this objection. Nottingham and Rochester then argued that the union was a threat to the church, but the government met the cry of 'the church in danger' by pointing out that the Archbishop of Canterbury had already been directed to draw up a bill guaranteeing the Church of England, similar to that already conferred on the Scottish establishment. Another Tory peer, Haversham, condemned the proposed union because in the nature of things it could not be entire, and pleaded for a federal union that would, he believed, be more acceptable to public opinion in Scotland. Haversham held that forcing an incorporating union on an unwilling Scotland was asking for trouble and might well provoke rebellions.[61] Federalism, however, was roundly rejected by the Lords not just because it was believed to be a cumbrous and inefficient system of government but also because it could not give the essential guarantee of permanency to the union or, even more important, to the successsion.

The delay in the Lords was contrived by the ministry in order to give the Commons time to complete and send up their union bill.[62] When the bill finally arrived in the upper house it was hurried through all its stages in less than three days, and in spite of the protests of about twenty Tory peers the Act of Union passed both Houses on 4 March, received the royal assent on 6 March, was finally ratified on 19 March and came into operation on 1 May 1707. Godolphin in a letter to Marlborough expressed his relief when he called this 'the best sessions of parliament that England ever saw'.[63]

The treaty's easy passage through the English parliament showed that, quite apart from masterly management, there was no great opposition to it there. Of all the remarkable changes of the time this was the most remarkable. At the beginning of Anne's reign there had been strong aversion in England to the idea of union with Scotland, but by 1707 it was English insistence that made union possible. There is no mystery about what caused this change in attitude – it was brought about by fears for the security of England. A disgruntled Scotland raised the spectre of French intervention and the opening of the old 'Northern postern', which, the Civil Wars apart, had been lockfast for over a century. Nor were these fears and changes in attitude confined to the parliamentarians. They were widespread among all classes. The people of the northern counties of England, for example, were greatly alarmed by the Act of Security and had openly expressed their relief when the negotiations for union got under way.[64] And while the treaty was under consideration by the parliaments there were no anti-union outbursts in England, though Scottophobia did not miraculously vanish in 1707. It was far otherwise in Scotland where the mood of most people in 1707 was sombre if not sullen. On 1 May Harry Maule wrote to Mar, who was in London, describing the black mood in Scotland which contrasted so sharply with the jubilation in England.[65] Most Scots evidently felt that there was little to celebrate at 'the end o' an auld sang', as Chancellor Seafield had drolly described the winding up of the Scottish parliament.

NOTES

Abbreviations used in the notes

APS   *Acts of the Parliaments of Scotland*
HMC   Historical Manuscripts Commission

1 George Lockhart, *Memoirs* (1714), 218–19.
2 Daniel Defoe, *History of the Union between England and Scotland* (edn. 1786), 236. For the cause of Hamilton's indisposition, see Duke of Argyll, ed., *Intimate Family Letters of the Eighteenth Century* (1910), I, 55, Leven to Godolphin, 26 October 1706.
3 Lockhart, *Memoirs*, 222.
4 Defoe, *Union*, 236–84; Lockhart, *Memoirs*, 215 *ff.*, esp. 218–29.
5 H.M.C., *Mar and Kellie Papers*, I, 329.
6 Defoe, *op cit.*, 237–8; Lockhart, *op cit.*, 223–8; A.P.S., XI, 309–10; Hume of Crossrigg, *Diary*, 176–7.
7 *Edinburgh Review*, October 1892, 518.
8 Sir William Fraser, ed., *Melville and Leven* (1890), II, 205.

9 *A.P.S.*, XI, 305–6.

10 P. Hume Brown, ed., *Lord Seafield's Letters, 1702–1707* (S.H.S., 1915), 93; Hume, *Diary*, 172–3.

11 Lockhart, *Memoirs*, 221. On the first day of the session the government had a majority in an election dispute, which Seafield took as a good omen – *Seafield Letters*, 93; but Mar was more circumspect – H.M.C., *Mar and Kellie*, I, 283–4.

12 *Seafield Letters*, 94–8.

13 *Ibid.*; Defoe, *Union*, 230.

14 *A.P.S.*, XI, 307; Hume, *Diary*, 173–4; Lockhart, *Memoirs*, 220–2; Defoe, *Union*, 288–90.

15 *A.P.S.*, XI, 311–12; Hume, *Diary*, 178–9.

16 Defoe, *Union*, 308. This work is at its best for the session of 1706, which is given lengthy if rather partisan treatment.

17 *A Speech in the Parliament of Scotland, the Second Day of November, 1706*, by William Seton of Pitmedden, junior (1706).

18 Belhaven's speech is in Defoe, *History*, 317–28; for its effect, *Seafield Letters*, 100. It was printed as *The Lord Beilhaven's Speech in the Scotch Parliament Saturday the Second of November* (1706), and frequently reprinted thereafter.

19 Frank H. Ellis, ed., *Poems on Affairs of State: Augustan Satirical Verse, 1660–1714*, VII (1975), 216.

20 Lockhart, *Memoirs*, 252–3.

21 For the incident, Hume, *Diary*, 179; for Mar's interpretation, H.M.C., *Mar and Kellie*, I, 313.

22 *A.P.S.*, XI, 313.

23 *Ibid.*, 312–13.

24 *Ibid.*, 313–15.

25 Hume, *Diary*, 179.

26 *Ibid.*, 182–3.

27 *The Lord Bellhaven's Second Speech in Parliament, the Fifteenth Day of November, 1706, on the Second Article of the Treaty* (1706).

28 *A.P.S.*, XI, 326–7.

29 *Ibid.*, 322.

30 *Ibid.*, 333–4.

31 *A.P.S.*, XI, 328; Defoe, *Union*, 354–5, for Annandale's speech; Hume, *Diary*, 183–4, for Hamilton's.

32 Defoe, *op. cit.*, 360–3.

33 J. M. Gray, ed., *Memoirs of the Life of Sir John Clerk of Penicuik* (S.H.S., 1892), 49.

34 Defoe, *Union*, 364.

35 *A.P.S.*, XI, 329–30.

36 *Ibid.*, 332.

37 *Ibid.*, 375–6.

38 Lockhart, *Memoirs*, 285–90.

39 *A.P.S.*, XI, 371–2.

40 Lockhart, *Memoirs*, 325.

41 *Ibid.*, 293–327.

42 *Ibid.*, 235.

43 *A.P.S.*, XI, 386–7.

44 *Ibid.*, 402–14.

45 H.M.C., *Mar and Kellie*, I, 367–9, 370–2; *Correspondence of George Baillie of Jerviswood 1702–8*, Bannatyne Club, (1841), II, 183–9.

46 H.M.C., *Mar and Kellie*, I, 379, for the Squadrone's expectations; Clerk, *Memoirs*, 67–9, for the commission.

47 H.M.C., *Mar and Kellie*, I, 389.

48 Reg. Ho. (S.R.O.), P.C. 1/53, 507–8.

49 James Mackinnon, *The Union of England and Scotland* (1896), 326.

50 George Eyre Todd, *History of Glasgow*, III (1934), 66–71.

51 Rosalind K. Marshall, *The Days of Duchess Anne* (1973), 220.

52 Reg. Ho. (S.R.O.), P.C. 1/53, 492.

53 William McDowall, *History of Dumfries* (1867), 548–54.

54 Lockhart, *Memoirs*, 283.

55 See Andrew Lang in *The Union of 1707* (1907), chs. VII and VIII.

56 Annie A. Mackenzie, ed., *Orain Iain Luim* (Scottish Gaelic Texts Society, 1964), 'A Song Against the Union', 225–6.

57 H.M.C., *Mar and Kellie*, I, 353.

58 Defoe, *Union*, 481.

59 Abel Boyer, *History of Reign of Queen Anne, 1706–07* (1707), 439–40.

60 See *Commons Journal*, XV, 272–317 *passim*; *Parliamentary History*, VI, 543–83.

61 *Parliamentary History*, VI, 563–5.

62 Gilbert Burnet, *History of his own time* (1838), II, 802; *Parliamentary History*, VI, 555–6.

63 Coxe, *Marlborough*, II (1818), 180.

64 *Parliamentary History*, VI, 477; G. M. Trevelyan, *Ramillies and the Union*, 247–9.

65 H.M.C., *Mar and Kellie*, I, 389.

The 'Forty-Five: Jacobite Tactics

Extracted from JM Hill 1986 *Celtic Warfare, 1595–1763*, Edinburgh (John Donald), 127–56.

Despite the poorly conceived and implemented strategy of the Jacobites in the 'Forty-five uprising, their tactics under irregular battlefield conditions were extremely effective. The old Highland charge continued to be the centrepiece of Jacobite tactical doctrine and it succeeded remarkably well against regular British troops in the early stages of the uprising. Although between 1715 and 1745 the British had concentrated on diminishing the shock value of the charge, they were unable to stand up to the Highlanders in the first two major battles of the campaign. In January 1746 General Henry Hawley, a grizzled old veteran familiar with Gaelic warfare, instructed his men as to the proper way to defend against the Highland charge. He told them to fire by ranks, three deep, when the clansmen were ten or twelve paces away. Hawley went on to caution his soldiers that if they fired too soon, they probably would miss their target and have no chance to reload before the Highlanders were upon them.[1] By 1745 both sides realized that if the clansmen were allowed to make effective use of their traditional weapons, the broadsword and target, the British regulars could not defeat them even with the new flintlock musket, enhanced as it was by the iron ramrod and socket bayonet, and the platoon firing system.[2] A key to breaking the Highland charge was defense in depth. At both Killiecrankie and Sheriffmuir the Highlands had smashed the enemy's single line. The three-deep formation proposed by Hawley was little more than a single line reinforced for more platoon firepower, but the refined concept ultimately rendered the Highland charge ineffective. The British at Culloden drew up in a true two- or three-line defense in depth and, consequently, found it much easier to absorb the shock of Gaelic offensive tactics . . .

The Jacobites at the battle of Prestonpans (21 September 1745) faced an enemy in possession of an extremely strong defensive position. The day before the battle General Sir John Cope's army was drawn up just to the east of the town. Its back was to the sea; its front was protected by a flat, marshy stretch fronted by ditches and walls; its left was fronted by a morass; and its right was protected by high garden walls.[3] . . .

To neutralize Cope's strong defensive position, Charles decided to march before sunrise around Tranent and to the eastern flank of the enemy. Enlisting the aid of a local guide, the Highlanders set out and crossed the marsh to the south-east of Cope's position. The first column traversed the narrow track across the bog undetected, but Cope's sentries spotted the second column and the general wheeled his army to the left. Their sudden move disorganized the government troops. As the clansmen passed from the marsh and turned sharply to the left near Seton House, they disappeared silently about 800 yards from Cope's army into a thick morning mist. Cope had underestimated the Highlander's ability to cross the bog between Tranent and Seton House and, consequently, had not posted a guard in that vicinity. Even though the march was detected and the Jacobites had some difficulty in forming their battle lines, it was a brilliant and daring move that allowed the clans to stage their traditional charge against an enemy who was in no position to defend against it.[4] . . .

The Highlanders emerged from the mist less than 200 yards from Cope's front line, their war cries piercing the morning silence. The clansmen broke into a trot, muskets in hand, and formed up into the tightly packed wedges that gave the Highland charge its tremendous impact. A government officer described the horde that would in a moment smash the ranks of his hapless regiment:

> . . . most of them seemed to be strong, active, and hardy men; . . . and if clothed like Lowcountry men, would appear inferior to the King's troops; but the Highland garb favoured them much, as it showed their naked limbs, which were strong and muscular; . . . their stern countenances, and bushy uncombed hair, gave them a fierce, barbarous, and imposing aspect . . .[5]

The execution of the Highland charge over the final 100 yards was marred by just one potentially disastrous error. Murray had ordered the Camerons on the extreme left of the Jacobite front line to fan out farther to the left to avoid being outflanked by Cope's dragoons. As Lochiel's men drew off in that direction, they left a wide gap in the center of the Jacobite line. The gap between the two Highland wings might have allowed the center of a better army than Cope's to set up a coordinated crossfire that surely would have taken a heavy toll of the attackers. Before the opportunity became readily apparent to the government army, however, Charles's second line came forward to fill the gap. Now that the Highlanders had reordered their ranks as they advanced (a most unusual accomplishment for an irregular army), they bore down with characteristic swiftness upon Cope's flanks amid harmless musket volleys fired too soon by the impatient government infantry. The clansmen responded with a volley of their own and then flung away their muskets in favor of the broadsword and target. Murray had personally led the Camerons across the last few yards that separated the lines and saw the enemy dragoons and infantry struggle in vain to reload before the Highlanders reached them.[6]

Despite the overwhelming preponderance of firepower contained within the artillery, infantry, and dragoons, the government army learned (as had MacKay at Killiecrankie) that modern firearms alone were not capable of stopping the Highland charge. Cope's six pieces of artillery on the right wing might have caused a great execution of the attackers, but they were poorly serviced and managed to fire only once before being overrun by Murray's men.[7] The performance of the government infantry, too, was inept, reflecting their unfamiliarity with the Highland charge. Though some of them were veterans of continental war, they were unable to execute their much-heralded system of platoon firepower against a rapidly advancing enemy. Few men in Cope's front line fired more than one round before the Highlanders were upon them. Curiously, they did not have their bayonets fixed and had no time to attach them after expending their first load.[8] When the Highlanders hit, the government infantry buckled and broke instantly, threw down their muskets, and fled from the battlefield. An observer noted that '. . . none of the soldiers attempted to load their pieces again, and not one bayonet was stained with blood . . .'[9] In the pursuit that followed, many of Cope's men ran into the enclosure that had served as their camp the night before and were cut down by the clansmen. Others gave themselves up at once.

The destruction of Cope's army cannot be blamed solely on the lack of firepower from the infantrymen, since the dragoons failed to protect the infantry's flanks. The dragoons put up an effective fire at the outset of the battle, and consequently drew the attention of the clansmen. Seeing confusion among the attacking Jacobites, the government horse advanced, firearms blazing, into the ranks of the Highlanders. Before they got well under way, however, the clansmen greeted them with a counter-volley. The dragoons turned to flee, and the Highlanders charged into their midst, slashing at the horses' heads and legs.[10] On both flanks the Jacobites drove the dragoons from the battlefield, leaving Cope's infantry unprotected: '. . . the two Regiments of Dragoons who should have supported the Infantry . . . shamefully deserted their Commanders, and fled without once looking behind them.'[11] With the dispersal of the dragoons Cope's hope of victory vanished.

Prestonpans illustrated the Gaels' tactical superiority over an opponent not sufficiently trained or led and unfamiliar with the Highland way of war. The battle lasted no longer than fifteen minutes,[12] and the performance of his troops so impressed Charles that thereafter he '. . . entertained a mighty notion of the Highlanders, and . . . imagined they would beat four times their number of regular troops'.[13] Charles, however, deceived himself in equating Cope's rabble with the best regular troops in the British army. The government dragoons were poorly disciplined, many of the infantrymen were fit only for guarding baggage, and the artillery arm was inadequately staffed with sailors. As it was, Cope's bedraggled outfit was routed by about 1,900 to 2,000 of Charles's front-line troops, who were unsupported by artillery or horse. The Highlanders did their job so quickly and thoroughly that the Jacobite second line had no reason to join the fray.[14] A Jacobite officer described the effect of the Gaelic offensive: 'The field of battle presented a spectacle of horror, being covered with heads, legs, and arms, and mutilated bodies; for the killed all fell by the sword.'[15] Cope's losses confirmed the superiority of Highland arms: 300 to 400 killed, including five or six officers; 400 to 500 wounded, including sixty to seventy officers; and 1,400 to 1,600 captured, including seventy to eighty officers.[16]

Charles's easy victory at Prestonpans obscured several fundamental drawbacks in Highland tactics. Flushed with success, Charles did not pause to consider what might have happened had the impetus of his undisciplined attack been blunted by an effective fire from the enemy's artillery and musketry. At no time during the battle were the Jacobites able to coordinate the movements of their two wings; therefore, if they had suffered a setback on either flank it is unlikely that they could have made the necessary adjustments to regroup and stage a further attack. In addition, the principal Jacobite officers and chiefs led the assault. If they had fallen in a withering fire, their regiments would have been left without direction. Though the clansmen executed a nearly perfect Highland charge, their victory was not based on tactical acumen. Charles certainly had some idea of Cope's deficiencies before the battle, but he could not have been sure how the Highlanders would perform against a regular British army, and the cheap victory definitely left him over-confident and gave him unrealistic expectations of their capabilities . . .

The battle of Culloden (16 April 1746) not only ended the 'Forty-five, but also witnessed the ascendancy of modern conventional British tactics and weaponry. The road to Culloden had begun, from a tactical standpoint, a century earlier with the alliance of MacColla and Montrose and the subsequent introduction of the Highland charge into Scotland. Since the 1640s the clans had experienced a true military 'golden age'. They had proved themselves to be masters of the battlefield time and time again against enemy armies that, on paper at least, should have given them a good fight. On all but a few occasions the Highlanders swept away the opposition with relative ease. From Inverlochy to Prestonpans and Falkirk, the wild, unbridled clansmen had refused to change their tactics even though the British army slowly had evolved into a formidable opponent and by 1746 was no longer unfamiliar with or overawed by the

Highland charge. But even then, improvements in British tactics and weaponry alone could do no more than diminish some of the shock of the charge if it was carried out under irregular battlefield conditions. To blunt it effectively required something more – a conventional scenario in which the two armies faced one another across ground favorable to the employment of cavalry and artillery. At Culloden the Highlanders' very serious strategic mistake led them finally to give battle under circumstances that negated every tactical advantage they had ever enjoyed. Culloden, like Kinsale a century and a half earlier, pointed up the Gaels' most telling weakness – their inability to adapt to the dictates of modern tactical warfare.

When Prince Charles decided on the morning of 16 April to fight on Culloden Moor, the Jacobites could only await the enemy's approach and then array themselves in response to the Duke of Cumberland's alignment. At about 10:30 the British army marched into sight about two miles east of the Jacobite camp. There Cumberland formed his troops up in two lines, with most of his cavalry on the left, and then resumed his advance. At that point it was too late for the Jacobites to make any major adjustments in their position. They were so fatigued from their abortive night march that they were not able to move eastward to the area they had occupied the day before; therefore, they were forced to draw up a mile farther to the west on unfamiliar ground. On their right stood a stone enclosure which could have served to protect the clan regiments on that flank. To hold the enclosure, however, would have required a large number of Charles's men to be detached from the main body and arrayed in a defensive alignment – a move that would have weakened the Jacobites' offensive strength. Lord George Murray proposed that the enclosure's walls be pulled down. The officers debated that course of action but realized they were out of time. With the enemy only a mile away, the Jacobites attempted to put their regiments into some sort of fighting order before it was too late.[17]

Once Charles became aware of the size and disposition of Cumberland's army, he took measures to align his own forces as advantageously as possible. According to the muster rolls, the Jacobites had about 8,000 men on the day of the battle; however, of this total only about 5,000 to 6,000 were available to take the field. The army was drawn up in two lines, with the few cavalry troops in the rear on either flank and the dozen or so pieces of artillery in the center and on either end of the front line. The front line numbered about 3,000 to 3,500 clansmen, while the rear echelons contained some 1,500 to 2,000 foot and about 200 horse. As a precaution against a flank attack from the enclosure, Murray had moved a small body of foot and a few horse to cover the right side of the entire formation.[18]

Considering the short time they had to put their troops in line of battle, the

Jacobite officers did a commendable job; when the composition of the Jacobites' alignment is scrutinized, however, it is apparent that something was amiss: the MacDonalds did not hold their traditional post on the right wing of the front line. The slight put the proud men of Clan Donald into a sullen mood, but Murray refused to concede the honor that he claimed Montrose had bestowed on the Athollmen a century before. Now, instead of concentrating on the enemy, the clansmen quarrelled among themselves. Charles had no knowledge of the dispute,[19] but Murray, who had perpetuated the split between the MacDonalds and his Athollmen, must have remembered Clan Donald's occupation of the right wing at Prestonpans and Falkirk. He himself had commanded the MacDonalds on the right of the line at Falkirk! He apparently saw that the right wing at Culloden, which was flanked by the enclosure, would be the most critical area of the field, and he probably wanted to command there because he believed no one else could be trusted to oversee operations at such an important point.

While the Jacobite officers struggled to settle the argument concerning the post of honor, Cumberland's regiments moved steadily forward to take their final positions for the impending battle. The government army, between 7,000 and 8,000 strong, was divided into fifteen regiments of infantry and three regiments of dragoons. Cumberland drew up his army in two lines and, because of his numerical superiority, outflanked the Jacobites on both wings. He kept the lines about fifty yards apart. Then, if the Highlanders broke through the advance regiments, the second-line units would have ample time to respond to the attackers. Cumberland's intent was to provide a true defense in depth to stop the Highland charge.[20]

Cumberland's army advanced in line formation and looked as though it would reach the battlefield in good fighting order; however, when it came within 600 yards of the Jacobites' front line, the artillery train got stuck in a bog. Cumberland halted while his soldiers threw down their muskets and wrestled the cannon from the mud. This delay broke the rhythm of the advance and disordered the infantry regiments. More importantly, it rendered temporarily harmless the most potent weapons in Cumberland's army.[21] The Highlanders might have attacked the enemy before they regrouped and negated Cumberland's overbearing military strength in artillery and musket firepower, but they made no move. The ill feeling and confusion within their own ranks perhaps kept the Highlanders from attacking at this critical juncture. At any rate, the Jacobites lost an opportunity to take on the enemy on the flat moorland under the most advantageous circumstances.

Once the government army had extracted the artillery from the bog and the moment of danger had passed, Cumberland re-formed his lines and advanced to his final position about 400 yards from the Highlanders. The left flank was covered by two dragoon regiments and the eastern section of the park enclosure, while the right was protected by a small morass. Cumberland posted his sixteen pieces of artillery along the front line. As his officers checked their regiments to make certain they were battle-ready, Cumberland must have known that he had the Highlanders where he wanted them. The clansmen were not only out-numbered, outgunned, and outflanked on ground ideal for conventional tactics, but they would also have to fight with sleet and rain blowing hard into their faces. The Jacobites appeared to be disorganized and uncharacteristically hesitant to move forward from their posts. As Cumberland's gunners prepared their pieces and his infantry and cavalry steeled themselves for the coming battle, he could not have envisioned the effect that his preponderance of firepower would have on the previously almost invincible Highlanders.[22]

It was too late for Charles and his lieutenants to do anything but fight. Under less than ideal circumstances the Jacobites had done all that they could to prepare themselves tactically for the most important contest of their lives. The clansmen were to stage the traditional Highland charge. They had been instructed to stand their ground until ordered to attack; there was to be no repeat of the confusion that had cost them a complete victory at Falkirk. As they awaited the signal to advance, the Highlanders must have sensed that the battlefield scenario was unlike any that they had seen before. Cumberland's well-ordered infantry and dragoon regiments and his ominous artillery batteries stood poised across the moor. The relentless wind blew sleet and rain into the Jacobites' faces, and the clansmen waited to execute an attack that many of them perhaps feared would be their last.[23]

Charles's artillery began the battle at about one o'clock with a barrage that was intended to bring on an enemy attack. He apparently believed that Cumberland would launch an assault since the wind was at his back, but the Jacobites' inaccurate fire was answered only by a steady and effective report from the enemy artillery.[24] The solid shot from Cumberland's guns '. . . did great execution, making lanes through the Highland regiments'.[25] Cumberland hoped that the effect of his cannonade would force the High-landers to stage a disorganized attack where he could then stage a counter-attack. As he witnessed the devastation caused by the artillery, however, Cumberland realized that he need not move at all. If he could keep up the barrage until the clansmen were cut to pieces and fled from the field, he could win an inexpensive victory. In the first few minutes of the artillery duel the Highlanders indeed suffered tremendous casualties. Many threw themselves to the ground in desperation, all the while awaiting the signal that would allow them to rush ahead and silence their tormentors. It finally became clear to

Charles that the clan regiments must attack immediately or they would be destroyed where they stood.[26]

Before the charge could be staged, however, the Jacobites had to secure their right flank. When the cannonading began, Murray noticed a squadron of enemy cavalry and a large body of Campbells moving from the left wing down toward the river Nairn. Presently, these forces came upon Murray's flank. The Campbells threw down the park walls to allow Cumberland's dragoons passage to the rear of the Jacobite ranks. Murray had already taken precautions against just such a move, so he was able to frustrate the enemy's intentions.[27] However, the few minutes spent in further securing the right flank delayed Charles's attack and allowed Cumberland's artillery to continue its deadly fire. When Charles was assured that his flank had been covered adequately, he sent word for Murray to begin the attack. Murray, however, delayed, believing that the Highlanders '. . . were as yet at too great a distance, and that what vigour the men had left would be spent before they could reach the enemy'.[28] Murray apparently also feared that the Campbells lying behind the enclosure walls would put up a strong flanking fire and reasoned that it would be best to wait until Cumberland advanced past that point before risking an attack. Each minute that Murray waited, the clansmen grew more impatient. Old Cameron of Lochiel left his regiment and hurried to Murray to ascertain the reason for the delay. Murray despatched a runner to Charles, who again urged his officers to attack at once. Amid all the confusion and noise the Jacobites finally were set to launch what they hoped would be a coordinated charge. Murray received word that the attack should begin with an advance by the MacDonalds on the left (as they were the farthest regiments from the enemy), but he looked ahead and saw the MacIntosh regiment in the center of the line lurch forward. The weary Highlanders had taken all the punishment they could bear. Now they took matters into their own hands without waiting for orders.[29]

The attack by the Highlanders on the right wing ran into difficulty at once because of the close proximity of the enclosure. A strong body of Campbells was posted behind the walls, but just before the attack got underway, Cumberland moved the infantry regiment on his extreme left to a position at right angles to the rest of the front line.[61] From this position they fired volley after volley into the unprotected flank of the Highlanders as they advanced across the 400 yards of open terrain that separated them from Cumberland's front. To add to the clansmen's misery, the British artillerymen began loading their pieces with grapeshot, which had a deadly effect on their line. The enemy artillery fire forced the clan regiments in the center of the field to veer sharply to the right and push the already crowded Athollmen, Camerons, and Appin Stewarts nearer to the enclosure and to the enemy musket fire.[31] Murray, however, doggedly pressed home the charge, prompting an enemy officer to note that 'Nothing could be more desperate than their attack . . .'[32]

Despite the heavy and accurate musket and artillery fire from the enemy regiments on the Jacobite right, Murray's Highlanders rapidly closed in on Cumberland's front. As the clansmen drew nearer, however, the English quickened their fire to the point that it '. . . was so terrible, that it literally swept away, at once, whole ranks'.[33] Cumberland's infantry then began a slow and orderly advance to meet the Highlanders, who, seeing the enemy coming, fired their traditional volley, threw down their firearms, and drew their broadswords. Murray's troops had such a narrow track over which to carry out the Highland charge that the speed of their advance was affected. The clansmen were within thirty yards of the enemy infantry when they received a particularly heavy hail of musket, grape, and cannister. Those who escaped death or injury now would reach Cumberland's troops before they could reload; thereafter the outcome on the Jacobite right was determined by the sword and the bayonet.[34]

Jacobite chances of victory depended upon reaching Cumberland's front line with enough strength to employ the broadsword and target at close quarters. The clansmen were not the only ones to understand this: Cumberland and his officers did as well. Besides positioning the regiments for defense in depth, Cumberland had trained his troops in the proper manner of dealing with the Highland broadsword in hand-to-hand combat. British soldiers previously had been easily defeated by the Highlanders using blade weapons. If the Highland charge could not be broken, the enemy had virtually no chance of survival. Cumberland would take no such chances. He would do what he could to destroy the clan regiments before they reached his line; and, if the fighting became confined to close quarters, as it almost certainly would, Cumberland's men had been instructed not to take on the Highlander immediately before him, but to thrust with their bayonets toward the clansman to their right. The Highlanders were expert at absorbing a bayonet thrust with their targets on their left forearm, extending that arm to the side, and then slashing with the broadsword in their right hand at the unprotected British soldier. By focusing attention on the clansman on the right, Cumberland's infantrymen would render useless the target and wound the Highlander in his right side with the bayonet. While it is difficult to assess the frequency or effectiveness of this particular tactic at Culloden, the performance of the British infantry in standing firm before the Highland charge suggests that their level of training and discipline far surpassed that of their predecessors at Prestonpans and Falkirk.[35]

Murray intended to bring the battle to close quarters on the Jacobite right wing before Cumberland's firepower weakened the clan regiments to the point

where their shock tactics would lack impact. Murray knew that if the Highlanders did not overpower the enemy with their initial attack all would be lost.[36]
With the officers and clan chiefs at the head of the clans, it would be impossible
to rally the troops in the event of a repulse. Murray, then, led his men on
'. . . with all the bravery imaginable . . .',[37] fully aware of the consequences
should the Highland charge succeed or fail.

As Murray's regiments slammed into the left of Cumberland's front line, the
two infantry regiments posted there (Barrel's and Munro's) wavered. Here the
most furious action of the day occurred. When the clansmen had come within
ten yards of the line, they were met with grapeshot and cannister from a battery
of enemy artillery brought forward from the second line. The clansmen
nonetheless emerged from the smoke, reached the enemy's bayonets, and
literally flung themselves onto their adversaries. The best of Murray's clan
regiments, the Camerons, hit Barrel's formation on the extreme left so hard that
the British infantry gave way. For a moment it appeared that the charge had
enough impact to carry the day, but as the Camerons and the Athollmen waded
through the enemy front line, Cumberland's two infantry regiments on the left
of the second line advanced some fifty paces in good order, knelt, and poured an
accurate volley into the ranks of the Highlanders. The impetus of the charge was
broken and the battle on the Jacobite right wing turned into a life and death
struggle for the Highlanders. The few who remained standing pressed on
toward the second line, but soon found themselves surrounded by the remaining elements of the front-line regiments that had regrouped.[38]

The Highlanders probably would have destroyed the entire left wing of
Cumberland's army if he had not provided for defense in depth. Once the front
had been pierced, the clansmen could not turn their attention to Barrel's and
Munro's regiments because of the hail of fire they received from the second-line
units. At that moment Murray realized that he must overwhelm the second line
as well if he hoped to win the battle. But by the time he had reorganized his
troops, they were set upon by the four enemy infantry regiments to their front
and rear. The fighting between the lines was so fierce that a government witness
wrote that the battlefield was '. . . bespattered with blood and brains'.[39] The
Highlanders' attempt to hack their way through the two enemy lines, either
back toward their own comrades or forward through the British regiments, was
in vain. Still, many Highlanders fought on; others fell '. . . spitted with the
bayonet . . . [or] torn in pieces by the musquetry and grapeshot . . .'[40]
Cumberland's disciplined regiments and his defense in depth had broken the
Highland charge on the right side of the field where most of Charles's warriors
were engaged.[41]

While Murray's Highlanders on the right carried out their furious assault on the enemy infantry, the MacDonalds, Farquharsons, and the regiment of John Roy Stewart on the left hesitated until it was too late to execute an effective Highland charge. The left wing of Charles's army was farther from Cumberland's front than was the right, so that it should have advanced first. As it was, however, the order to attack did not reach the left wing until after the right had charged ahead; therefore, when Murray's clansmen made contact with the enemy, the MacDonalds and their comrades on the left were just beginning to advance. There was some speculation as to whether the MacDonalds had refused to attack because they had been denied their traditional post on the right wing. Such a contention is utterly ridiculous. Since the 1640s the MacDonalds (along with the Camerons) had been the real fighting strength of the various Highland armies. It is unlikely that they would have allowed an insult to their honor to keep them from doing their part in the battle. On the contrary, they perhaps would have fought even harder than usual to prove to Murray and the others that Clan Donald was indeed the elite element of the army. Their initial hesitation probably resulted from moving across the field to an unfamiliar position on the left end of the line.[42]

The delay of the Jacobite left proved fatal to their cause, and this was noted by one of Charles's officers, who wrote that '. . . the only chance the Prince had for a victory that day, was a general shock of the whole line at once . . .'[43] If the MacDonalds and the others on the left had begun the attack, or at least had advanced simultaneously with Murray's regiments, it is entirely possible that Cumberland's front line would have been unable to stand up to the impact of a coordinated Highland charge. Cumberland's left wing had been pierced; had his right been broken at about the same time, the second line might not have had nerve enough to advance and repulse the charging Highlanders. The MacDonalds' late start gave the enemy an opportunity to pick off the Jacobites piecemeal, and the sight of the clansmen being cut down near the enclosure no doubt bolstered the spirits and confidence of the government forces opposite the MacDonalds. Conversely, the same spectacle must have demoralized the Jacobite left wing and impressed upon them the futility of repeating the same scene on their end of the line.[44]

Though the MacDonalds and others on the left finally did advance, they did not carry out the Highland charge. Instead, they moved ahead slowly and cautiously, firing their muskets indiscriminately into the solid ranks of Cumberland's infantry regiments. When the MacDonalds were within fifty to a hundred yards of the enemy front, they halted, swords drawn, and cast nervous glances to their left where they expected to be outflanked and attacked momentarily by a regiment of enemy cavalry. From then until their final retreat from the moor, the MacDonalds vacillated between making an attempt to pierce the British formations and falling back to their starting point. While they wavered, the outcome of the battle was being decided on the right side of the moor. Seeing that decisive action was necessary to prevent a total rout, MacDonald of Keppoch, the chief of his clan, tried to persuade his men to make a mad dash toward the enemy and thus bring on a struggle at close quarters. He bravely advanced with sword and pistol but was immediately wounded by a musket ball. Against the advice of a subordinate, Keppoch pulled himself to his feet and pressed on. He moved ahead a few more yards, was hit again, and fell to his death. With Keppoch's fall the MacDonald regiments left the battlefield demoralized and heavy-hearted. Cumberland now saw both wings of Charles's army in flight and ordered his infantry to advance and take possession of Culloden Moor, while his cavalry rode down and butchered the fleeing Highlanders.[45]

Charles's strategy at Culloden had placed the clan regiments on an ill-chosen field that greatly favored conventional British tactics and weaponry, but the performance of the individual Highlanders might have made up for this disadvantage if they had been given a sound tactical plan and been effectively commanded during the battle. Despite the shortcomings on the part of the Jacobite leadership, the clan rank and file who engaged the enemy gave a good account of themselves. Of the 5,000 to 6,000 Jacobites on the field that day, only about 2,000 ever came to blows with the British.[46] Almost all of the 1,000 to 1,200 casualties that the Jacobites suffered came from the ranks of the front-line Highland troops. When the Jacobite casualty figure is compared to the total number of troops that Charles had on the field, the loss comes to between sixteen and twenty percent killed and wounded; however, if that figure is divided by the total number of Highlanders engaged, the casualty rate jumps dramatically to more than fifty percent.[47] If Charles had found a way to bring the full strength of the army to bear on Cumberland without delay, the Jacobites might still have suffered the same high casualty rate, but a swift and coordinated attack by the entire host of clan regiments would have inflicted much higher losses on the enemy than the 300 or so killed and wounded that the British actually suffered.[48]

The Jacobite front line regiments that engaged Cumberland were not able to carry out the Highland charge largely because Charles and his officers and chiefs delayed the attack and thus permitted their men to be subjected to Cumberland's artillery. During the terrible artillery barrage the Jacobite officers could not keep their undisciplined regiments in the proper alignment to execute the charge. An officer wrote that the Highlanders were eager '. . . to come up with an enemy that had so much the advantage of them at a distance . . .' and consequently they forged ahead '. . . with the utmost violence, but in such confusion, that they could make no use of their firearms'.[49] Therefore, not only was the general, coordinated advance absent from the Highlanders' attack, but also the musket volley that served to disorder the enemy formations. Also, according to one of Charles's lieutenants, many of the clansmen did not have their targets, which reduced their chances of defending themselves when and if they reached the British infantry.[50] The blame for all of these defects and shortcomings must not be placed on the Highlanders themselves, for they did all that Charles and his officers realistically could have expected them to do.

The Jacobite performance at Culloden was flawed because of a lack of battlefield direction from the commanders. Once the clan regiments were committed to an attack, they could not be called back or redirected. This course had been attempted half-heartedly at Falkirk and resulted in the escape of a significant part of the enemy's army. It is not known whether Charles had forbidden his officers and clan chiefs to issue any orders to their men after the charge had been launched, but it is likely that Charles cautioned them against attempts to issue complicated orders through the noise and confusion. It is known that all of the front-line regiments were led into battle by their officers or chiefs, most of whom fell during the initial stages of the conflicts.[51] It goes without saying that the practice of the captain's personally leading his troops into battle made it almost impossible for a Gaelic army to fight in a coordinated fashion after the attack was under way. If Charles had intended to fight a conventional battle on Culloden Moor, he would have been well advised to provide his officers and men with a well-defined tactical plan. Charles simply turned loose his seeming invincible Highlanders to win the day as they had done repeatedly over the previous century . . .

NOTES

1 General Henry Hawley's Description of Highland Warfare, 12 January 1746, quoted in David, Lord Elcho, *A Short History of the Affairs of Scotland in the Years 1744, 1745, 1746*, ed. Evan Charteris (Edinburgh: David Douglas, 1907; reprinted ed., Edinburgh: James Thin, 1973), p. 460.

2 By 1745 British infantrymen were armed almost exclusively with the new firelock or flintlock musket, the socket bayonet, and the steel ramrod. This new musket was a.85–inch caliber weapon about five feet long without bayonet and weighed about eleven pounds. A well-trained soldier could fire a round every thirty seconds at an effective range of sixty yards. Greater rapidity of fire was made possible by the use of pre-packaged paper cartridges that held both ball and powder. The socket bayonet could be attached without sacrificing firepower and provided the soldier with an effective weapon for close-quarter combat. Steel ramrods replaced the old wooden ones that were prone to snap. These improvements made the British infantryman a much more formidable opponent in 1745

than he had been in 1689 or 1715. Peter Young and J. P. Lawford, eds., *History of the British Army* (New York: G. P. Putnam's Sons, 1970; London: Barker, 1970), p. 29; J. W. Fortescue, *A History of the British Army*, 13 vols. (London: MacMillan and Company, 1910–1930), I: 586–87.

3 MacDonald of Lochgarry, 'Lochgarry's Narrative,' in *Itinerary of Prince Charles Edward Stuart from his landing in Scotland July 1745 to his departure in September 1746*, ed. W. B. Blaikie (Edinburgh: Scottish History Society, 1897), p. 115; Andrew Lumisden, 'A Short Account of the Battles of Preston, Falkirk, and Culloden,' in *Origins of the 'Forty-Five and other Papers Relating to that Rising*, ed W. B. Blaikie (Edinburgh: Scottish History Society, 1916). pp. 405–06; Elcho, *Affairs of Scotland, pp. 266–67.*

4 John Home, *The History of the Rebellion in the Year 1745* (London: T. Cadell, 1802), pp. 115–16; James Maxwell of Kirkconnell, *Narrative of Prince Charles of Wales' Expedition to Scotland in the Year 1745* (Edinburgh: The Maitland Club, 1841), pp. 39–40; Lumisden, 'Preston, Falkirk and Culloden,' pp. 406–07; Robert Chambers, *History of the Rebellion of 1745–1746*, (Edinburgh: W. R. Chambers, 1869), p. 125; Elcho, *Affairs of Scotland*, pp. 269–72; The Chevalier de Johnstone, *Memoirs of the Rebellion in 1745 and 1746*, 2nd edn. (London: Longman, Hurst, Rees, Orme and Brown, 1821), pp. 33–34; George Lockhart, *The Lockhart Papers Containing Memoirs and Commentaries upon the Affairs of Scotland from 1702 to 1715, by George Lockhart, Esq. of Carnwath, His Secret Correspondence with the Son of King James the Second from 1718 to 1728, and his other Political Writings; Also, Journals and Memoirs of the Young Pretender's Expedition in 1745, by Highland Officers in his Army*, 2 vols. (London: William Anderson, 1817), II: 489–90.

5 Home, *History of the Rebellion*, p. 104.

6 James Ray, *A Compleat History of the Rebellion from its first Rise in 1745, to its total Suppression at the glorious battle of Culloden, in April, 1746* (London: James Ray, 1754), p. 35; W. A. S. Hewins, ed., *The Whitefoord Papers Being the Correspondence and Other Manuscripts of Colonel Charles Whitefoord and Caleb Whitefoord from 1739 to 1810* (Oxford: The Clarendon Press, 1898) p. 91; Samuel Boyse, *An impartial history of the late rebellion in 1745. From authentic memoirs; particularly, the journal of a general officer, and other papers, yet unpublished. With the characters of the persons principally concerned. To which is prefixed, by way of introduction, a compendious account of the royal house of Stuart, from its original to the present time* (Reading: D. Henry, 1748), p. 80; Andrew Henderson, *The History of the Rebellion, MDCXLV and MDCCXLVI*, 5th edn. (London: A. Millar, 1735), p. 82; Maxwell, *Narrative*, p. 41; Johnstone, *Memoirs*, pp. 35, 39–40; Lumisden, 'Preston, Falkirk and Culloden,' pp. 40–08; Elcho, *Affairs of Scotland*, pp. 271–72; Lord George Murray, 'Marches of the Highland Army,' in *Jacobite Memoirs of the Rebellion of 1745*, ed. Robert Chambers (Edinburgh: William and Robert Chambers, 1834), p. 40.

7 General Wightman to Lord President Forbes, 26 September 1745, in *Culloden Papers: Comprising An Extensive and Interesting Correspondence from the Year 1625 to 1748*, ed. H. R. Duff (London: T. Cadell and W. Davies, 1815), pp. 224–25; Home, *History of the Rebellion*, pp. 119–20.

8 Ray, *Compleat History*, pp. 35–36; Hewins, ed., *Whitefoord Papers*, p. 91; Henderson, *History of the Rebellion*, pp. 82–83; Maxwell, *Narrative*, p. 41; Elcho, *Affairs of Scotland*, pp. 271–72; Lumisden, 'Preston, Falkirk, and Culloden,' pp. 407–08; Johnstone, *Memoirs*, pp. 39–40.

9 Home, *History of the Rebellion*, p. 120.

10 Maxwell, *Narrative*, p. 41; Lockhart, *Lockhart Papers*, II: 490; Lumisden, 'Preston, Falkirk, and Culloden,' pp. 407–08; Home, *History of the Rebellion*, pp. 119–20; Boyse, *An impartial history of the Rebellion*, pp. 80–81; Johnstone, *Memoirs*, p. 35; Elcho, *Affairs of Scotland*, pp. 271–272; Henderson, *History of the Rebellion*, pp. 82–83; Hewins, ed., *Whitefoord Papers*, p. 91; Ray, *Compleat History*, pp 35–36.

11 Boyse, *An impartial history of the rebellion*, pp. 80–81.

12 Rev. Dr Alexander Carlyle, *Autobiography of the Rev. Dr. Alexander Carlyle, Minister of Inveresk, containing Memorials of the Men and Events of his time*, 2 vols. (Edinburgh: William Blackwood and Sons, 1860), I: 142; Johnstone, *Memoirs*, pp. 36–38; Elcho, *Affairs of Scotland*, pp. 271–73; Hewins, ed, *The Whitefoord Papers*, p. 91; Lumisden, 'Preston, Falkirk, and Culloden,' pp. 407–08; Murray, 'Marches,' p. 40; Home, *History of the Rebellion*, pp. 119–20; Ray, *Compleat History*, pp. 35–36.

13 Elcho, *Affairs of Scotland*, p. 277.

14 Major-General Alexander B. Tulloch, *The '45 From the Raising of Prince Charlie's Standard at Glenfinnan to the Battle of Culloden*, 3rd ed. (Stirling: Eneas MacKay, 1908), p. 51; Lumisden, 'Preston, Falkirk, and Culloden,' pp. 408–09.

15 Johnstone, *Memoirs*, p. 38.

16 Lumisden, 'Preston, Falkirk, and Culloden,' p. 409; Johnstone, *Memoirs*, p. 38; Home, *History of the Rebellion*, pp. 120–21; Boyse, 'An impartial history of the rebellion, pp. 80–81; Murray, 'Marches,' p. 41; Ray, *Compleat History*, pp. 35–36; Elcho, *Affairs of Scotland*, pp. 274–76; Maxwell, *Narrative*, p. 42; Hewins, ed., *The Whitefoord Papers*, p. 59; Lady George Murray to Duke of Atholl, 22 September 1745, in *Jacobite Correspondence of the Atholl Family during the Rebellion, MDCCXLV-MDCCXLVI*, ed. J. H. Burton (Edinburgh: The Abbotsford Club, 1845), p. 22; Katherine Tomasson and Francis Buist, *Battles of the '45* (London: B. T. Batsford, 1962; reprint ed., London: Book Club Associates, 1978), pp. 67–69; List of Killed and Prisoners at the Battle of Prestonpans, 1745, Edinburgh, Edinburgh University Library, Laing MSS.

17 Colonel Ker of Gradyne, 'Colonel Ker of Gradyne's Account of Culloden,' in *Jacobite Memoirs*, ed. Chambers, pp. 140–41; Lockhart, *Lockhart Papers*, II: 520, 530–31; Elcho, *Affairs of Scotland*, pp. 431.

18 Elcho, *Affairs of Scotland*, pp. 423–24; Home, *History of the Rebellion*, p. 332; Gradyne, 'Account of Culloden,' pp. 140–41; Lockhart, *Lockhart Papers*, II: 520, 531–32.

19 Maxwell, *Narrative*, p. 149; Winifred Duke, *Lord George Murray and the Forty-Five* (Aberdeen: Milne and Hutchinson, 1927), p. 187.

20 Lockhart, *Lockhart Papers*, II: 520; Henderson, *History of the Rebellion*, p. 323; Sir Robert Strange, *Memoirs of Sir Robert Strange and Andrew Lumisden*, ed. James Dennistoun, 2 vols (London: Longman, Brown, Green, and Longmans, 1855), 1: 62–63; Elcho, *Affairs of Scotland*, pp. 424–25n.

21 Home, *History of the Rebellion*, p. 230; Chambers, *History of the Rebellion*, p. 289–90.

22 Henderson, *History of the Rebellion*, pp. 325–26; Tulloch, *The '45*, p. 41; Chambers, *History of the Rebellion*, pp. 287–90; Elcho, *Affairs of Scotland*, p. 432; Gradyne, 'Account of Culloden,' p. 141; Lockhart, *Lockhart Papers, II: 520.*

23 Elcho, *Affairs of Scotland*, pp. 431–32.

24 Boyse, *An impartial history of the rebellion*, p. 160; Lockhart, *Lockhart Papers*, II: 520; Strange, *Memoirs*, I: 62–63; Ray, *Compleat History*, pp. 334–35; Elcho, *Affairs of Scotland*, p. 431; Hewins, ed., *The Whitefoord Papers*, p. 78; Suppression of the Rebellion, 22 April 1746, Laing MSS, II. 502.

25 Home, *History of the Rebellion*, p. 230.

26 Elcho, *Affairs of Scotland*, pp. 431–32; Home, *History of the Rebellion*, pp. 230–31; Tulloch, *The '45*, p. 42; Lockhart, *Lockhart Papers*, II: 531.

27 Maxwell, *Narrative*, p. 151; Elcho, *Affairs of Scotland*, pp. 431–32; Sir James Fergusson, *Argyll in the Forty-Five* (London: Faber and Faber, 1951), p. 172.

28 Maxwell, *Narrative*, pp. 151–52.

29 Gradyne, 'Account of Culloden,' p. 142; Lockhart, *Lockhart Papers*, II: 521; Maxwell, *Narrative*, pp. 151–52; Home, *History of the Rebellion*, pp. 231–32.

30 Home, *History of the Rebellion*, pp. 230–32; Lockhart, *Lockhart Papers*, II: 531; Chambers, *History of the Rebellion*, p. 296.

31 Peter Anderson, *Culloden Moor and Story of the Battle, with description of the Stone Circles and Cairns at Clava* (Stirling: Eneas MacKay, 1920), p. 64; Elcho, *Affairs of Scotland*, p. 431; Hewins, ed., *The Whitefoord Papers*, p. 78; Maxwell, *Narrative*, p. 152; Lockhart, *Lockhart Papers*, II: 521; Home, *History of the Rebellion*, pp. 231–32.

32 Hewins, ed., *The Whitefoord Papers*, p. 78.

33 Johnstone, *Memoirs*, p. 189.

34 Henderson, *History of the Rebellion*, pp. 327–29; Chambers *History of the Rebellion*, p. 286; Elcho, *Affairs of Scotland*, pp. 432–33; General James Wolfe to Major Henry Delabene, 17 April 1746, quoted in J. T. Findlay, *Wolfe in Scotland in the '45 and from 1749 to 1753* (London: Longmans, Green, and Company, 1928), p. 106; Suppression of the Rebellion, 22 April 1746, Laing MSS, II. 502.

35 Chambers, *History of the Rebellion*, pp. 286–87; Anderson, *Culloden Moor*, p. 56.

36 James Maxwell of Kirkconnell wrote that the Highlanders were '. . . more impetuous on their first onset than any other troops . . .' Maxwell, *Narrative, p. 143.*

37 Lockhart, *Lockhart Papers*, II: 521.

38 Ray, *Compleat History*, pp. 338–39; Chambers, *History of the Rebellion*, pp. 296–97; Duke, *Murray and the Forty-Five*, p. 189; Home, *History of the Rebellion*, pp. 232–33; Lockhart, *Lockhart Papers*, II: 521, 531; Henderson, *History of the Rebellion*, pp. 327–32; Tulloch, *The '45*, p. 43; Suppression of the Rebellion, 22 April 1746, Laing MSS, II. 502; Gradyne, 'Account of Culloden,' p. 142; Lumisden, 'Preston, Falkirk, and Culloden,' pp. 418–19; Boyse, *An impartial history of the rebellion*, p. 159; Wolfe to Delabene, 17 April 1746, quoted in Findlay, *Wolfe in Scotland*, pp. 106–07.

39 Suppression of the Rebellion, 22 April 1746, Laing MSS, II. 502.

40 Hewins, ed., *The Whitefoord Papers*, p. 78.

41 Ray, *Compleat History*, pp. 338–39; Chambers, *History of the Rebellion*, pp. 296–297; Lockhart, *Lockhart Papers*, II: 521; Home, *History of the Rebellion*, pp. 232–33; Tulloch, *The '45*, p. 43; Boyse, *An impartial history of the rebellion*, p. 159; Henderson, *History of the Rebellion*, pp. 327–32; Edward Weston to Robert Trevor, 25 April 1746, quoted in Findlay, *Wolfe in Scotland* pp. 111–12; Elcho, *Affairs of Scotland*, pp. 432–33.

42 Chambers, *History of the Rebellion*, pp. 297–98; Duke, *Murray and the Forty-Five*, p. 189; Johnstone, *Memoirs*, p. 189–90; Maxwell, *Narrative*, pp. 152–53; Lockhart, *Lockhart Papers*, II: 510; John Roy Stewart, 'Another Song on Culloden Day,' in *Highland Songs of the Forty-Five*, ed. John Lorne Campbell (Edinburgh: John Grant, 1933; reprint ed. Edinburgh: The Scottish Gaelic Texts Society, 1984), pp. 179–80.

43 Maxwell, *Narrative*, p. 153.

44 Chambers, *History of the Rebellion*, pp. 297–98; Home, *History of the Rebellion*, pp. 233–34.

45 Ray, *Compleat History*, pp. 334–35; Hewins, ed., *The Whitefoord Papers*, pp. 78–79; Duke, *Murray and the Forty-Five*, p. 189; Henderson, *History of the Rebellion*, p. 326; Johnstone, *Memoirs*, p. 192; Home, *History of the Rebellion*, pp. 233, 235, 239; Lockhart, *Lockhart Papers*, II: 531; Maxwell, *Narrative*, pp. 152–153; Chambers, *History of the Rebellion*, pp. 297–98, 300–01.

46 Tulloch, *The '45*, p. 45.

47 John Prebble, *Culloden* (London: Martin Secker and Warburg, 1961; reprint ed., Harmondsworth: Penguin Books, 1967), p. 112; Peter Young and John Adair, *Hastings to Culloden* (London: G. Bell and Sons, 1964), p. 229; Hewins, ed., *The Whitefoord Papers*, pp. 78–79; Elcho, *Affairs of Scotland*, pp. 434–35.

48 Hewins, ed., *The Whitefoord Papers*, pp. 78–79; Elcho, *Affairs of Scotland*, pp. 434–35; Lumisden, 'Preston, Falkirk, and Culloden,' pp. 418–19; Tomasson and Buist., *Battles of the '45*, p. 178; Home, *History of the Rebellion*, p. 237; Chambers, *History of the Rebellion*, pp. 311–12.

49 Maxwell, *Narrative*, p. 152.

50 Elcho, *Affairs of Scotland*, pp. 433–34.

51 Home, *History of the Rebellion*, pp. 238–39.

The Disruption
and the Union

MRG Fry 1993, *in* SJ Brown and MRG Fry (eds), *Scotland in the Age of the Disruption*, Edinburgh (Edinburgh University Press), 31–43.

The Disruption seldom figures among the historical episodes fondly recalled by Scots of their recalcitrance towards the British state in which a unionist destiny has placed them. It was doubtless not bloody or proletarian enough for modern political taste. Yet it turned out to be one occasion when hundreds of thousands of ordinary men and women in Scotland challenged the authority set over them. And unlike other Scottish rebellions, it succeeded, up to a point. It created a Church, enjoying the allegiance of a large section of the people, which denied the assertion by the British state that religion, along with everything else, was subject to its absolute parliamentary sovereignty.

Yet the challenge also failed in a major respect. The Free Church was visibly not a continuation of the old Kirk, a Church of Scotland entire. It was rather a secession, much like previous secessions in nature if not in scale, and that soon came to be reflected in its outlook and actions. Some of its leaders had hoped that the whole Church, or nearly the whole Church, would break with the state, which might then be forced to deal with it on its own terms. But that did not happen. If the state was shocked at the outcome, it was not shaken into changing its ecclesiastical views or policies. And if it came to regret the Disruption, it finally felt able to put the affair down to the fissile nature of Presbyterianism, something to be counted therefore as of no wider importance.

All this helps to explain why the Disruption had so little obvious secular effect. It might have united Scotland in a political sense, against the Conservative Government in 1843, but the Whig opposition was wary of taking sides, and real religious partisans were found mostly on the radical fringe. The conflict could thus not readily take on a political colour. Scotland might have been united in a nationalist sense, against English abuses of the Treaty of Union. During the Ten Years' Struggle the spirits of Wallace and Bruce were from time to time evoked, and the cry of 'Scotland for ever!' had been heard.[1] But, because of the domestic disunity, sharp lines were hard to draw between Scottish and English interests, and the conflict could thus not readily take on a nationalist colour either. Instead, it would be turned inwards, into bitter sectarianism within Scotland, and cease to cloud relations with England.

Yet the Disruption did alter the constitutional relations of the two countries. In other words, it altered the Union and probably gave us a different Union from the one we would otherwise have had. It brought to an end a key element of the compact of 1707, designed to preserve a semi-independent Scotland. In effect, it devised a new compact, with terms that would allow Westminster to become the centre of Scottish affairs. Since the turn of the century Scotland had anyway been subjected to ever greater pressure, internal and external, to be assimilated into the rest of Britain under centralising government in London.[2] But the formal nature of the assimilation remained open till it was decided by events, of which the Disruption was the greatest.

The most independent part of that semi-independent Scotland had been the Kirk. It held a peculiar constitutional position, essentially an inheritance from the Middle Ages, from the prevalent theory then that there were present in every polity two kingdoms, two types of sovereignty, the temporal and the spiritual, neither superior to the other, each supreme in its own sphere. In England any such idea had been indignantly repudiated during the Reformation. But John Calvin and John Knox had in this respect innovated conservatively, and bequeathed to Scotland what they conceived as a purified version of the medieval system.

Scottish historical experience had given it a still more federal character. In the temporal kingdom, the Crown shared even the seat of justice with its greater subjects, the holders of heritable jurisdictions, and did so for forty years after the Union. It might be argued that this was just a case of deficiency, of failure by any central authority to establish its power, for which English intervention through a joint sovereignty was a remedy which could never have been supplied by the Scots alone. But when administration of the law was then concentrated in Edinburgh, for the rest of the eighteenth century the Court of Session acted much as the Supreme Court acts in the United States today. It was not itself much interfered with by the Parliament at Westminster, since the volume of statute law was small. Rather the court itself met changing conditions by reinterpreting, reshaping, reforming the law, and this in no authoritarian spirit but usually with reference to the parties concerned, a coherent framework for the whole being maintained by the institutional writers. The law thus developed in line with national traditions and kept Anglicising influences at bay.[3] That was in varying degrees true of the other secular institutions perpetually guaranteed by the Treaty of Union.

In the spiritual kingdom, too, Presbyterianism diffused authority in a hierarchy of courts. But the Kirk's real constitutional peculiarity lay in its enjoying a guarantee more special than the rest: the Act of Security antecedent to the Treaty, passed by both Parliaments as a precondition of the United Kingdom. If, in the novel environment of the Union, it was to rely on secular legislation, that did not amount to an admission by it of civil supremacy, any more than to an assertion of its supremacy over the state. The admission was rather by the state, at the moment of its birth, that it accepted the Kirk's view of its own situation. On this the Scots Parliament and the English Parliament alike seem to have believed themselves to be laying down a fundamental law with as much solemnity as they could muster.[4] A treaty resting on that basis could not be an expression of absolute parliamentary sovereignty. It stipulated that wherever else this sovereignty might extend, in Scotland the sphere of religion, morals and welfare was to be yielded to the Church. There was of course bound to be some argument about the delimitation of the two kingdoms. It arose, however, not out of assertions of supremacy by one over the other, rather out of the problems of co-ordinating them.

Semi-independence thus extended over most internal affairs. English indifference to them was natural, indeed welcome, for it handed to Scots the prime responsibility for maintaining the delicate balance by which the settlement of 1707, with its many silences and lacunae, was made to work. The achievement looked the more remarkable because the Union's formal guarantees started to break down almost at once, notably with the Patronage Act of 1712. Scots still argued they were real. Robert Dundas of Arniston, later Lord President of the Court of Session, called the articles of the Union 'unalterable' in the 1720s, even while recognising he could do little to prevent alteration of them. Thus the heritable jurisdictions were to be abolished in 1747, though in a reform this time at least negotiated and paid for. Arniston's son, Henry Dundas, sought as Scottish manager in 1785 the King's express permission to reorganise the Court of Session, a device which might have set a useful precedent but in fact did not. The government was still asserting in the 1820s that the royal burghs' constitutions rested on chartered rights placed by the Treaty beyond the reach even of the royal prerogative.[5] By now, however, the institutions preserved in 1707 were coming under severe strain, stretched on a Procrustes' bed of an emergent industrial society. Even so, many Scots refused to concede that this was reason enough to submit them to parliamentary regulation. The Claim of Right by the General Assembly in 1842 asserted that the Kirk's constitution was 'reserved from the cognizance and power of the federal legislature'[6] created by the Treaty.

The Scottish tradition behind the Claim of Right was logical and consistent in itself. To be sure, its stream had not run unsullied since 1707, and logical consistency had at several points yielded to political expediency. The result was not its negation, though, rather a state of affairs where nobody could be quite certain if it was constitutionally proper to regard the Treaty as just another Act of Parliament, amendable at will, or if there was indeed something federal about the British constitution, at least by virtue of its comprehending Scotland. Scots holding the latter view were by no means unusual or eccentric. It was understandable, as the crisis in the Kirk deepened, that men soon to be branded Presbyterian fanatics should hold it. That it should be held by a man like Sir George Clerk of Penicuik – a pillar of the old Scots Tory establishment, a friend of Sir Robert Peel since their days together at the university of Oxford and by 1843 a minister in his government – was not easy to explain except on grounds of his genuine conviction, formed by assessment of Scotland's true constitutional position. Sir George was no natural rebel and would remain loyal to his party and to the old Kirk. Yet in 1839 he had declared plainly to the House of Commons: 'The Church of Scotland does not refuse to render unto Caesar the things that are Caesar's, but it will not allow of an interference with its spiritual and ecclesiastical right.'[7] His view stood close to that of the high Presbyterians. He was in effect denying the doctrine of absolute parliamentary sovereignty.

Again, the Moderate party in the Kirk found itself often pilloried as servile to the state. Yet the Revd George Cook, its leader in 1843, explicitly held with the theory of the two kingdoms. He spoke of 'a great and sacred corporation, possessing ample power for its own internal government, but restrained from exercising that power to the prejudice of the community, or in excess of its appropriate jurisdiction.' His qualification here was that disputes between the two kingdoms had to be justiciable, and in practice could only be so in the courts: 'When any law is declared by the competent authorities to affect civil right, the Church cannot set aside such a law . . . So to do would be to declare ourselves superior to the law of the land'. Yet such cases would never have occurred but for the false pretensions which the church courts have put forward . . . The jurisdiction of the civil courts has been invoked to meet claims before unheard of, and when such claims are abandoned all such interference will immediately cease. [8]

There he put his finger on the weakness in the Evangelicals' argument, that they were bent on restoring to pristine purity an ecclesiastical constitution in reality profaned by time and events, rather than defending an actual constitution. But in any case the basic question was the same, whether Parliament had jurisdiction over everything.

It was a momentous question on which hinged the performance of a formidable task, and one might ask why Scots felt the exertion so compelling. An obvious reason was that the means of restoration were to hand, after an era in which they had been wanting, by virtue of an Evangelical majority appearing in the General Assembly from 1832. The deeper reason was that the Kirk felt called to apply these means to a much greater end than mere manipulation of majorities, to the redemption of the new society rising round it. The Revd Thomas Chalmers tried to put all this over to the English in the series of lectures he was invited to give in London in 1838. Already a renowned churchman, he was able to draw a distinguished audience including many peers of the realm and the young William Gladstone. It was also a conservative audience, expecting from Chalmers a conservative theory of Church and state. What it heard instead must have struck it as a bizarre brew indeed, composed of a medieval theory (that of the two kingdoms) and an almost radical concern for modern problems (those of the Industrial Revolution).

Chalmers meant to show how these disparate notions were connected by arguing for the continued necessity of an established religion, which had been coming under attack from sundry political and religious quarters. He argued that the best way for modern society to fulfil its Christian duty and show compassion for suffering humanity was through a national Church. It was not yet generally thought a duty of the state to offer such succour, and the dominant secular ideology of political economy decreed that it ought not to be. Nor could the voluntary exertions of competing sects ever suffice. Parliament had to choose one Church or another – and he naturally expected the choice to fall on a protestant one – as the vehicle for promoting the spiritual and material well-being of society as a whole. This need not be uncongenial to the secular ideology, at least if the Scottish model was adopted: 'There might be an entire dependence on the state in things temporal, without even the shadow of a dependence upon it in things ecclesiastical.' Such freedom was preferable from the Church's point of view too, just so that it could be at its most effective in its own kingdom.[9] The thesis was clearly meant to challenge Englishmen, and not only with the notion that Jesus Christ rather than Queen Victoria was head of the Church, but also with a call to reflection on how else the ends Chalmers set out were to be achieved, if not by the means he specified. Gladstone, at any rate, was so shocked that he went home and sat straight down to write his own tract on Church and state, vindicating the English view.[10]

This episode proved significant in showing that, if the Kirk was to be renewed, then the so far indifferent English would have to be enlightened about the Scottish doctrines concerning it.

'I have never yet met an Englishman who could understand, or even conceive, that idea of the relation between Church and State which was embedded in the constitution of Scotland. John Bull, with all his qualities, is a very parochial creature.'[11]

This was with justice written by the young Marquis of Lorne, a Whig nobleman who would exert himself in vain to avert the crisis. Indeed, whatever Englishmen may have thought of the empirical evidence for the theory of two kingdoms adduced from Scottish history, they certainly disliked the argument for it from first principles. What would really annoy Chalmers was their reluctance, after the Auchterarder case had turned the tensions into conflict, to accept that he had a valid point at all:

> 'The question of whether each court might not have its own proper and certain limits prescribed in the constitution, or whether these limits might not possibly, yea, have been actually transgressed – this is a question which they have not looked at, and will not listen to.'[12]

It was hardly the best start for a trial of whether the problem of relations between Church and state was to be resolved by an English or a Scottish interpretation of the constitution. If Englishmen had conceptual difficulty with any other model of established religion than the Anglican one, this was because England remained in essence an absolute monarchy. It had been so since 1534 when the Act of Supremacy swept away the two kingdoms and made the Crown the sole fount of sovereignty in a unitary state. While the Glorious Revolution of 1688 had rendered the monarchy less absolute, it did not create a constitution federal in the Scottish sense. It merely specified that the sovereignty should be exercised constitutionally, with the advice and consent of the Crown's subjects represented in Parliament. This expression of the doctrine of parliamentary sovereignty was thus beyond doubt recent. Contrary to English assumptions, it owed little to an ancient constitution, and embodied political notions quite the opposite of medieval ones.[13]

Still, just as the Scots tradition was somewhat sullied, so before 1843 the exercise of Westminster's sovereignty had never been absolute in practice, but modified through choice or necessity by English pragmatism. For more than a century England had, after all, put up with special arrangements in the same state for a Scotland of alien constitutional principles. Meanwhile, the muddy self-seeking of politics in the eighteenth century had left Parliament ill-equipped for the first serious test of its sovereignty, the revolt of America, a test that it miserably failed. As late as 1832 it was granting a Reform Act more in terror at the prospect of revolution than out of serene exercise of its sovereignty. In the aftermath, nobody pondered how Scotland might fit into what in effect was a new constitution, a question of no triviality when Scottish resistance to reform rested on defence of the settlement of 1707. The English jurist, William Blackstone, had already been wondering in the 1770s if its guarantees possessed any meaning under a doctrine of absolute parliamentary sovereignty. The answer was that they had meaning so long as they lasted in practice, and they did last till the 1830s and 1840s. The full doctrine would really come into its own only as a reinvention of the high Victorians, reflecting their confidence in their state.

The Disruption was formative in the re-invention and, if nothing else, answered the question of how Scotland would fit in with the new constitution, which was to say, by complete abandonment of her old one. Up to that point, though, English politicians did not impress with the quality of the ideas they advanced in answer to the points raised by the Scots. On the contrary, they were plainly unsure of the ground in their bemused search for a workable solution. Sir James Graham, Home Secretary in 1843, had earlier told Gladstone how he hoped the antagonists might 'without a sacrifice of principle, have devised some middle term'. In the same correspondence, Gladstone wrote to say that the difficulty was caused 'by principles really embodied in the presbyterian polity, though disclosed and valued in very various degrees at various periods . . . If the postulates of presbyterianism be granted the right is not all on our side.'[14]

While such men wanted to uphold Established religion, they had never reckoned with the Established religion now confronting them in Scotland. It insisted that for the sake of renewal the Kirk should be enabled to set priorities different from, even at odds with, secular ones, a far cry from the deference to the state of the old Moderate regime or of the Anglicans. Conservatives had already induced in themselves a thoroughgoing pessimism about the politics of the future. Now it seemed they must do the same with religion. Graham wrote in 1840: 'I am not blind to the political consequences of this struggle. I foresee its fatal effect on the peace of Scotland.' He forecast that religious radicals would come together with their political counterparts in a potentially revolutionary alliance: 'Scotland will be convulsed; and the issue no man can confidently predict.'[15]

Politicians regarding the times as so dangerous were unlikely to be absolutists. And it is not clear that their leader, Peel, asserted absolute parliamentary sovereignty in the modern form. He did distinguish between an Established and a Voluntary Church:

'If a Church chooses to have the advantage of an establishment and to hold those privileges which the law confers – that Church, whether it be the Church of Rome, or the Church of England, or the Presbyterian Church of Scotland, must conform to the law.'

Consequently it could not set the limits of its own jurisdiction, which might only be done in 'the tribunal appointed by Parliament, which is the House of Lords'.[16] His theory was, then, that while a Voluntary Church might possess the rights claimed by the Kirk, an Established Church surrendered them. If dissatisfied with the results, it could only break with the state.

Peel also conceded, though, that since the repeal of the Test and Corporation Acts the state had given up trying to control non-established religion. Yet today the argument would be that not even a voluntary association was independent in this sense, and that Parliament could without doubt enforce its will on an unestablished Church if it wanted. Peel's views show us a doctrine of parliamentary sovereignty still in process of reformulation, not yet absolute. Even in this tentative shape, however, it was thoroughly unpalatable to Chalmers and his colleagues. Peel was of course set on a quite different task from theirs, on restoring Conservatism in a polity which after 1832 was reshaped on Liberal lines. From the new dispensation he accepted severe restraint of the political kingdom. He stipulated only that it should be strong in what remained to it. Liberal philosophy, however, allowed no other kingdom to exist. Beyond its bounds lay a state of nature, subject only to the laws of political economy. So on Peel's interpretation, Churches could choose where to place themselves in relation to the bounds, but not beyond them have a second kingdom of their own.

Still, this was just a statement of position, and the attitudes of other English Tory leaders do not imply that they would have spurned a compromise if available. Prominent Scots laymen, in and outside the government, exerted themselves to propose one. Their efforts often owed a good deal to Lord Jeffrey's dissenting judgment on the Auchterarder case, which appealed for a view of statutes taking some to be less absolute in their applicability than others. Conflicts between Church and state, he pointed out, could not all be as exceptional and momentous as the one then before the Bench. There were many more minor examples of ecclesiastical actions with civil consequences, as when a man felt aggrieved at his exclusion from communion. How the courts might discriminate among such cases was by weighing the civil loss against the ecclesiastical loss. At Auchterarder, Lord Kinnoull's loss was less than the Kirk's loss. The decision ought therefore to be in the Kirk's favour. This was a pragmatic theory of law, on a constitutional view containing some element of the federal. 'In the theory of the constitution,' Jeffrey sensibly observed,

> 'the supreme courts of the country are held to be as nearly incapable of doing wrong as the sovereign herself, and, though known to be fallible in fact, are presumed to be so equally fallible as not to be trusted in the correction of each other's errors.'[17]

The Earl of Aberdeen afterwards busied himself in quest of a corresponding technical solution, but of greater interest were the exertions of Lorne, about to succeed as Duke of Argyll, who unusually for a nobleman was also an intellectual. He undertook to coax the English towards an appreciation of the depth of the issues at stake. In particular, he tried to develop Jeffrey's view with a definition of the term 'unconstitutional', in relation to statutes passed by Parliament, which was 'not altogether strange or unintelligible to the English ear'.[18] What he wanted was to establish a hierarchy of statutes, in which one like the Act of Security would rank high, 'laws which the united Parliament of Britain were in future to respect, and which, under the guardianship of a national treaty, and the Sovereign's oath, were in future to be preserved inviolate'. By contrast, a more ordinary statute would rank low, especially in the form it took by dint of the Auchterarder judgment as just a judicial interpretation. This would make explicit a 'distinction between a mere civil statute, and constitutional law and principle'. But the task, Lorne stressed, would have to be consciously undertaken by the government, and not left to haphazard collisions among the national institutions.[19]

The Kirk was not utterly uncompromising either. Though deadlock ended the talks in 1838 between Peel's predecessor as prime minister, Lord Melbourne, and Chalmers, the latter went into them ready to accept that Parliament might statutorily confirm the General Assembly's own legislation since 1832, a potential concession on the point of spiritual independence. Though it became ever harder for him to control the Evangelical hotheads, even in 1843, we should recall, the Moderate party remained powerful in the General Assembly. With the Middle Party, formed for the sole purpose of compromise, it had an actual majority. Right on the brink, with the different parties polarised, a way back could still be sought. The Kirk was not entirely friendless in Parliament, where seventy-six votes were cast in support of a committee on the Claim of Right. On the strength of that the Scottish philosopher James Ferrier told ministers they had been wrong to give up their livings unless ejected; they should have hung on till Church and state felt obliged to deliberate together, as they surely must do in the end.[20] English pragmatism might thus have been brought to concede that there was not just one kingdom in Scotland, but two. Nobody at any rate should have lost from sight the purpose of vindicating Scottish rights without disrupting the Kirk, or given up all appeal to Caesar to rely on religious enthusiasm for the upholding of spiritual independence, in what Ferrier's modern interpreter calls 'a spirit of pietistic laissez-faire'.[21] For in this case the seceders were by implication agreeing with Peel: that only one kingdom existed, with a state of nature beyond it.

Ferrier wrote with the benefit of hindsight, but it might be granted that till quite a late stage the situation ought to have been more fluid than it appeared. Opinions on each side were not yet cast in the inflexible mould of dogma, and genuine hope of compromise still existed. In fact, the stumbling block that rendered all such hope vain was already there. Strangely, it is to a Scottish, not an English source, to the Court of Session's judgement on Auchterarder, that we have to look for the introduction of a truly uncompromising spirit. It is there we must go – long before anyone at Westminster had intervened or been asked to – for the most comprehensive and contemptuous rejection of the Kirk's claims and for the idea that society must have a sovereign without equal or superior, so that, with the Act of 1712 before it, the Bench simply did not have the option of judging lay patronage to be a matter for the General Assembly.

Here is Lord Gillies, dealing with any reservations that may have arisen on grounds of the Act of Security:

> 'There can be no compact, properly speaking, between the legislature and any other body in the state. Parliament, the King and the three estates of the realm are omnipotent, and incapable of making a compact, because they cannot be bound by it.'

And here is Lord President Hope: 'The Parliament is temporal head of the Church, from whose acts and from whose acts alone, it exists as a national Church, and from which alone it derives all its powers.' There could be no conflict because 'an Establishment never can possess an independent jurisdiction which can give rise to a conflict . . . It is wholly a creature of statute.' Altogether, 'that our saviour is head of the Kirk of Scotland in any temporal or legislative or judicial sense is a position I can dignify by no other name than absurdity.'[22] It was only when thus prompted by the Bench in Edinburgh that the House of Lords, on the appeal, threw its weight behind this most extreme of the available positions. And it was the two Scots sitting in Westminster Hall, Lords Brougham and Campbell, who then went the furthest of all. Campbell could apparently see no real difference between the Kirk and the Church of England: 'While the appellants remain members of the Establishment, they are, in addition to their sacred character, public functionaries, appointed and paid by the state; and they must perform the duties which the law of the land imposes on them.'[23] So the Lords just confirmed what had been, from Scotland, unqualified assertions of parliamentary sovereignty and unqualified denials of the theory of the two kingdoms. How could this have happened? In 1785 the idea that the Court of Session itself might be reformed at Parliament's unfettered discretion had been repudiated. Did it now refuse to the other institutions the same safeguard? The integrity of Scottish society depended on balance and compromise among them. Was it the court's intention to destroy that?

Judges are no better than the times they live in, and perhaps the answer has to be sought from what had changed in Scotland at large to justify the application of, by Scottish standards, novel principles. The judiciary, for example, had indeed been several times reformed by statute meanwhile, so that the reservations of 1785 evidently no longer held. Moreover, the whole of the surviving political constitution had been toppled since 1832. Most Scots assumed that the old Scotland was simply passing away. They regretted it, but thought it unavoidable if they were to have their rightful place in the United Kingdom and the empire. And the process seemed irrevocably bound up with the transfer of powers to the imperial Parliament and government. In the spirit of the age there was something anomalous about the Kirk alone seeking to stand out against the state.

Testimony to this effect came from the Lord President's son, John Hope, who played a yet bigger role in the Disruption. The Tories' last Solicitor General before 1832, then Dean of the Faculty of Advocates, he did much to bring the Auchterarder case to court and was an adviser of notable intransigence to Sir Robert Peel from 1841. Consciousness of a new, British context to events is often evident in his views, as here on the Veto Act: 'The changes contemplated cannot be confined to Scotland. The consideration of these cannot be regarded merely as a Scotch question even if their importance to society in Scotland did not demand the most anxious consideration.' He deplored nationalistic attempts to draw a comparison between Presbyterian tradition and what was now at stake, for in these days such exertions in the name of Scotland could be 'alarming sources of disturbance and confusion to the social system'.[24]

It would be easy to dismiss Hope as extreme and biased, except that key points of his were echoed by others of different convictions. Henry Cockburn stood at the opposite end of the political spectrum, yet he also appreciated what difference a British perspective might make:

'There never was such an instance of the habitual ignorance and indifference of Government (all governments) to Scotch affairs as in this of patronage . . . Yet because it was as yet merely Scotch, and conducted without turbulent agitation, it was impossible to get any line whatever adopted by ministers'.[25]

When a Scotch affair at length became more than Scotch and a line had to be adopted, ministers were happy to grasp at the ready-packaged solution from the Scotch Court of Session, a doctrine of absolute parliamentary sovereignty. The judges may have thought they had defined the law as it ever was. They were in truth giving expression to a great change that had come over Scotland, an acceptance that it was the British context, not the native tradition, that mattered most.

The judgement certainly ruled out any chance of finding a modern form of semi-independence, of renewing the concepts of 1707, even if obligations towards Scotland were thus disregarded. Everything was declared simply subordinate to Parliament, without further qualification. It was incompetent of the highest courts of the land to declare that Parliament had erred, let alone to correct the error, or consider the strength of another body's case. There could be no superior theory of law, because the law was simply what had been passed by Parliament. To have ruled in any other sense would, of course, have defined parliamentary sovereignty as non-absolute, and have granted that Church and state might exercise some form of co-ordinate jurisdiction.

From this point, the British constitution must have started to elaborate a new theory of itself. Peel's observations even indicate that there might have been scope to do so. But at the decisive moment, it was the Scots judges who took a view allowing no ambiguity. Surely this was an outcome more absolutist than the circumstances called for, or politicians in London could ever have intended or has been altogether good for Scotland and the Union since.

The Kirk could not believe it anyway and reacted in a manner eventually matching the judges' extremism, with a conscious polarisation that made the Disruption unavoidable. In defence of it, one should recall how fantastic the idea must have seemed that the Church of Scotland was a mere creature of Parliament, enjoying rights only at its pleasure – the Church of Scotland of all Churches, whose entire history and tradition spoke of its independence, its capacity to stand alone if need be, whatever the world did to it! Even if by the middle of the nineteenth century it was hard-pressed to maintain its kingdom, still it felt that its wholeness in industrial society could somehow be restored: *nec tamen consumebatur*. Independence, wholeness – it was impossible with these purposes for the Kirk to perceive in society anything other than a federal structure, where sovereignty could not be attributed exclusively to one part.

Over that perception the unitary state did formally prevail, in what can, however, hardly be called a victory. Graham said just before the Disruption: 'These pretensions of the Church of Scotland as they now stand . . . appear to me to rest on expectations and views so unreasonable, that the sooner they are extinguished the better.'[26] This was the same man who later admitted that he 'never would cease to regard it with the deepest regret and sorrow, as the saddest event in his life, that he should never have had any hand in that most fatal act.'[27]

The state invited moral defeat by its very insistence that there was no superior theory of law, so that law must then have the primacy over conscience. This, a free people could not be made to accept. Consequently, the state had just to look on while great numbers walked out of the national Church, the established position of which it was in principle committed to defend. As a result, there existed no real national Church in Scotland. This was undesirable given the problems of the age, quite apart from the fact that it smashed the compact of 1707.

Yet it did not – as it might have done and as some hoped it would – bring a rapid, let alone ultimate, assimilation of Scotland into England. People saw clearly enough that if Scots had been able in any degree to decide for themselves, the Disruption could never have happened. There might have been a clash between Kirk and courts, but Scottish statesmanship and Scottish public opinion would have ensured a better outcome. For reasons already explained, this realisation generated no strong nationalist reaction. But still in major respects it did make the Scots more Scottish, more rigid, vehement and intransigent, more concerned with the logic of a position than with its practical effects, though also more respectful of democracy than of hierarchy, above all more resolved to be themselves than to truckle. This was no doubt necessary in a Union which for the sake of its material benefits none wanted broken, but which had changed all the same against the Scots' will. It would in future assert over historical or particular interests new interests of its own, and do so by means of a new doctrine of absolute parliamentary sovereignty. This, like so much else in Victorian Britain, seems ironically to have been in its highest form an invention of Scotsmen, of the judges who pressed home a logical rigour for which Englishmen left to themselves might have had little taste. Whether the resulting Union is better than what a different course could have produced is not for this chapter to answer: enough to observe that the tension within it of Scottish particularism and absolute sovereignty remains unresolved.

The dilemmas of the future were already visible on 18 May 1843. The Revd Thomas Brown tells in the *Annals of the Disruption* how the Revd Walter Wood of Elie had visited Langholm in January of that year, as a member of one among a number of missions sent out by the General Assembly on tours round Scotland to prepare the faithful for an event which all now knew to be inevitable. He addressed a meeting, and complained to it that at Westminster the voice of the Scottish members had been overborne by the English majority:

'I said, on the spur of the moment, that such injustice was enough to justify Scotland in demanding the repeal of the Union. With that, to my surprise, and somewhat to my consternation, the meeting rose as one man, waving hats and handkerchiefs and cheering again and again. No doubt the enthusiastic feelings of the people assisted our object, but I took care not to speak of repeal of the Union at our subsequent meetings.'[28]

NOTES

1 From the Revd Thomas Guthrie, quoted in Anon., *Practical Remarks on the Scotch Church Question* (London, 1841), p. 56.

2 M. R. G. Fry: *The Dundas Despotism* (Edinburgh, 1992), chs. ix, x.

3 Lord Cooper of Culross, 'The Central Courts after 1532', in Stair Society, *An Introduction to Scottish Legal History* (Edinburgh, 1958), p. 44; T. B. Smith: *British Justice, the Scottish contribution* (London, 1961), pp. 61, 68.

4 H. J. Laski: *Studies in the Problem of Sovereignty* (New Haven and London, 1917), p. 28.

5 Fry, *The Dundas Despotism*, pp. 7–8, 142–3, 334.

6 Quoted in full in R. Buchanan: *The Ten Years' Conflict* 2 vols (Glasgow, 1849), vol. ii, pp. 633–47.

7 Hansard, 3rd ser, vol. xxxv, pp. 575–81.

8 Buchanan, *The Ten Years' Conflict*, vol i, p. 481 and vol. ii, p. 21; R. W. Vaudry, 'The Constitutional Party in the Church of Scotland', *Scottish Historical Review*, lxii (1983), 42–3.

9 T. Chalmers, 'Lectures on the Establishment and Extension of National Churches', *The Collected Works of Thomas Chalmers*, 25 vols. (Glasgow 1835–42), vol. xvii, pp. 264–5.

10 W. E. Gladstone, *The State in its Relations with the Church* (London, 1838).

11 Duke of Argyll, *Autobiography and Memoirs* (London, 1906), p. 174.

12 Buchanan, *The Ten Years' Conflict*, vol. ii, p. 364.

13 C. McIlwain: *The High Court of Parliament and its Supremacy* (New Haven, 1910).

14 C. S. Parker: *Life and Letters of Sir James Graham 1792–1861* (London, 1907), vol. i, pp. 374–5.

15 *Ibid.*, p. 321.

16 Hansard, 3rd series, vol. lxvii, p. 502.

17 C. Robertson (ed.), *Report of the Auchterarder Case* (Edinburgh, 1838), pp. 361–96; G.W.T. Omond: *The Lord Advocates of Scotland*, 2nd ser. (Edinburgh, 1914), p. 58.

18 Marquis of Lorne: *A Letter to the Reverend Thomas Chalmers* (Edinburgh, 1842) p. 18.

19 Duke of Argyll: *Letter to the Peers* (Edinburgh, 1842), p. 79.

20 J. F. Ferrier: *Observations on Church and State* (Edinburgh and London, 1848), p. 20; J. Bulloch & A.L. Drummond: *The Scottish Church 1688–1843* (Edinburgh, 1973), p. 222.

21 G. E. Davie: *The Democratic Intellect* (Edinburgh, 1961), p. 306.

22 Robertson, *Report*, pp. 1–20, 21–52.

23 Quoted in T. Brown (ed.): *Annals of the Disruption* (Edinburgh, 1893), pp. 27–8.

24 J. Hope: *A Letter to the Lord Chancellor on the Claims of the Church of Scotland* (Edinburgh, 1838), pp. 7, 11.

25 Quoted in I. Maciver, 'Cockburn and the Church', in A. Bell (ed.), *Lord Cockburn: a Bicentenary Commemoration* (Edinburgh, 1979), p. 94.
26 Hansard, 3rd series, vol. lxvii, p. 502.
27 Parker, *Life and Letters*, p. 395.
28 Brown, *Annals of the Disruption*, p. 69.

Born again at Cambuslang: New evidence on popular religion and literacy in eighteenth-century Scotland

TC Smout 1982 in *Past and Present* 97, 114–127.

> I had attended frequently at Camuslang in March and April, and was made to see I had need of convictions and converting grace, and that I must be born again.
>
> – J. Hepburn, 'a young man aged about 21'[1]

Cambuslang lies five miles south-east of the modern centre of Glasgow, embedded now in a great city, but in the 1740s still a typical north Lanarkshire rural parish. It was untouched, as yet, by the great agrarian and industrial changes associated with the modernization of Scotland. Its farms lay runrig and unenclosed, oats was 'almost the only grain sown', two-thirds of the land was possessed by the duke of Hamilton, and most of the tenants were small men. Weaving of 'holland, or fine linen' had just begun and 'gave employment to a few looms'. There were old-established small-scale coal-mines and a few traditional crafts like masons and wrights.[2] It differed in no obvious respect from its neighbours.

Here, however, in the first half of 1742, there occurred a religious revival that was to make its name known not only throughout Scotland but in England, America and the Low Countries as well. In January the minister, William M'Culloch, responded to a petition signed by 90 heads of families to give a weekly lecture on spiritual regeneration. Dramatic conversions occurred from the middle of February, and for six months Cambuslang became the focus of great spiritual excitement, reaching its climax at the two outdoor communions on 11th July and 15th August, when tens of thousands from miles around gathered to hear the famous English evangelist George Whitefield address the multitude. Many publicly declared themselves moved by the spirit of the Lord:

some went into a trance-like state of ecstasy. To its friends it was a manifestation of the Holy Ghost: to its enemies it was a dreadful example of religious hysteria. Its effect on the Church of Scotland was profound and long-lasting, not least in stiffening the resolve of many leading church politicians to do all in their power to prevent this sort of thing from happening again.[3]

The most recent historian of the Cambuslang revival, Arthur Fawcett, has given an admirable account of what happened.[4] He has demonstrated not only its links with the Methodist revival in England and the Great Awakening in America, but also its deep Scottish roots both in older popular Presbyterianism and in newer local pietistic enthusiasms for praying societies. Fawcett has also drawn attention to a remarkable source, two bound manuscript volumes now in New College Library, Edinburgh, that contain a record of the spiritual experiences of 110 individuals as taken down by the minister. It is unclear why he chose these individuals rather than others, though only the first volume appears to contain his final selection for publication. It is quite likely that there were also other papers, or even volumes, containing other cases, now missing.[5] But M'Culloch explained how his subjects: 'gave me very particular accounts of God's dealings with their souls, in their first awakenings and outgates, with their following soul-exercises . . . distresses, deliverances and comforts . . . I set down very many of these from their own mouths, always in their own sense and very much also in their own words'.[6] In fact he seems to have given them structured interviews, asked them a series of questions, and scrupulously recorded what followed.[7] He then submitted the first volume (but not the second) to other well-known ministers of the evangelical party to make marginal comments with a view to publishing, ultimately, an edifying book on the born-again experience.[8] It was, in fact, the first Scottish oral history project.

The interest to the general social historian is twofold: first, the 110 interviews give an excellent impression of who was attracted by a religious revival of this sort and, secondly, because the minister evidently enquired systematically about it, they throw a unique light on the nature and meaning of popular literacy in Scotland.

Who were attracted to the Cambuslang revival? Of 110 cases reported, 75 were women: they were rather oddly divided between the two volumes, with 25 (out of a total of 46 accounts) in the first volume, and 50 (out of 64) in the second – as the first volume is the only one annotated by the other ministers with a view to publication, it must be regarded as M'Culloch's choice of converts to bring before the public eye. The smaller proportion of women probably reflects a subconscious element of male chauvinism entirely characteristic of his age and creed, and one would be safe in the assumption that at least two-thirds of the 'converts' were women, always supposing that his 110 cases are a fair sample of the total converted. The average age was three years younger for women than for men, but the more significant difference was the greater attraction to teenage girls than to boys, and a greater attraction again for women in the thirties age-group. (See Table 1.)

TABLE 1: AGE OF 'CONVERTS' AT THE CAMBUSLANG REVIVAL 1742*

	WOMEN	MEN
13–19	19	4
20–29	36	20
30–39	12	3
40–49	3	6
50–59	0	1
60–69	1	0
not known	4	1
mean age	24.9	27.9

* Source: 'Examination of Persons under Scriptural Concern at Cambuslang during the Revival in 1741–42 by the Revd. William Macculloch, Minister of Cambuslang, with Marginal Notes by Dr. Webster and Other Ministers': New College Lib., Edinburgh, MS. W. 13.b.2/2.

The strength of the appeal to unmarried women (about half the total cohort of 110 cases) is also apparent. (See Table 2.) The mean age of the unmarried women was 21.8, of the married 33.5, and of the widowed 40.5.

TABLE 2: MARITAL STATUS OF 'CONVERTS' AT THE CAMBUSLANG REVIVAL 1742*

	WOMEN	MEN
unmarried	56	4
married	14	4
widowed	4	0
not known	1	27

* Source: As given in Table 1.

The second volume alone contains systematic evidence on occupations. The information on the men relates to their own jobs, that on women to their husbands' (if they are married) or fathers' (if they are not). Of 36 unmarried women, 10 were the daughters of tenants (presumably these were mostly quite small farmers or peasants in this part of Scotland before the agricultural revolution). Another 16 were the daughters of low-status craftsmen (4 shoe-makers, 3 weavers, 2 smiths and one each of fuller, wright, shipwright, cooper, tailor and maltman). Five were the daughters of 'unskilled' fathers (collier, 2 gardeners, sailor and workman). Only 4 were what would now be called 'middle-class', from mercantile or professional backgrounds (merchant, 'wool merchant', schoolmaster, writer). One was a 'packman' of mercantile background but very low status. The overwhelming majority of these unmarried girls were living-in servants at the time of the revival, as is clear from incidental remarks in the autobiographical details of many of the accounts: we know one was a seamstress.

Of 8 married women, 2 were wives of tenants, one of a shoemaker, one of a weaver, one of a labourer, one of a soldier, one of a carter; one was the wife of a baillie of Hamilton. Of 16 men, 2 were tenants, 8 were craftsmen (4 weavers, 3 shoemakers, a waulker and a mason), one was a collier, one a gardener, one a servant; 2 had high status, a baillie of Hamilton and a 'serjent'.

Thus 40 of the accounts, two-thirds of all those where the occupation was specified, came from the background of small tenants or generally low-status craftsmen, 13 from still more humble backgrounds, and 7 at most, one in nine, from anything that could be regarded as 'middle-class'.

A profound dislike of the propertied for the revival was indeed obvious from other sources. Sir John Clerk of Penicuik wrote to his brother-in-law blaming George Whitefield for inducing men to idleness by 'a gading after conventicles', and estimating the national loss of one day's work in the week at 'eight million of sixpences'.[9] The duke of Hamilton, who held the patronage of Cambuslang and had resisted M'Culloch's call initially, took care after his death to insert in his place a moderate who would pour cold water on excessive popular zeal – even though he could only do this with great difficulty and after three years' delay due to local opposition.[10] Even at the time some local heritors bitterly opposed what was happening, as the following account from the 'Examination' makes clear. The account is by John Napier, aged twenty-one:

Next day, the Gentle Man in whose ground I lived sent his Officer for me and another lad. And when we came before him he discharged us to go to Cambuslang, threatning that if we did he would arreist our crop and turn us out of his land: for that he was informed that when we came home we could not work any next day, an he particularly abused a certain minister George Whitefield with his tongue, calling him a Mountebank and a Damn'd Rascal, who was putting all the people mad: that he put on his black gown to fright people out of their wits, and that when he put on his black gown and black cap at night he frighted them terribly. He added, that if we could read our catechism we needed no more religion: and that if we would stay more at home at our work and go less to Cambuslang to hear that Damn'd Rascal and get our brains crack'd we might pay our rent better and work better.[11]

The two young men defied their landlord, insisted on going again to the preaching, and were duly evicted.

This is dislike of popular religion carried to the level of persecution, but sentiments against it are echoed by many in the ruling classes through the century – *vide* Adam Smith, when he speaks of 'the delusions of enthusiasm and superstition, which, among ignorant nations, frequently occasion the most dreadful disorders'.[12] Excessive religious zeal was widely seen as a social danger in Scotland for the excellent reason that it had, in the 1640s, undoubtedly occasioned 'the most dreadful disorders', and in the next half-century had clearly been the main threat to stability. Clerk did not use the term 'conventicle' accidentally. Another girl who went to Cambuslang was rebuked by her employer, 'saying we were a party of Mad people that went there; and we would never rest till we would get a parcel of Dragoons to scatter us', a clear reference to Covenanting history.[13] When the Lords of Session were hearing a lawsuit relating to the disposal of the poor's money at Cambuslang in 1752 they wished to add a rider severely condemning the practice of preaching in the fields, and had to be reminded by one of their number that such would be *ultra vires*.[14] Active popular participation in religion was thus clearly not seen as socially desirable, but as socially dangerous. Those who attended were often in real danger of falling foul of their superiors.

There is also information on the geographical location or origins of 57 individuals, 20 of whom were either married women or men, and 37 of whom were unmarried women. The first group should give an impression of where the participants in the Cambuslang revival were living at the time. Seventeen of the individuals lived within seven miles of Cambuslang (though only 2 within the parish); the mean distance was five miles. Of the remainder, one lived in Paisley (ten miles), one in Kilmarnock (twenty miles) and one in Girvan (forty-five miles). It is likely that the source is biased in favour of recording those who lived fairly near at hand, since the record is based on subsequent examination of the people concerned by the minister, who was unlikely to be able to interview many who lived at a distance and made, say, a single memorable visit to Cambuslang. Certainly some were prepared regularly to go long distances to other communion services, or to hear preachers of their choice: a twenty-year-old servant girl spoke of going to the Seceders' services – 'sometimes seven miles, and sometimes to Stirling which was twelve miles from the place where I lived to hear them'.[15]

In the case of the 37 unmarried women the information tells not where they were living, but where their fathers lived, which may not necessarily be the same thing as most in this group were servants living away from home. Nevertheless, 30 lived within seven miles of Cambuslang (though only one in the parish); the mean distance was again about five miles. The others may possibly have been in-migrants: 3 came from Dalserf, Campsie and Shotts, in the ten- to twelve-mile radius, 3 from Airth, Greenock and Roseneath, in the twenty- to thirty-mile radius, and 2 beyond – one from Girvan and one from Edinburgh whom we know, however, to have been living with her widowed mother at Lesmahago fifteen miles away.

Of previous religious experience the 'examination' made careful enquiry. It emerges as crystal-clear that the 'converts' were anything but infidels plucked from the burning. Each, without exception, was in the habit of attending religious ordinances with some regularity before the revival, though many had done so in a half-hearted manner: 'I always used to go to the Kirk when I could get it done; but I went only to see and be seen', was one typical comment. Another girl admitted to spending the sabbath forenoon dressing rather than preparing herself by prayer before church unless 'some aufull despencation had not mov'd me to it such as thunder or ye like'. A third, only thirteen years of age, confessed that to her a short sermon had been 'a good preaching because I soon got away; but a long one was always a bad one'. In 70 cases they had been taught to pray 'in secret' as young children; only in 13 cases is it known they had not been so instructed, though several admitted having allowed the practice to lapse when they left home. On the other hand, many were avowedly already seeking after a more rewarding religious life at the time of the revival, perhaps by joining a local prayer society, perhaps by attending other parish communion services in the area after the Scottish fashion (for example at Glasgow, Calder and Paisley), perhaps, like one girl, by reading religious books and hearing sermons: 'I thought I got no benefit at all by them, but rather turned still more dead stupid and hard hearted: yet I thought I would still wait on and ly at the pool side of ordinances and possibly I might sometime or other meet with a cast of grace'.[16]

There is a single moving example of a man assailed by religious doubt, though he had resolved them long before the revival. He was David Logan, a collier and old soldier living in Cambuslang, aged fifty-one. He explained how:

When I was about 22 years of age, I fell under dreadful unbelieving apprehension (whether proceeding from Satan or my own heart I know not) relating to the Bible: I heard that the Turks had their Alcoran, the Papists their Traditions, and all sects pretended to what they received for their rule to be from God, and yet all was but from man; and I thought, so might the

Bible which I and others lived among, be, for anything I knew to the contrary. I was much perplex'd about this matter, but kept all within my self, fearing that if I should mention such thoughts to any I would be taken for an Atheist, and I did not know but the Laws of man might take hold of me and put me to Death.[17]

His apprehension was understandable: as recently as 1696 an Edinburgh student, Thomas Aikenhead, had been executed for allegedly denying the divinity of Christ.

M'Culloch was also concerned to ask what special 'sins before the world' his examinees thought they had been guilty of in their unregenerate days. Many could think of none, though they might still be oppressed with a general sense of their sinfulness 'as if it had been a sclate house, and my sins were represented to me as the sclates on the house, set in ranks, and one rank rising higher than another'[18]. When they could be specific, the women most often admitted to fondness for idle or frivolous company, with an occasional swearer, liar or sabbath-breaker. The men often admitted to drinking to excess, swearing, sabbath-breaking, playing at cards and – in one case – breaking into orchards as a boy. One tenant had been a positive alcoholic: he had once met the Devil in his stable 'like a long black man before me', and heard him 'whisper to me, What are thou going to do? Is there such as thing as a God?' He took to drinking heavily: 'And once, I remember, I wrought each lauful day of the week, and drank every night of that week out and out without sleeping at all till Saturday night'.[19] Very few of either sex (under half a dozen) admitted to fornication, though one was the mother of an illegitimate child.

In regarding the evidence on literacy it is important to consider to what degree these 110 individuals can be taken as a representative sample of the ordinary Scot, at least of those who lived in the north Lanarkshire area. There is no obvious bias in terms of status, though the least skilled may be under-represented in comparison to the distribution of the population as a whole. It is hard to be sure: certainly one would not expect many labourers in the context of the small family farms of the district. There may well be a bias in favour of the most earnest in the community, and those who were earnest in their religious habits may perhaps have been earnest readers and writers as well. Again, it is hard to be sure: we simply do not know, for example, what proportion of Scots normally went to the kirk on Sundays in the first half of the eighteenth century, let alone what proportion were set to private prayer as children, or got drunk, or broke into orchards, or had pre-nuptial sexual intercourse. The overall tone of the examination, however, gives the strong impression that these were not markedly abnormal people. It would certainly be dangerous to assume that because they were religious converts they had nothing in common, in other respects, with those around them.

It is clear from the 'examination' that McCulloch began his interviews by asking one or more questions about education, probably whether his subjects had been taught to read and write, and whether they had learned and retained the catechism, though the exact form in which the queries were put is uncertain. Unfortunately he did not always give an indication of the replies: there are 14 cases in volume 1 and 6 cases in volume II where the answer is not immediately apparent from prefacing notes, though by searching in the text it is possible to establish certain facts about at least reading ability in 109 cases out of the 110 under review. A second drawback is that even when the answers are given, they are not always provided in exactly the same form, so that one cannot be absolutely sure that the person in question was in fact unable to write – though it is unlikely that there would be many omissions in the 90 cases where M'Culloch has prefaced his account with a specific note on literary skills.

As Table 3 shows, an interesting and striking pattern emerges from counting the number of cases where reading and writing are recorded. From this, certain conclusions can be drawn. First, all the women and men could read. Secondly, probably over a third but perhaps not as many as three-quarters of the men could write. Thirdly, there is no evidence that much above a tenth of the women could write. There proves to be little connection between ability to read and ability to write. Perhaps this is the most significant conclusion of all: for better or worse, reading and writing are no more closely or necessarily associated than horses and carriages, or lovers and marriages.

TABLE 3: LITERACY OF 'CONVERTS' AT THE CAMBUSLANG REVIVAL 1742*

	TAUGHT TO READ	TAUGHT TO WRITE
Using a total of 109 cases		
Women	74 (100)	8 (11)
Men	35 (100)	21 (60)
Using 90 cases with prefacing notes		
Women	61 (100)	7 (11)
Men	29 (100)	21 (72)

* *Note and source: The source is as given in Table 1. Figures in parentheses denote percentages.*

Rab Houston, in a challenging study of Scottish literacy, has come to the conclusion that in the lowlands in the mid-eighteenth century about 70 per cent of Scottish women and almost 40 per cent of Scottish men were 'illiterate', using as evidence the ability or otherwise of deponents and witnesses in lawsuits to sign their names.[20] But what does illiteracy mean? If the inability to write a signature indicates no more than that a woman or a man has not been taught to write, then the Cambuslang evidence supports Houston in a fairly satisfactory way, though it seems a shade more optimistic about men and more pessimistic about women. Any further suggestion, however, that inability to sign might also be an indication of inability in what Rosalind Mitchison has called 'the more significant side of literacy, ability to read and understand', is demolished by the Cambuslang evidence.[21] It shows a population universally able to read, but with almost all the women and a substantial minority of men unable to write.

This picture also fits in remarkably well with recent evidence from Scandinavia. In Sweden, the excellence of the parish examination books, or *husförhörslängder*, allows a uniquely close inspection of reading and writing abilities. By 1750, 80 per cent or more of the population had, in many areas, attained reading ability, while writing ability limped behind at 5 to 20 per cent, only making up the leeway in the nineteenth century.[22] In Denmark, the latest research suggests that most of the population could read by the late eighteenth century, but that a general ability to write was the effect of the important education acts of 1814.[23] And the English evangelical Sabbatarians of the late eighteenth and early nineteenth centuries were sure that one skill could be taught without the other, as they were quite prepared to teach reading in Sunday schools, but not writing.[24]

The evidence from Cambuslang that Scots were able to read also squares well enough with much eighteenth-century comment, not least by Englishmen contrasting Scotland with their own country. Defoe in 1707 remarked in 'a hint to English hearers' that 'in a whole church full of people, not one shall be seen without a Bible . . . if you shut your eyes when the minister names any text of scripture, you shall hear a little rustling noise over the whole place, made by turning the leaves of the Bible'.[25] George Whitefield himself, on visiting Scotland first in the summer of 1741, spoke in a similar vein of preaching 'to a very thronged assembly. After I had done prayer, and had named my text, the rustling made by opening the Bibles all at once, quite surprised me – a scene I never was witness to before'.[26] It also fits well with Laslett's picture of a Scotland where people of humble status were often keen to subscribe to the publication of the collected sermons of their favourite divines,[27] and with the comment of Burns's first biographer (at least if that is taken to apply to males) that 'In the very humblest condition of the Scottish peasants every one can read, and most persons are more or less skilful in writing . . .'[28] There could be a real and pressing enthusiasm for reading, obviously of the Bible and other religious books but also for ballads and chap-books,[29] but it might not be at all accompanied by equal writing skills. This seems exactly to be the mid-eighteenth-century Scottish position.

It was Adam Smith's opinion in 1775 that 'the establishment of . . . parish schools has taught almost the whole common people to read, and a very great proportion of them to write',[30] but another of Houston's iconoclastic contributions has been seriously to call into question the role of schools in the educating process, and to argue that much may have been achieved in less formal ways. Unfortunately M'Culloch does not record as systematically as we would like whether or not his subjects attended school, though for 36 individuals (16 women and 20 men) he is explicit that they did attend, and only for 5 (a highland man and 4 lowland women) is there a statement or a strong implication that they did not. Of these known school attendees, at least 13 men (but only 3 women) were taught writing, but all were taught reading, and of many it is remarked that they were taught to memorize the catechism. Indeed, to enable the child to repeat the catechism by heart appears to have been almost the first aim at school,[31] and it may be a measure of attendance that in volume II, where childhood learning of the catechism is recorded more systematically, over 80 per cent had had this experience.

Some other impressions of the schools can be gained from these accounts. One relatively advanced task was attending church to take note of the sermon to repeat to the master in class next day: 'when at school I gave ear to sermons till once I got my note . . . after that I was for ordinary no more concerned'.[32] The books explicitly mentioned as being taught were the catechisms, the psalm book and the Bible, though occasional references refer to an ability to 'read any other English book', and one girl confesses that out of school 'I used to read the Bible at my parents desire tho' I had more delight in reading story books and ballads'.[33]

Much was implied about how little was learned in school. Several deplored their own inattention, like the girl who 'was so much set upon my diversions and so much neglected that I learned little more than to read the Catechism', and the boy who 'would not apply myself to learn to read, only I learn'd the letters and to read the Catechism some way, and was entred in the Psalm Book when I left'.[34] For some, formal education was pathetically minimal, as it was for the girl who 'got some learning to read my Catechism but was only twenty days at school'.[35] An interesting sidelight on the Perthshire highlands is given by a young man educated at Kirkmichael:

When I was about 12 year old I was put to school and was taught to read the Bible in English and the Psalm Book in Irish or Highland language, being taught from my infancy to speak Irish and afterwards by hearing some

people about me speak English I came also to learn that language: but I
could have read most of the English Bible before I knew anything of the
sense or literal meaning of what I was rendering.[36]

At the other extreme was a girl who learned to read the Bible at school when she
was six, and a boy (later a weaver) who reported that 'when I was put to school I
inclined so much to reading that I would oftimes have stayed of my own accord,
with the master that taught me reading after the school was dismiss'd and the
rest of the scholars were gone away'.[37] Of the 8 women who could write, 4 are
of unknown status, one was the daughter of a tenant, and 3 were of higher
status – respectively the wife of a baillie, the daughter of a schoolmaster and the
daughter of a 'gentleman'. The last of these stated, in a sentence, that she 'was
put early to schools and taught to read and write and all other pieces for
Education that are ordinary in Big Towns for gentlemen's daughters or people
of fashion and station'.[38] The contrast with the servant girl who was only
twenty days at school hardly needs pointing.

It is also, however, extemely plain that education was not necessarily
confined to school, or even to childhood. Five of the women expressly mention
their parents in the process of acquiring literacy skills: one said 'I was taught to
read my question and psalm book at the public school, and learned to read my
Bible by both my parents at home'; a second said 'I was put to school when
young and learned there and at home to read the Bible'; a third used almost the
same words; another said 'I was taught by my Father to read the Bible by the
time I was six years of age'; yet another was 'put to school and taught to read
and write by my parents'.[39] Interestingly, no men relate this experience. Perhaps
supplementary home education was reserved for girls because it was cheap, and
the expense of obtaining what was presumably regarded as a better, extended
education in the schools was reserved for the boys.

Even more interesting is the evidence for young women and men seeking to
improve their literacy skills in their teens or later. It is not surprising to find in
this group a real enthusiasm for reading the Bible or other religious books, such
as William Guthrie's *Short Treatise of the Christian's Great Interest* (first
edition, Glasgow 1695) and Thomas Vincent's *Explicatory Catechism* (first
edition, Glasgow 1674), and a few were evidently driven to work at their
reading by a quickening in their religious life. Equally, however, some learned to
read after the usual school-leaving age because of more general social pressures.

There are 9 specific cases of post-school learning (3 men and 6 women),
each of them worth considering. For 2 of the women we have only very general
information – a girl of nineteen who 'only learned to read the Bible about four
years ago and can read it now pretty well' and another of twenty-five who 'was

learned to read when I was young, but thro my own carelessness and negligence could not read so distinctly till of late'.[40] Of the remaining 7, one, a young man aged twenty-eight who had not learned to read as a child, returned to school when he was about eighteen years of age, but 'even then I did not learn much, but I am just now gone to school again to learn to read more distinctly and to write some'.[41] None of the others tried to use the school as adults. Two girls were self-taught mainly by following the Bible in church. One, who had learned at school little more than to read the catechism, and later 'could not find leisure to learn to read', taught herself 'by following the minister with my eye on the Bible'.[42] The other, who was also taught only to read the catechism at school, had been indifferent until the revival, when she became upset at her inability to read Scripture. She then applied herself carefully, 'and by reading much and oft in it when I hear passages of it cited, as I am hearing Sermons, I can now turn to them . . . And O how wonderful is the change now with me . . .'[43] This is the only clear instance of the revival effecting desire for literacy.

The remaining four learned to read while in service or as apprentices. One married man aged about thirty-eight related how he:

> was born in the High-lands; and my parents, living far from any place where there was a school, I was not put to it, nor could I read till I was about fourteen years of age: and then, in time of my Apprenticeship, I got lessons from some about: and so came at length to read the Bible. I also got all the Catechism by heart, and have it to this day.[44]

The girl who was only twenty days at school told how she was subsequently 'taught to read some in private houses where I served, and was brought the length of reading the Question book [the Catechism] exactly enough but I could not read my Bible till of late that I have been at great pains to learn'.[45] A tenant, who also had only had a very imperfect school education, explained how at the age of twelve he:

> took a fancy to learn to read, thinking I would not be like another man when I came to be of age if I could not read; and these with whom I liv'd seeing me incline to learn to read, both gave me liberty to learn and put me to it; and so I proceeded till I could read the Bible tolerably.[46]

This social pressure for reading is testified to by a woman who admitted that she used to read the Bible 'that I might have it so say that I read it as well as my neighbours',[47] and especially by the evidence of our last case, Margaret Clerk, a day-labourer's daughter from Girvan aged forty-two:

I used also to go to Kirk on Sabbath-days, tho' I think it was often only to see and to be seen; only I kept sometimes at home because I could not read and I was much ashamed that I could not make use of a Bible in the Kirk as others about me did. And therefore I set about learning to read when I was about 18 years of age, having never learn'd to read any before that; and it was one of the Terms of my agreement with those whom I serv'd that I should always get a Lesson every day; and by following it out in that manner, I came to be capable to read the Bible, and got part of the Catechism by heart, and retain it still.[48]

It is important to emphasize that the pressures referred to here are general societal ones, not specifically related to the revival and not to any particular religious group. As John Howard the prison reformer said of 'the southern parts of Scotland' (in contrast to England), here 'It is scandalous for any person not to be possessed of a Bible'.[49] And Robert Burns (not usually regarded as a poet of false social observation) draws a similar picture of the literate poor in the *Cottar's Saturday Night*. The overall impression given by the 'examination' is, indeed, of a society where it was normal to have reading skills, and quite exceptional and socially degrading not to have them. To achieve these skills it was normally regarded as necessary to go to school, but it was not always sufficient and parents and employers appear to have been more than willing to help plug the gaps.

For all the inadequacies of the system, especially in respect to writing, it thus appears from the Cambuslang evidence to be not totally wrong to designate rural society in lowland Scotland of the eighteenth century as having (in the words of Sir John Sinclair) 'a laudable zeal for knowledge', though whether it was also 'not generally found among the same class of men in other countries in Europe'[50] must be left to others to determine.

NOTES

* I am grateful to James Cameron, Rab Houston, Rosalind Mitchison, Geoffrey Parker, Sylvia Price and Keith Wrightson for helpful comments on an earlier draft; none can be held responsible for the shortcomings of the present paper.

1 'Examination of Persons under Scriptural Concern at Cambuslang during the Revival in 1741–42 by the Revd. William Macculloch, Minister of Cambuslang, with Marginal Notes by Dr. Webster and Other Ministers'. New College Lib., Edinburgh. MS. W.13.b.2/ 2, i, B.B. (see n. 5 below).

2 Sir John Sinclair (ed.), *The Statistical Account of Scotland*, 21 vols. (Edinburgh, 1791–9), v, pp. 245–58.

3 R. B. Sher, 'Church, University, Enlightenment: The Moderate Literati of Edinburgh, 1720–1793' (Univ. of Chicago Ph.D. thesis, 1979).

4 Arthur Fawcett, *The Cambuslang Revival: The Scottish Evangelical Revival of the Eighteenth Century* (London, 1971). See also Sinclair (ed.), *Statistical Account of Scotland*, v, pp. 266–74, for a less sympathetic view from the eighteenth century.

5 'Examinations of Persons under Scriptural Concern at Cambuslang'. The binding is later, and has resulted in some confusion: among the end-papers bound into the second volume are the index and key for the first volume, and among the end-papers for the first volume are the index, key and literacy notes for the second volume. There are also other papers bound in which seem to imply a third volume, and a good deal of repagination has taken place. In each volume the individual is identified by a two-letter symbol (A.A., B.C., etc,) and references in this article follow that system.

6 Quoted in Fawcett, *Cambuslang Revival*, p. 5.

7 Both volumes are in M'Culloch's hand and not, as Fawcett says (*ibid.*, p. 7) in the case of the second one, in a variety of hands. Only one case takes the form of a letter to the minister. There are 110 separate cases, not, as Fawcett says (*ibid.*, p. 6), 106.

8 Extracts (partly expurgated) have indeed been twice used for this purpose: James Robe, *A Faithfull Narrative of the Extraordinary Work of the Spirit of God at Kilsyth and Other Congregations in the Neighbourhood*, 2nd edn. (Glasgow, 1789); D. MacFarlan, *The Revivals of the Eighteenth Century, Particularly at Cambuslang* (London and Edinburgh, n.d. [*circa* 1845]).

9 Quoted in Fawcett, *Cambuslang Revival*, p. 145.

10 *Ibid.*, p. 200.

11 'Examination of Persons under Scriptural Concern at Cambuslang', i, A.W.

12 Adam Smith, *The Wealth of Nations*, 2 vols. (Everyman edn., London, 1910), ii, p. 269.

13 The ministers who annotated the first volume for publication were clearly sensitive about public reaction: they played down or edited out references to visions or fainting fits or to the interviewees missing hours of work (to attend the preaching) and altered most of the references to 'personal covenants'. The latter may, however, have been less for political than theological reasons: English Puritans, notably Richard Baxter, were associated with the idea of a personal covenant, and the ministers may not have wished any echoes of this concept. I am obliged to Professor James Cameron for this point.

14 Fawcett, *Cambuslang Revival*, p. 165.

15 'Examination of Persons under Scriptural Concern at Cambuslang', i, A.M.

16 *Ibid.*, I, A.N., and ii, M.S., B.R., B.H.

17 *Ibid.*, ii, C.R.

18 *Ibid.*, A.B.

19 *Ibid.*, C.H.

20 R. Houston, 'The Literacy Myth?: Illiteracy in Scotland, 1630–1760', *Past and Present*, no. 96 (Aug. 1982), pp. 81–102; see also R. Houston, 'The Development of Literacy: Northern England, 1640–1750', *Econ. Hist. Rev.*, 2nd ser., xxxv (1982), pp. 199–216.

21 Rosalind Mitchison, *Life in Scotland* (London, 1978), p. 45.

22 Egil Johansson, *The History of Literacy in Sweden in Comparison with Some Other Countries* (Umeå Educ. Repts., xii, Umeå, 1977).

23 Ingrid Markussen and Vagn Skovgaard-Petersen, 'Læseindlæring og læsebehov i Danmark, *circa* 1550 – *circa* 1850', in *Ur Nordisk Kulturhistoria* (Studia Historica Jyväskyläensia, xxii no. 3, Jyväskylä, 1981).

24 A. P.Wadsworth, 'The First Manchester Sunday Schools', *Bull. John Rylands Lib.*, xxxiii (1951), repr. in M. W. Flinn and T. C. Smout (eds.), *Essays in Social History* (Oxford, 1974), pp. 100–22. Useful surveys of the state of research into early modern literacy are provided by Geoffrey Parker, 'An Educational Revolution?: The Growth of Literacy and Schooling in Early Modern Europe', *Tijdschrift voor Geschiedenis,* xciii (1980), pp. 210–20; Geoffrey Parker, 'Early Modern Literacy Revisited' (forthcoming in *Tijdschrift voor Geschiedenis).*

25 Quoted in Fawcett, *Cambuslang Revival,* pp. 80–1.

26 *Ibid.*

27 Peter Laslett, 'Scottish Weavers, Cobblers and Miners who Bought Books in the 1750s', *Local Population Studies,* iii (1969), pp. 7–14.

28 *The Works of Robert Burns with an Account of his Life, Criticism of his Writings to which are Prefixed Some Observations on the Character and Condition of the Scottish Peasantry,* ed. James Currie, 2nd edn., 4 vols. (London, 1801), i, p. 3.

29 David Craig, *Scottish Literature and the Scottish People* (London, 1961), esp. ch. 4. Thus one contemporary recalled the first publication of Burns: 'I can well remember how that even ploughboys and maidservants would gladly part with the wages they earned the most hardly and which they wanted to purchase the necessary clothing if they might but procure the works of Burns': quoted in *ibid.*, p. 113.

30 Smith, *Wealth of Nations,* ii, pp. 266–7.

31 See Parker, 'Educational Revolution?', p. 218.

32 'Examination of Persons under Scriptural Concern at Cambulsang', i, B.R.

33 *Ibid.,* A.N.

34 *Ibid.,* ii, A.S., C.H.

35 *Ibid.,* i, B.U.

36 *Ibid.,* ii. A.I.; Annette Smith, *Jacobite Estates of the Forty-Five* (Edinburgh, 1982), pp. 34–5, suggests that although schools planted in the highlands by the S.S.P.C.K. and other bodies had as a prime aim teaching English they were often not the only, or the best, places for learning it: it was more often picked up by commercial exchanges with the lowlands which 'demanded and resulted in some knowledge of the southern language'.

37 'Examination of Persons under Scriptural Concern at Cambuslang', ii, B.C.

38 *Ibid.,* i, A.V.

39 *Ibid.,* A.C., A.J., A.N., A.V.

40 *Ibid.,* A.O., B.T.

41 *Ibid.,* A.E.

42 *Ibid.,* ii, A.S.

43 *Ibid.,* A.C.

44 *Ibid.*, i, B.D.

45 *Ibid.*, B.U.

46 *Ibid.*, ii, C.H.

47 *Ibid.*, i, A.H.

48 *Ibid.*, ii, A.W. Being able to read the Bible was regarded later as a superior skill to merely being able to read and write: 'A return to the Select Committee of 1816 on Children in Manufactories estimated that only a quarter of the children in the Manchester and Salford schools could read and write; one-sixth were learning the alphabet; a third were learning to spell; one-sixth could read the Testament; one-twelfth could read the Bible': Wadsworth, 'First Manchester Sunday Schools', p. 115.

49 John Howard, *The State of the Prisons*, 2nd edn. (London, 1780), p. 163. His observation relates to 1779.

50 Sir John Sinclair, *Analysis of the Statistical Account of Scotland*, 2 vols. (Edinburgh, 1825), ii, p. 99, paraphrasing Currie in *Works of Robert Burns*, i, p. 3.

Church attendance and the Kirk Session

Extracted from article by AA MacLaren 1967 in *Scottish Historical Review* 46, 115–139.

The Aberdeen [Religious] census returns [of 1851], by and large, do not substantiate a view of the smaller city differing greatly from the national pattern of attendance. But certainly in the case of Scotland it is doubtful whether the census returns could provide the means to do this.[1] Attendance figures may provide a fairly reliable indication of the relative strength of active support received by each denomination, but as far as being a gauge of 'religious feeling' such figures can be totally misleading. Certainly the Aberdeen attendance figure of 42.5 per cent offers little or no assistance in determining whether (to use one eminent historian's terminology) the city, or the nation for that matter, remained even 'nominally Christian'.[2] An earlier census carried out by the Aberdeen kirk sessions in 1837 and based not on attendance but on 'connection' found that only some 8 per cent of the population were not 'connected' to some church or other.[3] . . . Two questions naturally arise from such a situation: firstly why approximately 45 per cent of the population chose to stay away from church; and secondly why they nevertheless continued to believe themselves to be 'connected' to a church.

The problem of non-attendance can only to a limited extent be explained by religious apathy which in many ways is a symptomatic rather than a causal factor. Certainly in many presbyterian churches in the 1804s there was no lack of enthusiasm, if at times it descended to little more than inter-denominational rivalry. There was a wave of church-building led by the Free Church and followed to a lesser extent by the United Presbyterians. All of the presbyterian churches appeared to be aware of their shortcomings regarding the participation of the masses in public worship and in the Free Church particularly the matter was a subject of annual debate.[4] Nevertheless little if anything was accomplished, and the trend overall would appear to be one of deterioration rather than improvement.

The connection between non-attendance and lack of suitable clothing among poorer members has often been advanced as a reason for the failure of the churches to attract working-class participation.[5] Many who might otherwise have attended were undoubtedly deterred from doing so for this reason. One elder, looking back over nearly fifty years, commented thus on a revival meeting held in the church:

> One peculiarity of these meetings we have never observed in other gatherings of the kind . . . It was that many men attended in their working clothes, and crowds of young women without bonnets or caps, but with little shawls about their shoulders, which they put on their heads when they left church.[6]

A gathering such as this in a presbyterian church would appear to be virtually unique, and it might be argued from this occasion that where ragged rather than respectable clothes were the general rule the lower classes were prepared to participate. Few working people, however, were prepared to risk ridicule, and even kirk session censure perhaps, by attending thus on a normal occasion. Indeed lack of suitable clothes was accepted by some sessions as sufficient reason for non-attendance.[7] Agencies were set up by female members of congregations to provide clothes for respectable members of the lower classes.[8] In one church the session arranged that two girls share the same clothes at alternate services.[9]

But if lack of suitable attire undoubtedly deterred many from attending church it is perhaps equally true to say that it provided a ready and acceptable excuse for not doing so. Respectability of dress was in fact only a visible conformity to all the other requirements of religious respectability which was an integral part of church attendance. Any hint of violation of a whole catalogue of moral crimes brought the censure of the kirk session upon the individual.

Presbyterian kirk sessions were well-organised and integrated instruments for imposing a pattern of social, economic, and moral behaviour upon the church-going sections of the community.[10] Although the actions of these bodies were felt most profoundly by church-goers, their influence extended far beyond the immediate congregational bounds and tended to have the reverse effects of encouraging middle-class participation and deterring working-class attendance. Those who did not attend church but continued to believe in church 'connection' did not escape kirk session censure. A request for the sacraments of marriage or baptism led to moral enquiry by the session, which must have inhibited many from seeking more than this basic connection with a church. Working men and women were continually before the sessions on matters of moral behaviour, particularly with regard to the 'gross sin' of what was termed 'antenuptial fornication'. The child of such a premarital union was regarded in the same light as bastardy and unfit for baptism until the parents had fully submitted themselves to the discipline of the session[11] . . .

With the exception of church office-bearers,[12] the middle classes do not appear to have undergone any disciplinary action regarding sexual morality and intemperance. Presumably they either did not indulge in such excesses or were more discreet in the manner of their indulgence. The middle classes were, however, subject to close scrutiny in the realm of business morality, although here again it does not appear to have been the crime so much as the exposure which was regarded as the sin. Suspicion of financial insolvency led to immediate investigation. A member of Trinity Parish Church, who had the audacity to declare, when approached regarding his financial position, that 'Public Business and Kirk Sessions has little or no connection one with the other', was struck off the communion roll.[13] Even after meeting his creditors satisfactorily a bankrupt did not expiate his sin in the eyes of the session. One bankrupt who was a Sunday-school teacher was left by the session to determine for himself 'whether or not he should *immediately* resume the duties', the inference being that it was unbecoming for him to do so. Moreover the stigma of bankruptcy was attached not only to the bankrupt but also to his family. One undischarged bankrupt in 1860 was refused the sacrament of baptism for his child until he gave a more satisfactory account of his failure to the kirk session.[14] Another in 1865 was refused a certificate of church membership until he produced a written testimony from his creditors, although the session after due consideration agreed that they now had no objection to the granting of a certificate to the bankrupt's wife.[15]

But if the social pressures exerted on the middle classes differed radically in type from those applied to the lower classes, it could well be maintained that they also differed greatly in their effects. Church membership to the Victorian business-man was in many ways a mark of his continuing financial stability and social responsibility. No such positive advantages were attached to working-class membership, where fear of exposure or of mere perverted accusation acted as a disincentive to membership, as it inevitably resulted in humiliation and disgrace before a watchful session composed largely of employers acting in their capacity as elders . . .

Beyond attendance at religious worship working-class participation was negligible. Social respectability, and to a considerable extent financial expediency, dictated that the eldership be composed of middle-class socio-economic groupings. This in itself need not have been a deterrent to working-class attendance, but within the congregations there was little social integration and the socio-economic and financial requirements of office tended to produce office-bearers unwilling, or unable, to fulfil certain of the obligations of their office. Education, however inadequate its provisions, stood out as the one sphere where the presbyterian churches endeavoured with some success to fulfil their moral and religious obligations to society. But here again social segregation rather than integration resulted; what might have been achieved in the inculcation of religious principles was lost by the continuing lack of social contact at congregational level. The churches sought to embrace the spiritually destitute but their way was barred by the material poverty which they could not comprehend; and those whom they desired to help 'generally sneered at any attempt to help them'.[16] Churchmen worried over the problem: it was feared that 'some of them have not even rational knowledge of the fallen state of man ... Many of them become Chartists or Roman Catholics, or Unitarians, or have no profession of any definite religion.'[17] Yet what had the churches to offer the working class? The same minister who worried over the fallen state of the lower classes recorded in his diary in 1842:

> On Thursday evening I preached to labouring men, when few were present –
> below twenty ... I was somewhat grieved and discouraged. Perhaps I said
> some things inadvertently. I felt so. O forgive! What are the men?
> Thoughtless as children in the things of salvation. The veriest trifle will keep
> them away from church.[18]

This failure to communicate – both at the physical level of social contact, and at a more psychological one in attitude of mind – was the most dominant feature in the relationship between presbyterianism and the working class in mid-nineteenth-century Aberdeen.

NOTES

1 It is quite clear that the report on the census returns in Scotland was hurriedly and at times inaccurately prepared. The greatest weakness of the census as a source, however, is that the original schedules are no longer available for Scotland. This makes specific parish analysis extremely difficult.

2 G. S. Kitson Clark, *The Making of Victorian England* (London, 1962), 150.

3 *The Statistical Account of Aberdeenshire* (Edinburgh, 1843), 35. The writer himself questions the authenticity of these figures because many were included who never attended Church.

4 E.g. see reports of the committee anent the state of religion (*Free Presb.*, 7 May 1850; 13 Dec. 1859).

5 Inglis, *Churches and the Working Classes*, 59, 116, 130; Kitson Clark, *Victorian England*, 149; Briggs, *Age of Improvement*, 466.

6 W. Robbie, Bon-Accord Free Church, Aberdeen: A *Retrospect*, 1828–1887 [*Aberdeen* 1887], 21.

7 Greyfriars Parish Kirk Session Minutes [*Est. Greyf. Sess.*], 5 Sept. 1864; Free Trinity Church Session Minutes [*Free Trin. Sess.*], 19 Nov. 1854.

8 The Free Church were active in this field. However it was a Congregational church which claimed to have founded the first of these societies 'before 1843' (G. King, *Brief Historical Sketch of the Congregational Church* . . . [Aberdeen, 1870], 20.

9 *Free Trin. Sess.*, 18 Dec. 1854.

10 The kirk sessions co-operated on a national as well as a local level in matters of moral discipline and in exerting pressure over issues such as national education and Sabbath violation by railway companies. By 1850 denominational animosities had cooled to the extent of allowing limited co-operation over the problem of the moral investigation of members who had changed their denominational allegiance. In other matters, however, the sessions acted independently. For examples of their extensive sphere of interest, see rinity Parish Session Book [*Est. Trin. Sess.*], 21 Jan 1839; *Est. Greyf. Sess.*, 2 Dec. 1850, 4 Oct. 1852; Minute Book of the Free Presbytery of Aberdeen [*Free Presb.*], 26 Mar., 16 Apr., 3 Dec., 1850; Records of the Presbytery of Aberdeen [*Est. Presb.*], 10 Feb. 1847, 1 Feb. 1848; Register of the General Session of St Nicholas [*Est. Gen. Sess.*], 23 Apr. 1849.

11 All kirk session records abound with such cases – baptism of the child being refused until discipline was completed. Certainly with some sessions this was no mere formality. Trinity Free Church Session found it necessary, by visitation and prayer, to 'forcibly impress' on the mother that 'marriage subsequently cannot do away or atone for that sin' (*Free Trin. Sess.*, 31 July 1845).

12 Any hint of scandal among them led to investigation: deposition was not uncommon (e.g. *Est. Trin. Sess.*, 21 May 1840; Free West Church Kirk Session Minute Book [*Free West Sess.*], 26 Oct. 1863; *Free Trin. Sess.*, 21 July 1845).

13 *Est Trin. Sess.*, 12 Sept. 1842.

14 *Free Trin. Sess.*, 15 Sept. 1851; 4 June 1860.

15 *Free West Sess.*, 16 Oct. 1865.

16 A. S. Cook, *Pen Sketches and Reminiscences of Sixty Years* (Aberdeen, 1901), 188.

17 *Selected Portions from the Diary and Manuscripts of the Rev. Gavin Parker* (Aberdeen, 1848), 116.

18 Parker, *Diary*, 149.

Presbyterianism and social class in mid-nineteenth century Glasgow: A study of nine churches

Extracted from article by P Hillis 1981 in *Journal of Ecclesiastical History* 32, 47–64 (Cambridge University Press).

. . . This article attempts to analyse the relationship between the working class and several Presbyterian churches in Glasgow in the 1840s, 1850s and 1860s at the congregational level with a view to discovering whether working people were members or office-bearers of the church. In this area an attempt will be made to see if any differences arise between the Church of Scotland and the non-established Presbyterian churches. The findings should show that Dr MacLaren was incorrect in assuming that the social make-up of a kirk session was representative of the congregation.

The churches which were chosen to represent the Church of Scotland were Barony, Govan, St Stephen's and St George's. The non-established churches were Cambridge Street and Wellington Street United Presbyterian Church, Great Hamilton Street Reformed Presbyterian Church, St Enoch's Free Church and St Stephen's after 1843 when minister and congregation left the Church of Scotland and joined the Free Church. Passing reference was also made to Lansdowne United Presbyterian Church.

The social make-up of elders, managers and congregation was analysed using the following classification code:

A. Professional Group (generally university graduates)
B. Commercial Group
C. Large Merchant-Manufacturing Group
D. Retired-Rentier Group
E. & F. Public Servants
G. Small Merchant-Tradesmen Group
H. Artisans
I. Unskilled Workers

High Status Groups A, B, C, D
Low Status Groups E, F, G
Working Class Groups H, I

... A breakdown of the social make-up of kirk sessions in four non-established churches in the 1840s and 1850s is as follows: out of the total congregation of 117 (of whom 112 have been identified), 67 (57.3 per cent) were of 'high' status (groups A, B, C and D), 39 (33 per cent) of 'low status' (groups E, F and G), and 6 (5.1 per cent of 'working class' status (groups H and I). Three features stand out. Firstly, there is a very small working class presence on kirk sessions, secondly there is a reasonably high lower middle class representation, as shown by the low status category, and the third feature is the superiority of the upper middle class as illustrated by the high status division. Within this latter category section C, the large merchant-manufacturer group, is the most numerous of the four divisions.

However, these statistics hide the most important characteristic of these kirk sessions and the one which partly distinguishes them from the Church of Scotland. Within the high and low status groups in the non-established denominations many elders were on their way up the social and economic ladder and saw election to the session as a useful step up this ladder.

TABLE I

Status of elders in three established churches

CHURCH	TOTAL	IDENTIFIED	STATUS		
			HIGH	LOW	WORKING CLASS
Barony	15	15	13	2	0
Govan	23	18	13	5	0
St George's	49	43	36	5	2
Total	87	76	62	12	2
Percentage	100		71.3	13.8	2.3

The status of elders in these churches between 1840 and 1860 is shown in Table 1. When these figures are compared to the equivalent data for the non-established churches one feature stands out. This is the smaller number of low status elders in the Church of Scotland. The five in Govan may seem to contradict this, but of these five three were school teachers, a fact which illustrates the strong link between Church and education in Scotland.

Once again the working class is only noticeable by its absence and a possible explanation for this will be given below. As in the table for the non-established churches stark statistics hide the most interesting aspect of these established churches' kirk sessions. Elders came either from well-established middle class families or they were themselves firmly rooted in the middle class on becoming elders.

... Therefore, the middle class dominated the administrative posts of the church, a situation which largely arose out of the economic and social obligations attached to the office of elder and manager. However, this middle class hegemony is not reflected in the congregation as a whole.

The social composition of church members in four non-established churches between 1845 and 1865 and the equivalent figures for three Church of Scotland congregations between 1855 and 1865 are shown in Table 2. One statistic from these tables stands out and this is the fact that in every church the largest grouping is the working class category. A more detailed examination of this finding will be undertaken at a later stage. Before this we must turn our attention to the middle class section of the congregation.

TABLE 2

Status of church members

	TOTAL	IDENTIFIED	HIGH	STATUS LOW	WORKING CLASS
4 non-established churches (1845–65)	2663(100)	2397	457(17.2)	495(18.6)	1445(54.3)
5 Church of Scotland (1855–65)	1330(100)	1269	162(12.8)	109 (8.6)	998(78.6)

In contrast to the Church of Scotland, in the non-established churches the lower middle class outnumbered the high status members. Thus, the higher number of lower middle class elders and managers in the non-established churches compared to the Church of Scotland reflected the position at the congregational level. Moreover, it was common to find in the non-established churches, members, as we noted with elders, rising up the social scale during the period.

... Therefore, in terms of social composition all congregations were broadly based with the working class comprising the largest single percentage of members. However, the administrative offices of the church were in the hands of a middle class elite, a situation which resulted from the fact that only men of relatively high socio-economic status became elders or managers. It should be stressed that the social make-up of the kirk session was not representative of the congregation as a whole.

Historically, the non-established churches had a higher percentage of lower middle class adherents than the Church of Scotland, but the former were less successful in attracting the lower working class. This failure arose out of the stress they laid on living within strict moral guidelines and the heavy financial obligations of membership. Notwithstanding the relative failure of the non-established churches to appeal to the lower working class, the findings outlined in this article should go some way towards correcting the generally held misconception that the Church, in terms of the social composition of its membership, was a wholly middle class institution.

Was there a Scottish Agricultural Revolution?

G Whittington 1975 in *Area* 7, 204–6.

Summary: *The traditional and orthodox view that an Agricultural Revolution occurred in Scotland in the late eighteenth and early nineteenth centuries is challenged. An argument is put forward that the concept of a continuous evolution, of varied pace is preferable.*

In an earlier work (Whittington, 1973) attention was drawn to what has been considered for a long time to be the orthodox view of Scottish agricultural change in the late eighteenth and early nineteenth centuries. Perhaps the most recent expositions of this orthodox viewpoint are to be found in works by J. E. Handley (1963) and J. B. Caird (1964). The title of Handley's book *The Agricultural Revolution In Scotland* and a quotation from Caird's paper – *'Scotland's rural landscape is in fact a landscape of 'revolution' rather than one of slow evolution'* – serve to exemplify this viewpoint. Sporadic heretical outbursts against this orthodoxy occur from time to time and it is in an attempt to spread this heresy and to encourage further research into the whole matter that the following points are aired.

One of the linchpins for protagonists of the Revolution argument is that the Scottish landscape underwent a fundamental change as a result of enclosure. The old openfield system was replaced by squared and hedged or walled units of cultivation. There are several features, however, regarding enclosure which seem to have escaped such protagonists. In 1661 an Act of the Scottish Parliament made enclosure on a limited scale compulsory for many land holders and also made it much easier to achieve than for their contemporary English equivalents. The well-known Act of 1695 (Whittington, 1973, 538) reinforced the legal simplicity of enclosure. Lebon (1946) showed how enclosure had become common at an early date in the Western Lowlands and evidence for such activity could be forthcoming over a much wider area of Scotland; a search, which is long overdue, of estate documents could be the means of verifying this assertion. Enclosure certainly took place in the seventeenth century and probably earlier even on lay lands and this means that this activity was occurring over a period of at least two hundred years. That

the pace of enclosure quickened in its later stages is not denied but such a
lengthy period does suggest an evolution rather than a revolution.

There are two further points with regard to enclosure which need to be
made. It seems to be widely held that enclosure automatically brought into
existence what Caird (1964) calls *a landscape of geometrical lines*. This is far
from being universally true. The earliest known enclosures in the west and
south-west of Scotland merely put boundaries around some existing farming
units. These units had irregular limits and an examination of the first large scale
maps show the contemporary fields to have geometrical outlines only if the
projective rather than the Euclidean geometry is intended. In many instances,
however, enclosure was only taking place in the strictly legal sense of that word.
Pieces of land were exchanged and more compact holdings were achieved but
actual physical enclosure often did not occur at all.

The occurrence of enclosure and the extirpation of the infield-outfield
method of land exploitation are seen by the authors of the orthodox persuasion
as the twin pillars of their Revolution. Enclosure alone, however, did not mean
the end of infield-outfield agriculture; in many areas it merely meant that the
parts devoted to different intensities of arable farming remained that way but in
compact blocks for each cultivator rather than in scattered strips. Very little
difference had occurred in the landscape as a result of the earliest enclosure, nor
had former farming practices been abandoned overnight.

A fundamental feature of the infield-outfield method was the crop rotation
that this involved. The 'revolutionists' believe that there was a sudden striking
change in technology and attitude which led not only to the abandonment of the
infield-outfield method but also to the crop rotation pattern that they held to be
its underpinning. An examination of estate papers on a limited scale (the
Morton Papers from Aberdour in Fife and the Hay of Hays Papers from the
Carse of Gowrie) shows that different crop rotations in an infield-outfield
context occurred well before the supposed revolution dawned. The three-course
rotation of oats, oats, bere on the infield land had been superseded and
supplemented by the introduction of peas, wheat, beans and mashlum. Even
the technology which ushered in the new era had been in existence for a
considerable period. F. V. Emery (1959) drew attention to an unexploited
source of information on agricultural activity in the Lothians which dates from
the second decade of the seventeenth century. Analysis of this source shows that
the use of lime on the land was occurring widely by this date and was no doubt
responsible for the early appearance of the minimal areas of outfield and
unusually large coherent rural settlements to which B. Third (1955; 1957)
drew attention. The Lothians are merely an outstanding example of a gradual
improvement of agriculture and change in the landscape over a large area at an

early period which it is felt could be found to recur in other areas of Scotland once a more intensive search is made of the rentals in Scottish estate papers.

Revolution suggests that a previous system was overturned. Two further situations might be quoted which indicate that replacement over a long period is a more realistic approach to the changes in Scottish agriculture and the Scottish rural landscape. An investigation currently being undertaken on the location and continued existence of farms on the former Gordon estates in north-west Aberdeenshire shows that over three-quarters of the farms which the pre-enclosure maps of the mid-eighteenth century reveal were still in existence by the time of the publication of the first Ordnance Survey map at the six-inch scale. By that date enclosure had taken place. Where is the revolution? Surely this indicates that rationalization had been taking place before the date of the pre-enclosure maps (1776) and that a drastic change was unnecessary. One of the effects of the Agricultural Revolution according to Caird was the replacement of the fermtoun by individual farms. If the farms of the Gordon estates are considered to be examples of this then we have a change which is in an area not unduly environmentally favoured, which occurred in the pre-enclosure period and which led to so stable a system that over half of the farms are still in existence today. But even with enclosure there was not necessarily a change in the settlement pattern; the fermtoun layout was not always destroyed, indeed it survived in some instances well into the twentieth century. Compare the layout of a typical fermtoun, which can be found on hundreds of Scottish estate plans, with the layout of the houses of the agricultural communities described by Gibbon (1932) in *Sunset Song*. His communities were of very small scale farmers living in close proximity to one another and what is more they were not located in an area of climatic extremes but the Howe of the Mearns. How did a revolution miss an area which was environmentally and locationally so suitable for change?

In summary it can be said that there are available many *known* aspects of early (seventeenth century) changes and improvements in Scottish agriculture to throw considerable doubt on the wisdom of a continued usage of the term Agricultural Revolution. From at least the seventeenth century onwards farming methods, techniques and attitudes were changing; until much more work is done on the documentary sources the scale and distribution of these changes cannot be stated. When such work has been done it is the firm belief of the author that widespread evidence will be found of an agriculture in Scotland which was not as backward as was painted by many early nineteenth century commentators and indeed the death of the tradition of change and innovation, which is commonly believed to have taken place with the demise of 'high farming' upon the dissolution of the monasteries may never have occurred. That farming received a great setback at that period largely due to the reduction of *rich* estates may well be true but it is firmly held that attitudes did survive from the monastic period which made continuous evolution, albeit often with a varied pace, possible and a revolution unnecessary.

REFERENCES

Caird, J. B. (1964) 'The making of the Scottish rural landscape', *Scott. Geogr. Mag.* 80, 2, 73

Emery, F. V. (1959) 'A 'Geographical Description' of Scotland prior to the Statistical Account', *Scott. Stud.* 3, 1–16

Gibbon, L. G. (1932) *Sunset Song*

Handley, J. E. (1963) *The Agricultural Revolution in Scotland*

Lebon, J. H. G. (1946) 'The process of enclosure in the Western Lowlands', *Scott. Geogr. Mag.* 62, 100–10

Third, B. M. (1955) 'Changing landscape and social structure in the Scottish lowlands as revealed by eighteenth century Estate Plans', *Scott. Geogr. Mag.* 71, 83–93

Third, B. M. (1957) 'The significance of Scottish estate plans and associated documents', *Scott. Stud.* 1, 39–64

Whittington, G. (1973) 'Field systems in Scotland', in Baker A. R. H. and Butlin R. A. (eds), *Studies of field systems in the British Isles,* 530–79

The agricultural revolution in Scotland: contributions to the debate

IH Adams 1978 in *Area* 9, 198–205.

The capacity of *Area* to stimulate debate has been illustrated by three communications dealing with that hoary subject 'Agricultural Revolution'.[1] Most
English readers probably dismissed these contributions as an example of the
slow diffusion into the Celtic fringe of an academic debate which had enlivened
the English scene nearly a decade earlier.[2] Appearances are deceptive, for there
has emerged in the last decade a completely new evaluation of Scottish historical
geography based on our own indigenous resources which had laid so long
neglected.[3] Therefore, though we should be more than grateful to Whittington
for starting the hare, we must avoid the pitfalls that the earlier English debate
fell into. First we must define what we mean by 'revolution' and then develop
methods by which to measure it objectively.

Taking as a definition for agricultural revolution, 'a period in which
agrarian change took place at a rapid rate and on a large scale', both time
and spatial elements are suggested and are capable of measurement. Innovation
by itself, or its eccentric adoption, is not sufficient to qualify as revolution. One
thing must be remembered about revolutions: they are not undertaken by
theoreticians, but by men commanding the centre of power. These men will
use any tools to hand to further their objectives: the Americans used Paine and
Locke, the French the guillotine, and the Russians Marx. In Scotland, landowners, substantial tenants, professional men and burgesses saw nothing but
profit when they overthrew the old agrarian order in society. Nearly all the
innovations they applied were well-tried, but the revolution lay in their
simultaneous use across the face of the country.

To what extent can the English arguments be transcribed to Scotland? The
short answer is very little. Scotland's agriculture employed a different system of
cultivation, and the landownership structure was based on a legal system alien
to English common law. History too must be recognized – political stress of the
seventeenth century continued until 1746, creating an unfavourable atmosphere
for large-scale agrarian investment.

Seventeenth-century legislation. Whittington, in quoting an act of the Scottish Parliament making enclosure compulsory, makes a classic mistake in assuming that there was some tangible action thereafter. Dead letter acts sprinkle the statute book like clerk's sand. The Act of 1647 laid down principle but nothing else – Charles I, the Covenanters and Cromwell saw to that – and, like all the other legislation of this period, was annulled in 1661 by the Act Rescissory. Thereafter Parliament in the same year passed the 'Act for planting and incloseing of ground' but *no evidence* has been found to indicate that it had any effect.[4] Likewise the better known Acts of 1695 for division of runrig and commonty, which have been examined in detail, had little effect until economic circumstances became favourable.[5]

If Scotland had an extended agricultural revolution, where is the vernacular architecture showing the fruits of early agricultural advances? Show me a farmhouse dating from before 1750.[6] 'The Agricultural Revolution in Scotland', wrote Whyte, 'obliterated most traces of pre-existing agrarian landscape, and survivals of vernacular building from the first half of the eighteenth century are rare'.[7] Yet, as the same author has shown in the only doctoral dissertation written on seventeenth-century Scottish agriculture, some advances in agriculture had been assimilated in a piecemeal fashion.[8] Of course the agrarian innovations developed in the Netherlands were well known in Scotland, as many Scottish landowners sent their sons to Leyden for their education in law, medicine and theology. Yet the fact remains that in 1755 about 90% of the population were still in agriculture, and at least one half of these were cottars or labourers living on the margins of the system.

Divison of commonty. Commonty, the Scottish species of common land, extended over 650,000 Imperial acres, mainly in lowland counties (an area greater than the county of Warwickshire).[9] The division of these lands was undertaken, under a law passed by the Scottish Parliament in 1695, by a relatively simple legal action heard in the Court of Session.[10] So successful was this Act that hardly a piece of common land exists today. If one plots a simple bar graph of the dates of summons it is clear that the 1760s mark the most intensive attack on the common lands of Scotland (Figure 1A).

Enclosure. The building of dykes or hedges around fields, clearing stones, laying drains, levelling rigs and so on were rare events before 1750. In order to undertake these improvements the landowner required expert advice and this was available from the members of the land surveying profession who acted as agricultural consultants. Ideally, if one could plot all the plans made by these men, a picture of the intensity of their activities could be drawn. As this has only been undertaken on a very tentative basis another approach has been made, that of plotting the available land surveyors living in Scotland in any year (Figure

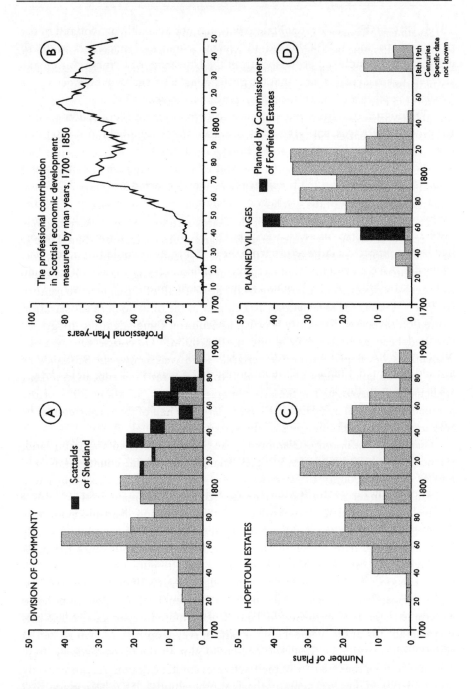

Figure 1. (Reproduced with permission from *Imago Mundi* 27 (1975))

1B). It is clear that professional talent was just not available in Scotland in the period up to the 1730s. Indeed in several instances landowners were so desperate they employed professors from the University of Edinburgh to make surveys. Again it is quite clear that the professional land surveyor emerged in the 1750s to reach his eighteenth-century zenith in the year 1770.

Whittington questions the existence of revolution on the Gordon estates. Revolution there was, for large areas of these estates were held in wadset and heritable bonds which were not redeemed until 1766–8.[11] Only when this had been done could the serious business be started of surveying the Gordon estates prior to enclosure. The main surveying activity occurred between 1769 and 1781 and full details of the survey, including a full transcription of the surveyor's instructions, have been published.[12] The Duke of Gordon would not have encumbered his estate with a bill of £1,265 13s 2½d for the surveyors had he not expected a large return from the higher rents he could command after enclosure. All the evidence points to him spending every penny the estate could yield on rebuilding Gordon Castle and his political ambition.[13] This is the *push factor* of agricultural revolution.

Whittington also cites from the Morton papers which show innovatory crop rotations well before the second half of the eighteenth century. With this one must agree, but acquaintance with the plans of the Morton estates at Aberdour around 1750 and 1785 can leave no doubt that a massive change in landscape occurred during this later period.[14]

Landownership. The control of improvement was closely supervised by the great landowners of Scotland.[15] Very few participated in any large-scale enclosure before the 1760s and those who did often found themselves bankrupt. 'This was an age of fast-rising rents, but it was also an age of insolvent landlords'.[16]

The landowner controlled the pace of enclosure through the system of leases or tacks. Mills cites the annual lease as a symptom of backwardness prior to enclosure. However, this is not the case; indeed the annual lease could be the mark of a *progressive* estate. From the seventeenth century farmers had been accustomed to leases of 7 or 9 years.[17] But when an estate was on the verge of enclosure, each lease as it ran out was continued on an annual basis. After the estate had been remodelled all the farmers would be put on long leases simultaneously; these would of course expire together, enabling the landlord to carryout any *future* remodelling without the long wait he was presently experiencing. Thus the annual lease in this circumstance was an example, not of rapacious, but of far-sighted landlordism.

Generally one can say that the speed and comprehensiveness of Scottish improvements stemmed from the landowners demanding maximum returns to support their conspicuous consumption. The bulk of the capital for improvement of land was supplied as time and labour by the tenant farmer and the landless cottar, for which the former was given security of tenure by the long lease plus ameliorations upon giving up the tenancy; the cottar's only reward was the delay of his rejection from rural society.

Forfeited Estates Commission. Scotland after 1746 was a country in political limbo, not unlike Germany and Japan after the Second World War. The setting up of the Forfeited Estates Commission and the annexing of Jacobite Highland estates gave an impetus for economic revival not unlike an eighteenth-century version of the Marshall Plan.[18] Through example and education and by providing extended employment for land surveyors and other agriculturalists the Commission engendered a new spirit of confidence which its members carried back to their own estates. One such man, the Earl of Hopetoun, was able to create a policy of improvement which affected lands from the shores of the Solway Firth to the wastes of Ross and Cromarty.[19] On his own estates the intensity of enclosure was concentrated in the 1760s as measured by the total production of enclosure plans in the Hopetoun House collection (Figure IC). Few countries had so much power concentrated in the hands of a few great landowners whose economic, political and social power was supreme.

Planned villages. Mills mentioned planned villages as a system of revolutionary settlement change. We are still a long way from discovering the total number planned, but work by Lockhart in north-east Scotland indicates the revolutionary objectives of these villages.[20] So far 268 planned villages have been identified.[21] If one plots these in a simple bar graph, again the 1760s stand out as a period of very active settlement formation (Figure 1D).

Marginal lands. Parry comes closest to giving some precision to the debate, with his table of establishment and abandonment of farms in the Lammermuirs.[22] In a recent paper he concludes that the period 1750 to 1770 represents the *beginnings* of farm amalgamation and that the pattern for 1770–1800 'also suggests that amalgamation was causing the redundancy of farmsteads *on a large scale*'.[23]

The marginal areas in many ways are critical in the measurement of revolutionary changes. The intensity of improvement became in some cases a 'fever of improvement' with over investment of marginal areas, leading to abandonment and bankruptcy. Landlords were happy to give leases for little or no rent to enable tenants (many of whom were the displaced cottars) to bring the waste into cultivation. Institutional factors like division of commonty and inflation during the Napoleonic Wars led men to invest in marginal lands. Equally the declining climatic situation, with the onset of the Little Ice Age, and the economic depression led to abandonment. Revolutions are very unstable times and the period from 1760 to 1820 was marked in Scotland by economic turmoil.

Contemporary opinion. Contemporary literature of the period from 1760 to the early-nineteenth century abounds in emphatic references to the large-scale changes of the age. Men at the time were in no doubt they were participating in a major upheaval: phrases like 'spirit of improvement', fever of improvement' and even 'revolution' are used unceasingly. John Ramsay of Ochtertyre, writing in 1804 of Lord Kames, the author of *The gentleman farmer* (1776) said: 'When Lord Kames invited a gentleman to visit him at Blair, soon after his accession to that fortune, he said he would show him sights that would make all his *een reel* [eyes pop out]. In fact, everything, *without* doors is going on upon a very great scale in office houses [farm buildings], cultivation, planting, roads etc. I had only to wonder, and wish success to the plans going on, without making any remarks, or obtruding hints which alwise imply officiousness or a display of wisdom. The *fever* of improvements, so common and malignant between 30 and 40 years ago, does not alwise appear in the same form, or produce precisely the same effects'.[24]

Let the last word be said by a scholar much nearer the events, reviewing a work by a man who had been very active at the period in question. James Ramsay McCulloch's criticism of the agriculturalist George Robertson's *Rural recollections* commended the author for 'confining himself to such changes in agriculture and in the condition of the agricultural population as fell under his immediate and very capable observation, and observed that the advances made by Scotland in industry, wealth, and their correlatives since 1765, when these recollections commence, has, we believe, been quite unprecedented in any old settled country, and is hardly, indeed, surpassed by anything that has taken place in Kentucky and Illinois'.[25]

Other indices of change. At this time landlord and farmer both recognized that to improve incomes from farming it was necessary to increase output per capita. Thus both had a vested interest in the removal of that group of people, the cottars, who made up about half the population. Their labour was required only periodically, for ploughing, threshing, herding and harvesting. Small's plough reduced the need for large teams of oxen and men; Meikle's threshing machine took over one of the most labour intensive tasks of the agricultural calendar; enclosures removed the need for the herd; only harvest itself needed extra hands and these were obtained by seasonal labour, first from the Highlands and then from Ireland. The cottage was effectively banned from much of the Scottish countryside and the bothy system instituted. This reduction of the rural population led to a great increase in emigration after 1760. Indeed it reached such epidemic proportions in the early 1770s that it was reported, 'the spirit of emigration is not confined to Scotland and Ireland: the English seem to have caught the infection'.[26] Most of the emigrants at this time complained about the high rents which were driving them from the land.

CONCLUSION

The Agricultural Revolution in Scotland was a real event recognized by contemporaries and is measurable with hindsight. English scholars have called into question its very existence in their own country, and this has proved a very profitable excercise; but we must not assume that the same circumstances prevailed elsewhere. I would support the contention that the agricultural changes in England were evolutionary rather than revolutionary. However, English revisionism can play no part in the understanding of the events in Scotland for, notwithstanding the Union of 1707, Scottish agriculture maintained its individual character, Scottish political life took its own wayward paths, the Scottish legal system remained feudal and in its influence upon agriculture differed completely from that of England. One could go on. So far, data have been assembled for a few aspects of agrarian change in the period in question, but it will be a long time before any definitive answer can be given. Theory and speculation can be erected very easily; the finding of precise proof is a more painstaking business.

NOTES

1 G. Whittington, 'Was there a Scottish Agricultural Revolution', *Area* 7 (1975), 3, 204–6; and correspondence relating thereto by D. Mills and M. Parry, *Area* 8 (1976), 3, 237–9

2 E. Kerridge, *The Agricultural Revolution* (George Allen & Unwin, London, 1967), and 'The Agricultural Revolution reconsidered', *Agric. Hist.* 43 (1969), 463–75; J. D. Chambers and G. E. Mingay, *The Agricultural Revolution 1750–1880* (Batsford, London, 1966); G. E. Mingay, 'Dr Kerridge's 'Agricultural Revolution', a comment', *Agric. Hist.* 43 (1969), 477–81; for a brief summary see I. H. Adams, *Agrarian landscape terms: a glossary for historical geography*, Inst. Br. Geogr. Spec. Publ. 9 (1976), 184–5

3 I. D. Whyte, 'Scottish historical geography: a survey and prospect', *Res. Pap. 8,* Dept of Geog., Univ. of Edinburgh (1976)

4 For a survey of seventeenth-century enclosure legislation in Scotland see I. H. Adams, 'Division of the commonty of Hassendean 1761–1763', *The Stair Society miscellany* (Edinburgh, 1971), 171–92

5 I. H. Adams, 'The legal geography of Scotland's common lands', *Revue de l'Institut de Sociologie* (Univ. of Brussels, 1973), 259–332

6 H. Fairhurst, 'The archaeology of rural settlement in Scotland', *Trans. Glasgow Archaeol. Soc.* 15 (1967), 139–58

7 I. D. Whyte, 'Rural housing in lowland Scotland in the seventeenth century: the evidence of estate papers', *Scott. Stud.* 19 (1975), 55–68

8 I. D. Whyte, 'Agrarian change in lowland Scotland in the seventeenth century', unpubd Ph.D. thesis, Univ. of Edinburgh, (1974)

9 I. H. Adams, *Directory of former Scottish commonties* (Scottish Record Society, 1971) (addenda maintained at the Scottish Record Office, Edinburgh, show a further 100,000 acres discovered since the publication of this work)

10 For example see Adams, 'Hassendean Common', *op. cit.;* and 'The division of Dunbar Common', *Trans. East Lothian Antiq. Field Nat. Soc.* 15 (1976), 75–86

11 V. Gaffney, *The Lordship of Strathavon* (Third Spalding Club, Aberdeen, 1960), 147

12 *See* introduction to I. H. Adams, *Descriptive list of plans in the Scottish Record Office* (HMSO, Edinburgh, vol. 2 1970)

13 Gaffney, *op. cit.,* 149–50

14 Scottish Record Office RHP 1022 and 1023 respectively

15 L. Timperley, *A directory of landownership in Scotland c. 1770* (Scottish Record Society, 1976)

16 E. Cregeen, *Argyll Estate Instructions 1771–1805* (Scottish History Society, 1964), xi

17 I. D. Whyte, 'The development of written leases and their impact on Scottish agriculture in the seventeenth century' (forthcoming)

18 V. Wills, *Reports on the annexed estates 1755–1769* (HMSO, Edinburgh, 1973); for details of the estate surveys see I. H. Adams *Descriptive list of plans in the Scottish Record Office* (HMSO, Edinburgh, vol. 3, 1974, introduction)

19 I. H. Adams, *The mapping of a Scottish estate* (Educational Studies Dept, Univ. of Edinburgh, 1971)

20 D. Lockhart 'Planned villages of north-east Scotland', unpubl. Ph.D. thesis, Univ. of Dundee, (1975)

21 A planned village index is maintained by the author at the Scottish Record Office, West Register House, Edinburgh. It is based on a list published by T. C. Smout and augmented by D. Lockhart and others.

22 M. L. Parry, 'Changes in the upper limit of cultivation in south-east Scotland 1600–1900', unpubl. Ph.D thesis, Univ. of Edinburgh, (1973)

23 M. L. Parry, 'The abandonment of upland settlement in southern Scotland', *Scott. Geogr. Mag.* 92 (1976), 56–7

24 B. L. H. Horn, *Letters of John Ramsay of Ochtertyre 1799–1812* (Scottish History Society, 1966), 121

25 James Ramsay McCulloch, *Literature of political economy* (London, 1845), 219

26 *Scots Mag.* 36 (1774), 161

The agricultural revolution in Scotland: contributions to the debate

ID Whyte 1978 in *Area* 10, 203–5.

Whittington's article[1] has brought to the surface a problem which has been widely discussed in Scotland in recent years. In his reply,[2] Parry points out that certain developments in Scottish agriculture such as enclosure were limited to particular areas before the mid-eighteenth century and even in these districts affected only a small proportion of the agrarian landscape, and Mills[3] comes down firmly in favour of the traditional view of the Scottish 'Agricultural Revolution'. However, I believe that Parry has viewed agricultural improvement upon too narrow a front while Mills has been misled by the sources he has quoted.

The changes which profoundly altered Scottish agriculture between the seventeenth and early-nineteenth centuries involved essentially the replacement of a subsistence-orientated farming system by a more commercialized one. They can be broadly divided into technical changes (for example, enclosure, new crops and rotations, improved implements) and organizational changes (the re-shaping of rural society and the modification of farm structures to produce more commercially efficient units of production).

To some extent these two facets of change could be introduced independently. However, for technical changes to be fully effective they had to be accompanied or preceded by some re-organization of rural society and farm structures. There is a strong case for viewing this as the most important contribution of the seventeenth and early-eighteenth centuries to agrarian change in Scotland. Limited technical innovations did occur,[4] but organizational changes were of greater importance in providing the groundwork for the more spectacular developments of the later-eighteenth century.[5]

Technical changes are easier to identify from historical sources than organizational ones. The former tended to catch the imagination of contemporary writers while the latter often passed unnoticed.[6] One reason why organizational change has received so little attention has been the tendency for historical geographers to rely upon later, secondary sources when seeking the origins of agrarian change in Scotland. The writings of the Improvers, the Old Statistical Account, the Board of Agriculture Reports all refer to pre-Improvement agriculture in Scotland. However, the Improvers had a vested interest in contrasting earlier farming systems unfavourably with their own and other writers of this period were not necessarily well informed about conditions a century or so earlier. Little progress has yet been made in analysing the abundant primary source material for the pre-eighteenth-century Scottish rural landscape,[7] but work by the author has demonstrated the importance of some aspects of organizational reforms in Scottish agriculture before the Union of 1707, particularly with reference to tenure and farm structure.[8]

The differences in the social distribution of land ownership between England and Scotland referred to by Mills[9] were important. However, the tenantry were not as insecure or downtrodden as has sometimes been suggested. A study of some 3000 written leases together with other estate documents indicates that the granting of written leases first became common on many Scottish estates in the early-seventeenth century. By the later-seventeenth century long leases of up to 19 years duration were quite frequent. Leases of over 10 years length comprised 45% of the total for the 1690s. That surviving leases are only a small proportion of those which once existed is shown by estate rentals where details of tenancy are given.[10] Tenants with written leases, often for substantial periods, were probably in a majority on many Scottish estates by the end of the century. On some estates proprietors were encouraging their tenants to take written leases. During the course of the century the bargaining power of the tenantry seems to have been strengthened by the trend towards commercial production. Instances occur of proprietors inducing tenants to accept 19–year leases by offering them some remission of rent.[11] By the early-eighteenth century the first 19–year improving leases had appeared.[12] The annual leasing of holdings on a verbal basis was uncommon by the late-seventeenth century in lowland Scotland.

The multiple-tenant farm has been seen as the standard model of farm structure for pre-Improvement Scotland, yet in many parts of the country such farms were already anachronisms by 1707. The importance of the large single-tenant farm cultivated not by the co-operative effort of several tenants but by hired labour is clear from estate rentals.[13] The Poll Tax records for Aberdeenshire show that in 1696 such farms were dominant in most of the lowland parishes of the county. It was mainly areas on the margins of the Highlands which perpetuated the old farm structures.[14]

Trends of this kind are only evident from detailed studies of the primary source material, few of which have so far been undertaken. More detailed work will be necessary before the picture becomes clearer and regional variations emerge. However, even this limited introductory work suggests the need to reassess the progress and nature of agrarian change in Scotland. It cannot be doubted that the second half of the eighteenth and the early-nineteenth century saw the most rapid and dramatic changes in the rural landscape. Nevertheless, the extent to which they were based on earlier, less spectacular groundwork requires further examination.

NOTES

1 G. Whittington, 'Was there a Scottish Agricultural Revolution?', *Area* 7 (1975), 3, 204–6

2 M. L. Parry, *Area* 8 (1976), 3, 238–9

3 D. Mills, *Area* 8 (1976), 3, 237

4 T. C. Smout and A. Fenton, 'Scottish agriculture before the Improvers – an exploration', *Agric. Hist. Rev.* 13 (1965), 73–93

5 I. D. Whyte, 'Agrarian change in lowland Scotland in the seventeenth century', unpubd Ph.D. thesis, Univ. of Edinburgh, (1974)

6 R. A. Dodgshon, 'The removal of runrig in Roxburghshire and Berwickshire 1680–1766', *Scott. Stud.* 16 (1972), 121–7.

7 I. D. Whyte, 'Scottish historical geography: survey and prospect', *Res. Pap.* 8, Dept of Geography, Univ. of Edinburgh (1976), 19–22.

8 I. D. Whyte, (1974) *op. cit.*, 247–327

9 D Mills, (1975) *op. cit.*

10 I. D. Whyte, (1974) *op. cit.*, 255–8

11 J. Dodds, *Diary and general expenditure book of William Cunningham of Craigends* (Scottish History Society, 1887), 4

12 *The Caldwell Papers* (Maitland Club, 1854), 300

13 I. D. Whyte, (1974) *op. cit.*, 294–5

14 *Ibid.*, 287–91

Scottish illegitimacy ratios in the early modern period[1]

L Leneman and R Mitchison 1987 in *Economic History Review* 40, 41–63.

This paper reports the findings of an attempt to measure illegitimacy in various regions in Scotland between the later seventeenth and the later eighteenth centuries. Illegitimacy came to the fore as a subject for social concern in Scotland with the start of civil registration in 1855, when figures were produced indicating both sharp regional variation in the percentage of births out of wedlock, and a level for Scotland as a whole for 1858–60 of 9.1 per cent, which appeared shockingly high to contemporary commentators. In spite of public concern, the relatively high regional figures changed only slightly during the later nineteenth century, a fact which suggested that they might be of long standing. This was one of the questions we set out to investigate: were these high levels of rural illegitimacy to be found in the eighteenth century and earlier? The other question in our minds was whether the level of illegitimacy rose in Scotland, as it has been held to in England, with economic development and changing marriage patterns from the mid-eighteenth century.[2]

Given the poor quality of most Scottish parish registers, the study could not be based on this primary source. However, illegitimacy was a matter of concern to the disciplinary courts of the Church, and the records of the lowest of the church courts, the kirk sessions, give evidence of the systematic handling of cases of sexual irregularity. The sessions were empowered, by statute as well as by church law, to exercise discipline on sexual irregularities, and had their records in this matter regularly inspected by the higher court, the presbytery. The ultimate sanction of church discipline was excommunication, which would lead to imprisonment by the sheriff. A well-kept kirk session register makes it possible to study the cases and quantify them, and so to study quantitatively and regionally this particular element in demographic history. Since even in the later nineteenth century Scottish fertility, both legitimate and illegitimate, reveals in its variety the cultural diversity of the country,[3] we decided to try to see if illegitimacy displayed a similar regional pattern in the early modern period.

The project involved an initial investigation into parishes which could supply long runs of kirk session registers. From regional lists, groups of parishes were selected which would give a substantial base population and then, decade by decade, the cases of unmarried pregnancy dealt with in the registers were collected, using only registers for which the internal consistency and quality were such as to give confidence of completeness.

An introductory section to our paper delineates the different Scottish regions and this is followed by an explanation of our choice of starting and finishing dates, and a list of the rules which we made for ourselves in assessing the records. A description of the procedure of kirk session meetings concludes this section. We then describe the decadal illegitimacy ratios which resulted from our work and discuss the conclusions to be drawn from the figures. Comments on other aspects of illegitimacy, e.g. 'repeaters', infant abandonment, and the social class of mothers and fathers, followed by a comparison of eighteenth- and nineteenth-century illegitimacy figures, round off the paper.

I

We divided Scotland into ten regions as shown in the map in appendix 1. Counties which were adjacent geographically might have quite different cultural patterns. West Lothian, Midlothian and East Lothian were grouped together as 'the Lothians.' Fife was treated as a different region. The 'Central Lowlands' comprised Stirlingshire and lowland Perthshire, the 'South-West' Dumfries and Galloway. Ayrshire was examined as a separate region. The Highlands were divided into 'Eastern' – Perthshire and Inverness-shire, and 'Western' – Bute, Argyll and Sutherland. The parishes grouped under 'Aberdeenshire' were all lowland, as were those in Caithness. Moray and Banffshire were classified as 'North-East'. Whenever possible the same parishes were used throughout the period, but this was often not feasible. Our rule was that in any one decade we would try to include at least four different parishes of the particular region, with a combined population of not less than 4,000.

Although some small burghs (e.g. Ayr, Dumfries, Thurso) were used in the survey, we have made no special attempt to study urban patterns of illegitimacy. In view of the sheer numbers involved in the larger urban centres a separate study would be necessary. Also, the difficulty which urban kirk sessions might have experienced in keeping track of the comings and goings of their parishioners means that illegitimacy figures from this source would be suspect. This decision may have been unduly cautious. It is clear from their co-operation with rural parishes in tracing women who ran away to the towns rather than face parish discipline that many urban ministers had a good grasp of what was going on in their parishes.

The population of Scotland was, and is, small, but it contains much cultural variety, sustained into the eighteenth century by difficulties in communication and the scale of the country, and persisting into modern times. The main cultural division, between a Gaelic-speaking Celtic area occupying the highlands, Western Isles and, at least in our period, part of the nearby lowland area, that was socially and politically tribal, and an English-speaking lowland population accepting the authority of a modernizing central state government, is well known, though there has been a general tendency to underplay the effectiveness of the protestant church structure in the Gaelic area for much of our period. Two of our regions were Gaelic-speaking – the Western and Eastern Highlands – though in the former the parishes are predominantly from the mainland and may therefore not be fully representative. There has also been a considerable Norse element, and we have used Caithness as a sample of this culture. Caithness has long been mostly English in speech and lowland in geology with prosperous arable farming.

Another area with a long tradition of separateness is the South-West – Galloway and Dumfriesshire. Galloway had its own separate law and justiciar in the middle ages and many Scots then regarded Galwegians as barbarians. Separateness and resistance to authority were manifested in the extremism with which in the seventeenth century it sustained the later convenanting movement.

The rest of our regions are all part of the main lowland culture of Scotland, yet had different political traditions and economic features. Fife was a county of small landowners, relatively poor farming and a coast dotted with small and active trading communities. Across the Forth lie the rich and influential Lothians, an area which accepted of necessity a close relationship with central government, a centre of good farmland and large estates, relatively good transport and profitable mining, and with the city of Edinburgh and its satellite town Leith giving the benefit of a large consumer market. The Central Lowlands of south Perthshire and Stirlingshire were also a prosperous region though, because of its exposure to highland incursion, less secure and conformist than the Lothians. The western coastal area of Ayrshire, combining a rich plain, hill country and a coalfield with numerous small ports is an area consciously separate from Galloway, but where poor communication reduced the impact of central government.

Finally we took two northern lowland regions, Aberdeenshire and the North-East consisting of the counties of Banffshire and Moray. Aberdeenshire provides the biggest single arable area in Scotland today: it has a long history of cultural individuality, including support for episcopacy; was under the political dominance of one great family in the seventeenth century; and by the late eighteenth century appears[4] to have had distinctive demographic features. Moray and Banffshire, west of the 'cold shoulder' of Buchan, with a coastal strip of rich soil and mild climate, combined with a mountainous interior, had a long tradition of separateness from southern Scotland, and an economy enriched by numerous small ports. In the nineteenth century it was an area of high educational provision and high levels of illegitimacy. The linguistic divide between the English-speaking North-East and the Gaelic-speaking areas of the highlands is still sharp.

Those who know Scotland today may feel that these regions over-emphasize the north. Today the great bulk of Scotland's population lives and works in the central valley, brought there by the early industrialization of this area and by its coal measures. But in the past the distribution of population was more even. Webster's 1755 census shows that over half of the population of the country was living north of the Tay and west of the Stonehaven/Dumbarton fault which defines the highlands. It seemed reasonable to take half our regions from north of these dividing lines. We would have liked also to have investigated the southern upland area of the Borders, an area distinct in social structure, economy and literary culture, but depopulation of this area, resulting from the early development of commercial sheep farming, gave us no grounds for thinking that the population figures available for the second half of the eighteenth century could give us reliable base figures for the decades on either side of 1700.[5]

In one important way the various regions of Scotland were less distinct than they are now: this was in their farming. Today it is obvious that the western areas, and the upland parts of Aberdeenshire and some other lowland districts, are predominately pastoral in their economy, while the south-east is a grain producing area, and Caithness also grows grain well. In the early modern period, as has been pointed out by Dodgshon, the relatively undeveloped transport system of Scotland could not provide flows of grain on a scale to permit specialization. All areas had to grow almost all their own food, even if the climate was inauspicious. Grain brought from a distance, except in the case of the supplies for Edinburgh, was always small in amount, even in the case of the highlands. Only the border area was, by the early eighteenth century, growing sheep for the market in a big way, and it had not yet abandoned grain.[6] Similarly, the export of pastoral products and animals from upland areas was on a small scale till the mid-eighteenth century. Agricultural improvement, when it arrived, was to change this, and in particular to encourage some specialized farming in the east of Scotland. By the mid-nineteenth century, as Smout has shown, in some districts high illegitimacy followed almost exactly the line of turnip husbandry[7] where there was plenty of work for women. But the turnip husbandry had not yet got beyond the south-eastern lowlands before 1770.

II

It was not feasible to begin our survey before 1660 in view of the turbulent state of the mid-seventeenth century. By 1661 the records indicate that most of the country had effective kirk sessions in operation. After 1690, when the episcopal establishment was replaced by Presbyterianism, there was a short period of turmoil, but for the most part the transition took place smoothly and in many parishes within two or three years the Presbyterian kirk sessions were running as efficiently as their predecessors. We noted no differences between the practices and procedures adopted by kirk sessions under the episcopal system and under Presbytery.

The cut-off date of 1780 was forced on us by the disintegration of kirk session discipline. The exact timing varied between parishes (and some could no doubt have been studied for a decade or two longer), but in the great majority of cases kirk session registers after 1780 would not sustain our inquiry. There can be no simple explanation for this phenomenon, but some contributory factors may be noted.

For much of our period the kirk was a more or less monolithic structure with undisputed control over all of its humble parishioners (the gentry were in rather a different category). But, starting with the Original Secession of 1733 the growth and spread of dissent meant that this was no longer the case in many parishes. It has been alleged that by 1765 dissenters numbered 100,000,[8] or about 7 per cent of the total population. Dissent tended to be concentrated in the large towns and the west-central area. Its existence may have had a more damaging effect on the authority of the established church than on the quality of its records, for it was the conclusion of Flinn's research team that protestant dissenting communities often used the rites of the establishment, particularly baptism, until 1783.[9] Certainly a kirk session regarded itself as responsible for the morals of the whole of the local protestant population, but since the dissenting bodies were more austere and puritanical than the Church of Scotland, there was not much occasion for investigation by the session of the established church into the affairs of dissenters.

The improvements made in transportation helped to erode the kirk's authority, for couples became less dependent on their parish ministers to marry them: from the 1740s onward the increasing number of 'irregular' marriages testifies to this. There may well have been other, subtler, forces at work too. By the 1760s in a number of parishes guilty couples could simply pay a fine and avoid having to make any public appearances at all. This represented a fundamental shift of attitude on the part of ministers and kirk sessions, although the reasons why this should have occurred cannot easily be found. We would stress that the changes in church structure were slow, and the decay in discipline patchy, so that we were able to find some parishes in all our regions sustaining discipline, at least for fornication cases, through the 1770s.

We are conscious that there is a serious hiatus between our information and that provided by civil registration from 1855 onwards, and that much may have changed in the regional pattern in this period. However, we are confident that even at the end of our period the figures are sound, and that the surprising lack of any rise in illegitimacy in most areas is a reality, not a reflection of a lack of zeal on the part of kirk sessions. In parishes which had become remiss by the 1770s this is clear in the tone and content of the record. We abandoned a number of registers where discipline had slackened; as a result the sample for the 1770s is markedly smaller than for most other periods.

To translate our catalogue of instances of the detection and investigation of unmarried pregnancy into an assessment of the number of illegitimate births, we had to make for ourselves a body of rules. These, which were based on the methodology of the kirk sessions, were as follows.

1. We counted as an illegitimate birth in a particular parish all cases where the couple made their penitential appearances in the parish church, regardless of where the child was born. Normally kirk sessions confined their disciplinary activity to cases for which the intercourse was thought to have taken place in the parish.

2. We did not count as illegitimate any case where the couple was already proclaimed for marriage or where the session accepted that it was contracted, as there was every likelihood the child would have been born after the marriage.

3. We have not counted any cases where the mother was married, even when the father was definitely not her husband, as the child was not legally defined as a bastard.

4. We have assumed that when a case led to public appearances in church for fornication (as opposed to scandalous carriage) it did result in an illegitimate birth. In some parishes in the seventeenth century pregnancy was not explicitly referred to, but it appears a very constant pattern in the eighteenth century that the allegation of fornication was not made until a woman was visibly pregnant, usually in the sixth or seventh

month.[10] In some cases there was reference to the child as already born before the first citation, in many to its birth during the inquiry.

5. We have recorded twins where the registrar makes explicit reference to a double birth, but since not all births occurred during the period of investigation, some multiple ones will have been accepted as single.

6. We made no allowance for stillbirths, and we have counted as an illegitimate birth any case where the mother claimed that the child had been born dead. In this our suspicion of the likelihood of infanticide is merely a reflection of that of the sessions. However, when it was reported that a mother had 'parted with the child', the phrase used for miscarriage, we have not counted a birth. These decisions were forced on us by the erratic timing of action by the kirk session, for though most sessions handled cases briskly, some met only monthly and some couples were difficult to get hold of, through illness, absence or recalcitrance. There were also cases which through successful concealment of pregnancy came to light only after the birth of a child. We had no acceptable figure for the likely level of stillbirths, and so no basis on which to draw a line between the probably natural death of a foetus and infanticide.

Kirk sessions, though they varied in the promptness with which they took up a case, acted in a remarkably systematic manner once an initial report was made. This is not surprising since they were acting under powers conferred by statute[11] and regularly supervised. An elder would 'delate' a particular woman as being with child. At the next meeting (usually a week later, but in zealous sessions it could be as little as two days while in more dilatory sessions it could be a month or more) the woman would appear and admit her guilt, naming a man at that time. At the next meeting the man would be cited to admit his guilt. If he did, the couple would then be ordered to pay a fine and begin public appearances before the congregation: three times for a first offence, six for a relapse, and many more for a 'trilapse' or for adultery; in the latter cases and if the man denied responsibility it would be referred to the presbytery. Unless proclaimed for marriage the couple would normally make their appearances separately.

There were, of course, variants of the above. In many parishes in the seventeenth century the man and the woman would be named together and would confess together. Even in the eighteenth century it was not unusual for the man to be named at the same time as the woman. From the 1750s onward in some parishes women (or couples) would come forward of their own volition to confess pregnancy. If a married man was involved the woman might make up a story about being ravished by a unknown man, but the session was usually able to get at the truth.

On rare occasions the woman would deny being pregnant. The local midwife might then be asked to examine her breasts for milk: a confession usually followed. Very occasionally a woman was able to convince the session that she was not and had not been pregnant. In the great bulk of the cases there was no suggestion that marriage would take place once church discipline was completed; economic and social factors would prevent such couples going forward for marriage.

III

We collected our figures by decades because we did not wish to be distracted by fluctuations from year to year. A decade began in January (Scotland's calendar did not suffer from the English uncertainty about the start of the year). Where registers gave information only for part of the year that year was not included. It was not always possible to get the full decade from an individual parish: the minimum number of years in a decade which made a parish acceptable was set at six. Cases were taken as belonging to the year in which they first appeared, so cases initiated at the end of a previous decade were not included in the new decade; cases instigated at the end of December in the decade being surveyed were included.

Our regional figures for the average annual number of illegitimate births by decade had to be set against figures for total births to give illegitimacy ratios, and so estimates of parish population and regional birth rates had to be made. The only available figures of parish population for any time within our period are those for Webster's census of 1755, and these we have accepted. It was the opinion of the Flinn team that Webster's census was honestly and carefully made at the date that he stated, and that his parish figures should be taken seriously. It was also the team's opinion that population growth had been slow between 1660 and 1690, and very slow between 1700 and 1740: however there invervened between these two periods the famine years of 1696–9 in which between 5 and 15 per cent of the population died, perhaps even more in the north-east.[12] The evidence being gathered in current research on the number of households in various rural parishes in the early eighteenth century supports the idea of a fairly static number of families in any parish, but clearly there will be distortions produced by using Webster's parish figures for the period before 1755. However, except for the 1690s, there are unlikely to be discontinuities in the amount of distortion.

For regional birth rates we have abandoned the figure of 41.8 per 1,000 derived from Webster's age distribution by Hollingsworth for the Flinn team.

Hollingsworth rationalized Webster's age distribution and compared it to parts of the North model tables in the Princeton life tables, in order to derive this relatively high birth rate.[13] However, some doubt must attach to this age distribution, for Webster both discounted as valid for Scotland, and then relied on, Halley's Breslau life table for calculating his total population, and in addition abandoned the basis of these calculations in his year by year age distribution. The ambiguity with which he expressed his age distribution has deflected criticism from its inherent inconsistencies.

In any case the calculation made by Hollingsworth depended on the assumption that Webster's age group 0–10 really meant 0–9: however Webster's figures for each year when added together show that he meant what he said.[14] If he is taken at his word, the age structure of his population has a smaller percentage in the juvenile groups and this implies a lower fertility. The same conclusion emerges from the information about the age of marriage of the rural population and from data about the intervals between successive births for the population of Kilmarnock. It is difficult to accept a birth rate of nearly 42 per 1,000 in an early modern population with fairly high mortality, a median age of women at first marriage of approximately 27 and birth intervals mostly over two years. Hollingsworth's figure also conflicts with the occasional information in *The statistical account of Scotland* (usually known as the *OSA*) where ministers gave retrospective summaries of decadal births, using the evidence of the old parish registers in their keeping.[15]

We were therefore forced to use the only other major eighteenth-century demographic compilation, the *OSA*, for the likely level of total births in a parish.[16] From this we worked out birth rates, ranging from 25 to 33, for each region based on all the material available in the *OSA* for all the parishes lying within the region.

Since the publication of Flinn's book, a major study of English population history has appeared, containing data reinforcing a belief in the need for revaluation of some of the conclusions about Scotland. England has now been shown to have had a 'low pressure' demographic system.[17] The birth rates there ranged from 29.7 in 1676–80 to 36.3 in 1776–80. A similar system, or at any rate a less 'high pressure' one than is implied by Hollingworth's estimate, may have existed for Scotland. It is easier to accept for Scotland birth rates lying in the 30s rather than one of nearly 42.

The main weakness of these base figures could be the absence in the *OSA* of information on the numbers of births to members of dissenting congregations. But these congregations within our period mostly used the ministrations and registers of the established church. Also, the *OSA* reports often state whether there was any sizeable presence of dissent in the parish. It seems, therefore, that the *OSA* material can be taken as giving the total number of registered births in the parishes, though an increase in the delay between birth and baptism in the 1770s will have increased slightly the shortfall between actual and registered births due to early infant death. It is unlikely that the ministers who gave information about the number of births in the *OSA* made adequate allowance for neo-natal mortality in the gap between birth and baptism. This gap was small until the 1770s, except for illegitimate children who would not be allowed baptism until their parents had completed church discipline. This is likely to make the *OSA* figures of birth rates slightly too low. This adds to the other features of our calculations which all tend to overestimate the share of illegitimacy in total births. A sample calculation of a regional decadal ratio is given in appendix 2.

For the 1760s and 1770s we are more confident of our figures of total births, for ministers would be using for their reports registers often kept in their own ministry.

IV

The decadal illegitimacy ratios which result from our work are set out in figures 1–4 which show the regional components of the total. These graphs demonstrate that illegitimacy was consistently low in the Lothians, Fife and the Central Lowlands. It was always under 4 per cent in these regions except in the Lothians in the 1770s and was under 2 per cent in Fife and the Lothians from the 1740s-60s. In the Western and Eastern Highlands the level was higher. For only one decade in the Western Highlands was it below 3 per cent. In both areas there was a marked downward gradient. A similar downward path can be seen in Aberdeenshire, Caithness and the North-East (Moray and Banffshire), progressing from relatively high levels, over 8 per cent, to between 3.5 and 6 per cent. The generally low level of illegitimacy by the second decade of the eighteenth century shows the completion of the establishment of church discipline. The only regions with upward trends are the South-West (Dumfriesshire and Galloway) and Ayrshire, where after a relatively stable pattern at a moderate level of about 4 per cent for most of the period there was a marked upward movement in the 1750s and after.

The figures suggest that in the central belt of lowland Scotland the population contained its sexual life within marriage throughout the period covered, either from assent to religious opinion or for other cultural reasons. The low level of the central lowlands is particularly interesting since for several decades the big parish of St Ninians received the impact of a regiment of the

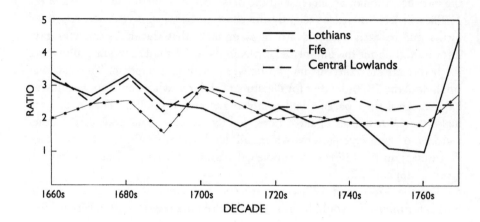

Figure 1. *Illegitimacy ratios, Lothians, Fife and Central Lowlands, by decade (percentage of estimated total births).*

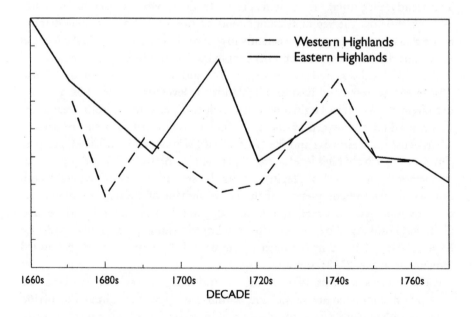

Figure 2. *Illegitimacy ratios, Western and Eastern Highlands, by decade (percentage of estimated total births).*

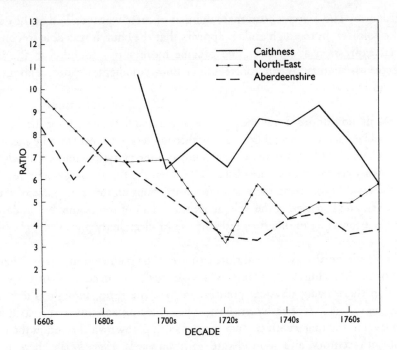

Figure 3. *Illegitimacy ratios, Aberdeenshire, the North-East and Caithness, by decade (percentage of estimated total births).*

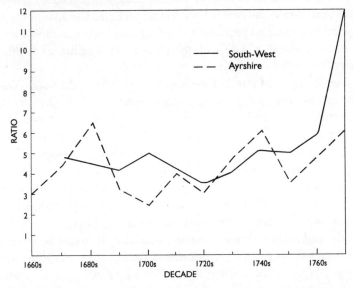

Figure 4. *Illegitimacy ratios, Ayrshire and the South-West, by decade (percentage of estimated total births).*

British army and a disproportionate number of cases was then laid at the doors of the soldiers. In the highlands it appears that the church was able to contain sexual expression as its discipline became more surely founded in the later seventeenth century. A late nineteenth-century commentator noted about the kirk session:

> Of all judicatories it was the most respected and best obeyed; for the Highlanders, remiss and careless in other matters, set great store by the ordinances of baptism and communion; and the cuttystool and sackcloth gown were much more dreaded in 1700 than the threats of law and 'tout' of the royal horn. Seeing there were few restrictions on the intercourse of the sexes, and considering the oblique idea they had of some other moral duties, it is astonishing to find how little the evil of illegitimacy prevailed.[18]

In the whole north-eastern and northern areas the picture is different. There is no doubt that church discipline was vigorously enforced in Caithness, the sanction there being physical punishment, yet the ratio, though falling, can never be called low. The North-East, where illegitimacy attained a strikingly high level in the nineteenth century, shows both a downward trend in the early eighteenth century and a moderate shift upwards after 1720: there is no indication on our graphs that the much higher mid-nineteenth-century level would be a natural extrapolation, but it is also clear that unmarried mothers can never have been rare in the North-East. In this area also there was little mention in the reports of unfulfilled promises of marriage – a fairly common allegation in other parts of Scotland. It is difficult therefore to see illegitimacy in this area as failed or uncompleted courtship.

The marked upward trend of the illegitimacy ratio in the South-West from the 1750s can be seen as suggesting a movement toward the high levels of the mid-nineteenth century. Work in England has suggested links between 'proto-industrialization' and earlier marriage, and between earlier marriage and a rising illegitimacy ratio.[19] In Scotland from the 1740s the linen industry was sustaining an increasing number of family incomes all over the country, but probably less so in Galloway than anywhere else, for the expansion of coarse linen manufacture is a development associated particularly with eastern Scotland. Linen was probably the most significant industrial product of late seventeenth- and early eighteenth-century Scotland; it would be unwise therefore to postulate the expansion of industry as a major contributor to illegitimacy in the South-West, since neither the timing of change nor the location of industry fit such a theory.

Another possible reason for rising illegitimacy has been put forward (for the whole of Europe) by Shorter. He argues that a change of mentality, causing what he terms a 'sexual revolution', took place amongst the labouring classes when the family ceased to be for them an agency of social control.[20] However, this supposed change in mentality still rests on an assumption of a radical change in work patterns, which, as we have noted, did not take place in Galloway in this period. The long-standing resistance of Galloway to all forms of authority is an element which might be expected to contribute to high illegitimacy: but there is no reason to see this resistance as increasing in the mid-eighteenth century.

The rise in decadal levels for the two regions of Ayrshire and the South-West was so marked that it seemed desirable to look more closely at the trends. The illegitimacy ratio of the parishes concerned was calculated year by year and seven-year moving averages were derived from them. The results are set out in figure 5. It is clear that the upward trend in the South-West was remarkably consistent and that in neither area were the decadal averages influenced by the exact divisions between decades; rather they show a genuine trend.

The unusual pattern of illegitimacy in this area should also be considered in relationship to the higher level of resistance to church discipline all through our period. In the South-West the percentage of men soon admitting responsibility was markedly lower than in most parts of Scotland, and if Ayrshire is taken as linked to the South-West these areas are conspicuous in that usually less than half the cases made this early submission, whereas elsewhere the 'admission rate' was usually over two-thirds. In their recalcitrance the men were aided by the women, who often determinedly refused to give names. There was also in these two regions a high proportion of cases where the women ran away rather than face discipline. It is of particular interest that Galloway, the base area of irreconcilable Covenanting sentiment and the only area of noted lowland resistance to agricultural improvement, should all through have shown resistance to the sexual discipline of the church.

V

The figures for Scotland as a whole (figure 6) have a downward trend to the 1720s, and after that they fluctuate. Since the study has to stop in 1780 we cannot be sure whether the slight rise in the 1770s was the start of an upward trend or merely a fluctuation. When set against the English quinquennial figures[21] what stands out is the markedly higher level of the Scottish ratios until the 1750s, in which decade the graphs cross. The English graph at this point is at an early stage of a marked upward acceleration. Though by the 1850s

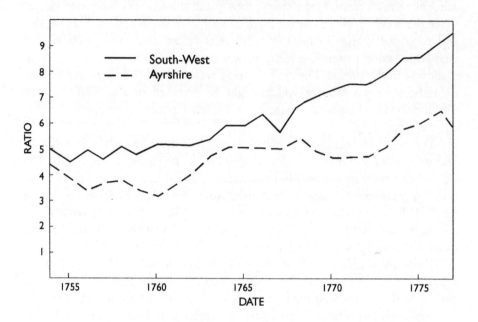

Figure 5. *Illegitimacy ratios, Ayrshire and the South-West, 1754–77 (7-year moving averages of percentages of estimated total births).*

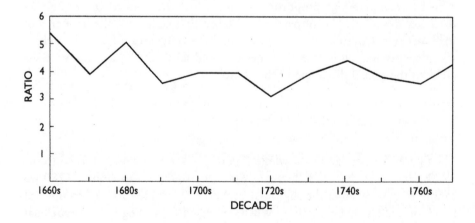

Figure 6. *Scottish illegitimacy ratios, all regions, by decade (percentage of estimated total births).*

the Scottish level [22] at 9.5 per cent is much higher than the English level of 6.5 per cent, our research does not give a clear indication from when the upward trend in Scotland can be dated. However, there is no reason to locate such a trend in the period of the expansion of the linen industry in the 1740s and 1750s.

The picture visible in the English ratios can be matched to some degree in the early decades with the levels of illegitimacy in the Lothians, Central Lowlands and Fife (figure 1), though in these regions it rarely fell below 2 per cent. What is striking in the national picture is that Scotland, with its clearly defined machinery for the forcing of sexual activity into marriage, and its uniform application by means of the supervision of presbyteries, did not match the low ratios found in England in the late seventeenth century, a period, when, apparently, registration there was good and the puritan discipline of the interregnum had been dissolved. Our calculations will tend to overestimate Scottish illegitimacy, but the distorting effect should be continuous and the constancy of illegitimacy ratios in the Lothians, Fife and the Central Lowlands, the area where the church's authority was most readily accepted, suggests that the levels of distortion did not change. The falling levels of illegitimacy in the later seventeenth century in the two highland areas support this view, since it was in this period that church discipline became effective.

It can be argued that the assumption of level population before 1750 is too crude a setting for our analysis. In figure 7 we offer alternative scenarios. It is possible that between 1660 and 1750 Scottish population increased by approximately the same amount now claimed for England, a little over 12 per cent. Line B gives the Scottish illegitimacy ratio on the assumption of a steady growth of 12.5 per cent. Line C is based on the assumption of a 25 per cent growth. Line A is deduced from a rough approximation to the most probable course of population change, a steady late seventeenth-century figure, falling by 15 per cent at the end of the century and regaining its earlier level between 1710 and 1750. In all cases the basic features remain, a ratio falling until the 1720s and then fluctuating between that low point and 4.5 per cent.

The choice of parish for a sample was based on the quality of the records rather than the centrality of the parish in its region. We were concerned that the regional structure, as we laid it down geographically, might obscure a social frontier, so we studied particularly the contribution of individual parishes to their regional totals to see if there were any that stood consistently much higher or much lower than the general regional level in their figures. For a few decades some were markedly higher than the rest of the region: this was the case for Forglen (North-East), Dailly (Ayrshire), Kilmartin (Western Highlands), and Kenmay (Aberdeenshire). By contrast Kilbirnie (Ayrshire) was usually lower.

Alvie (Eastern Highlands), notable in the mid-nineteenth century for its high illegitimacy, was also higher for the three decades for which its register could be used. The parish with the most consistently high level of illegitimacy was Westerkirk (South-West). The ratios for Westerkirk and the South-West region as a whole are set out in Table 1.

TABLE I. ILLEGITIMACY RATIOS FOR WESTERKIRK AND THE SOUTH-WEST

(percentage of estimated total births)

	WESTERKIRK	SOUTH-WEST
1691–1700	11.2	4.3
1701–1710	9.3	5.1
1711–1720	15.1	4.3
1721–1730	5.6	3.6
1731–1740	9.8	4.1

The aberrant nature of this parish lasted for several decades and is matched in the 1850s, with a level of 18.4 per cent when the regional figure was 14.5 per cent.

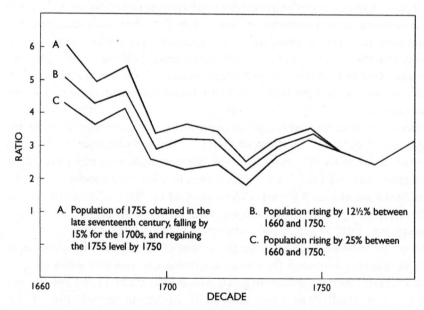

A. Population of 1755 obtained in the late seventeenth century, falling by 15% for the 1700s, and regaining the 1755 level by 1750

B. Population rising by 12½% between 1660 and 1750.

C. Population rising by 25% between 1660 and 1750.

Figure 7. *Scottish illegitimacy ratios, all regions, on varying population assumptions, by decade (percentage of estimated total births).*

Westerkirk was a small rural parish with a population, according to Webster, of only 544. The number of illegitimate births needed to produce a high ratio would therefore be modest. In such a setting a handful of illegitimate children in one decade might lead to the establishment of a structure of support, such as the availability of child minders, which would reduce the economic sanctions against illegitimacy. Without there being any weakening of the formal constraints, as expressed by the kirk session, bastard-bearing could thus become less stressful for the girls concerned.[23]

Bastard-bearing might also have a particular continuity of its own. As a check on this we collected the cases which were 'repeaters' – always noted by the kirk sessions because of the enhanced penalties laid down for this. Some women had a second, third, fourth or even fifth bastard. In *Bastardy and its comparative history* Peter Laslett writes that 'a rise in illegitimacy beyond a certain point is no longer a rise in the number of women who have bastards, but rather in the number of bastards borne by a minority of them'.[24] Our figures show no such correlation for any of the Scottish regions; illegitimacy levels appear to have risen or fallen with no corresponding rise or fall in the number of repeaters. It is noteworthy, though, that the percentage of all cases where the mother was a 'repeater' reached a low point in the 1720s, the period of most effective church discipline.

Laslett also postulates what he calls a 'bastardy prone sub-society', i.e. that the children of bastard-bearers were more likely than others to produce further bastards, in successive generations. The surname structure makes it impossible to test this theory for most of Scotland. However, amongst the numerous remarks made by ministers about deviant women which we have collected, in only one was there a statement that the woman's mother had also borne bastards.

We found that the percentage of 'repeaters' was consistently higher in the North-East (including Aberdeenshire and Caithness) than elsewhere in the country: apart from that there were no marked regional differences. In all the regions there appears to have been a peak in the early eighteenth century – somewhere between 1700 and 1720 – and after that a downward trend. Certainly by the 1770s fewer women than earlier were bearing more than one bastard.

One question which arose from the subject of 'repeaters' is to what extent the children involved were the offspring of couples who had stable unions, possibly even considering themselves married, albeit not in the eyes of the church. This could have been particularly significant in Scotland, where 'handfast' and other irregular forms of marriage have been thought to be prevalent and where Hardwicke's Marriage Act did not apply. As far as was possible we measured the number of 'repeaters' pregnant by the same man and those pregnant by a different man. In every one of the ten regions those pregnant by a different man far outnumbered those pregnant by the same man. The large component of untraceable cases makes this impossible to quantify absolutely, but the consistency of the evidence is unmistakable. To quote the figures from two very different regions: in Ayrshire out of a total 'repeater' figure of 84, 23 were with the same man, 39 were with a different man, and 22 were untraceable; in the North-East out of a total of 160, 42 were with the same man, 62 with a different man, and 56 were untraceable. Long-standing unions were more easily traced and the transgressors more easily identified than was the case with more casual unions, so we are confident that we have not missed any semi-marital relationships: our 'unknown' cases are likely to be liaisons with different men. The conclusion must be that while stable unions accounted for some repeaters (though when cited for fornification these couples did not claim to be 'married'), the majority did not fall into this category.

One sign of the level of stress for a mother was the desperate act of abandoning the child. Among 8,429 instances of illegitimacy there came to light in our records 78 cases of abandoned children in the parishes studied: some of these were found dead, but most were living, and some were successfully traced to their mothers. We have counted as illegitimacy cases only those where the mother could be found and shown to belong to the parish. A disproportionate number of these abandoned children occurred in the late seventeenth and early eighteenth century. None were recorded for the Western Highlands and only four for the Eastern Highlands. There were 11 in both the North-East and in Aberdeenshire. The highest figure was for the Lothians where 19 were mentioned. The low level of the total makes it clear that there was no general resort to this method of getting rid of a child and that it was relatively rare for a parish to have more than one foundling to support at any one time. The Poor Law material also available in session records shows that most foundlings were adequately cared for and sustained until they could be apprenticed out in their early teens. It was Calvinist theology rather than the risk of long-term support that maintained the system of church discipline on sexual offences, but in the matter of establishing parentage these two motives came together.

Recent work on English population history[25] has associated the English fertility increase (both legitimate and illegitimate) in the eighteenth century with a delayed response to higher wages. This is now being modified by a closer concern for the changing level of job opportunities.[26] Scotland also experienced a surge of economic growth from the mid-eighteenth century. There is uncertainty as to whether much of this occurred before the 1740s , but there is no doubt about the rapidity of change in the 1750s, 1760s and 1770s.[27] In the

1750s the tobacco trade moved into its most profitable stage and was increasingly able to use Scottish products in the return cargo. In the later 1750s the linen industry recovered from the setback resulting from the interruption of the export bounty, and expanded production enormously. In the 1760s there began the changes in agriculture that made up the agricultural revolution. Smout gives statistics which show these later decades as ones not only of economic growth but in particular of industrial expansion and therefore, in a world with few labour-saving devices, of proliferation of job opportunities.[28] We do not have the evidence to show whether legitimate fertility in Scotland was stimulated in the same way as it was in England,[29] but on our figures the economic developments apparently had no immediate effect on illegitimate fertility.

Ostensibly the church, and the laws of discipline which it exercised, made no distinction of class, but the cases that came before the session largely concerned those without property. Where the occupation of the woman was recorded it was most often 'servetrix'. Out of thousands of cases only a handful of women appear to have been of any higher status (whether such women were more virtuous, better guarded, or less likely to be found out is a moot point). The men belonged to a much wider range of categories. Many were fellow servants in the same household, but masters or sons of masters were also frequently cited. This does not necessarily mean they were of higher status in society, for girls were often placed as servants in the houses of kinsfolk. However, there were in addition a number of cases involving men belonging to the gentry; the extent to which the kirk session was able to exercise discipline over them varied considerably from area to area, but to say that recalcitrance was more usual than submission would be a fair summing-up of the situation.

Wrightson has quantified the positions of mothers and fathers of bastards in seventeenth-century Lancashire and Essex. He found that at least 28 per cent of Essex and 8 per cent of Lancashire fathers were fellow servants, and at least 23 per cent of Essex fathers and 14 per cent of Lancashire fathers were in a magisterial position vis-à-vis the mothers (masters, masters' kin or gentlemen).[30] We quantified this information for only one of our areas, the Lothians. Percentages varied greatly from decade to decade. In the 1680s at least 5.6 per cent of the men were fellow servants and 7.4 per cent were masters or sons of masters; in the 1700s 10.3 per cent are known to have been fellow servants and 5.2 per cent masters or masters' sons; in the 1720s the figures were 4.1 per cent and 14.3 per cent and in the 1730s they were 8.7 per cent and 17.4 per cent. In every decade a certain percentage of the total of fathers belonged to the same household as the mother.[31]

VI

The general conclusion of our research is that for most of Scotland the rise of illegitimacy to the level found in the mid-nineteenth century did not take place in the period of rapid expansion of domestic industry (table 2). The level of illegitimacy for the country as a whole was no higher in the 1770s than it had been in the 1730s. It is to the period of the industrial and agricultural revolutions, or to the decades after these changes, that the increase must be attributed.

There is also no reason to associate the areas of relatively high illegitimacy in eighteenth-century Scotland with economic growth. For much of the country the regional levels show a reduction of illegitimacy in the period 1660–1730 as church discipline gained in efficiency, but in the area where it already had considerable authority before 1660 relatively low levels had been established and were maintained. The anomaly of the rising trend after 1750 in the South-West and Ayrshire is more likely to have had its origin in local cultural features than in economic change.

TABLE 2. ILLEGITIMACY RATIOS, 1760S AND 1858–60*

(percentage of estimated total births)

	1760S	1858–60
Lothians	1.0	7.3
Fife	1.8	5.4
Central Lowlands	2.5	8.2
Eastern Highlands	4.0	7.5
Western Highlands	3.9	8.2
Aberdeenshire	3.5	13.7
North-East	4.9	12.1
Caithness	7.6	7.3
Ayrshire	4.8	8.8
South-West	6.1	14.6
Whole country from selected parishes	3.6	9.5

* *using the same parishes.*

We are continuing research to include an investigation into the level of premarital conceptions, since these can be seen as a complementary aspect of sexual behaviour also subject to church discipline. Indeed, Wrigley, discussing the high level of these in the England of the late eighteenth century, where some

39 per cent of first births occurred within eight months of marriages and the great bulk of these within six months, has offered the idea that the European marriage pattern should be seen as 'a repertoire of adaptable systems rather than as a single pattern'. At this period in England, when the illegitimacy ratio was over 5 per cent, it would seem that between 50 and 60 per cent of women who bore children conceived the first out of wedlock.[32]

It does not follow that the same pattern should be expected in another country experiencing economic change at a different pace, and with different institutions. Indeed Wrigley's own analysis of French fertility in the late eighteenth century, though it shows a sharp rise in unmarried conceptions, shows also a very different tradition from that of England and a different response to social discipline. In England when the age of marriage was high and the likelihood of marrying low, illegitimacy was low. When this pattern of enforced celibacy for many was relaxed and marriage became more universal and occurred earlier, illegitimacy rose. In France in the early eighteenth century the age of marriage was relatively low, and it rose through the century as did the proportion never marrying. As the prospect of marriage thus decreased the illegitimacy ratio rose.[33] Clearly different nations within the European system adopted different parts of the repertoire of systems.

Scotland was a country where it was technically very easy to get married, but the small amount of evidence we have, all of it from the later part of the eighteenth century, suggests that the rural population had a sizeable proportion never marrying and a high age of marriage. The pattern of local church discipline, backed by the sanctions of the state, exposed those anticipating marriage to financial penalties and to the type of public exposure used in England for only a short time in the seventeenth century. It does not appear that even in the 1760s and 1770s the level of premarital conception was as high as in England, nor does the evidence from the two regions which did experience a rise in illegitimacy after 1750 support Smith's conclusion that high illegitimacy was accompanied by a high level of repeater cases.[34] Just under 10 per cent of the cases were repeaters in Ayrshire and the South-West in the 1770s.

The kirk sessions' investigations into cases which the church called 'antenuptial uncleanness' covered all births occurring within nine calendar months of marriage: the period of gestation was defined in a very rigid way, and in cases where the parents claimed that an early birth was conceived within wedlock midwives would be called in to assess the apparent maturity of the child. The threat of this rigour is shown in the anxious notes recorded in the memoir of the minister of Penpont in 1694 about his recently acquired wife: 'all the time of her being with child I was still afraid lest she a very young lass, being but yet in her 19 year through her rashness or carelessness of herself, should bring forth before the due time, which made me put my request . . . often to God . . . that so he might not open the mouths of the Ungodly'[35]. There was no kirk session inquiry or comment by the ungodly because in the event the couple had 25 hours on the side of respectability, but the minister's fears provide an insight into the ethos of the day.

It should not, therefore, surprise that our figures show a story differing from that now established for England on a somewhat limited sample of parishes, and bear out the view of Teitelbaum that the political frontier between England and Scotland has also been a demographic one.[36] It took some time before the reformed church was able to reduce the relatively high level of unmarried sexual activity established in some regions, but by the 1720s church discipline was confining sexual activity to the married for the bulk of the population, though observance of this rule was never as rigorous in the north as in the south. The level of 'repeater' cases had also fallen to under 10 per cent of the total. Conformity continued into the third quarter of the eighteenth century except in Ayrshire and the South-West, even though by then other aspects of church discipline were falling into desuetude. The level of ante-nuptial pregnancy revealed in a sample of central and south-eastern lowland parishes which still investigated it in the 1770s, when brought into relationship with the illegitimacy ratio suggests that on the eve of the industrial revolution between 9 per cent and 24 per cent of women who bore children had conceived their first child out of wedlock. But even at this time many sessions were ceasing to enforce traditional discipline, and at some point during or after the onset of industrialization the power of social convention slackened.

University of Edinburgh

NOTES

1 This paper is based on research supported by a grant from the Economic and Social Research Council. Further research was supported by the British Academy. The archive used is kirk session registers in the Scottish Record Office (S.R.O.). Since this paper was written a number of these registers have been transferred to local and regional archives.

2 Laslett, Oosterveen and Smith, eds. *Bastardy*, p. 19.

3 Teitelbaum, *Fertility decline*, pp. 154–84.

4 Flinn, *Scottish population*, pp. 260–70.

5 Other areas not included are Nairnshire, because it spans the Celtic-lowland division, Angus, Mearns and Kinross-shire in eastern Scotland and Renfrewshire, Lanarkshire, Dumbartonshire and Clackmannanshire in western and central Scotland, because there seemed no strong and characteristic social features which would distinguish them from other parts of the lowlands. These areas are left blank in the map in Appendix 1.

6 Dodgshon, *Land*, p. 293. *Idem*, 'Agricultural change' p.80.

7 Smout, 'Aspects', p.80.

8 Flinn, *Scottish population*. p. 50; this is based on a General Assembly report in the S.R.O. CH/1/55.

9 Flinn, *Scottish population*, p. 207.

10 Davies, thesis, p. 83. Of 1981 cases of fornication found by Davies in Stirlingshire between 1637 and 1747, only 26 of the women were not pregnant.

11 A.P.S. III 541, *Act for abolishing of the actis contrair the trew religioun* (1592); VI ii 310, *Acts against Fornication* (1649) confirmed in VII 310 (1661); VII 99 *Act against Prophanes* (1672).

12 Flinn, *Scottish population*, pp. 58–64, 181, 260. We have also been fortunate in hearing a report on work on Aberdeenshire by R.E. Tyson.

13 Flinn, *Scottish population*, pp. 258–60; Coale and Demeny, *Tables*.

14 For Webster's age distribution, see Kyd, ed. *Scottish statistics*, pp.80–1.

15 Flinn, *Scottish population*, pp. 275–9, 287; Sinclair, *OSA*.

16 Flinn, *Scottish population*, p.285.

17 Wrigley and Schofield, *English population, passim*.

18 Campbell, *Lairds*, p. 113.

19 For the relationship between illegitimacy and age of marriage in England, Laslett and Oosterveen, 'Long term trends'. For the link with proto-industrialization, Levine, *Family formation*, pp. 58–87.

20 Shorter, 'Illegitimacy'. His thesis has been attacked by other authors, most notably L.A. Tilly, J. W. Scott and M. Cohen, W. R. Lee and C. Fairchilds, also in Rotberg and Rabb, eds, *Marriage*, pp. 121–43, 163–201, 219–48. Their conclusions, not all in agreement, rest on economic change rather than on sexual liberation.

21 Laslett, Oosterveen and Smith, eds. *Bastardy*, p.14.

22 This level has been worked out for all the parishes which contributed to this study, for the years 1858–60.

23 An explanation of this type might be used to explain the high level of illegitimacy in a larger parish, Terling, in the early seventeenth century, as shown in Levine and Wrightson, 'Social context', p.147.

24 Laslett, 'Sub-society', p.239. See also Smith, 'Family reconstitution', p.86, stating 'that as the bastardy ratio went up the proportion of women producing more than one bastard went up at an even faster rate'. See also Laslett, *Family life*, p. 147.

25 Wrigley and Schofield, *English population*, pp. 417–35.

26 Schofield, 'English marriage', pp. 2–20.

27 Morgan, 'Wage rates'.

28 Smout, 'Scottish economy', pp. 61–7.

29 Flinn *Scottish population*, p. 227.

30 Wrightson, 'Nadir', pp. 187–8. Wrightson also shows that couples not actually serving in the same household were likely to be near neighbours: this is not something which can generally be ascertained for Scotland.

31 This aspect raises the question of qualitative as well as quantitative evidence. We have

amassed considerable detail on subjects ranging from the behaviour of the gentry to attempted abortion, and hope to use it in further publications.

32 Wrigley, 'Marriage', pp. 157–63.
33 Wrigley, 'Marital fertility', pp. 48–51.
34 Oosterveen, Smith and Stewart, 'Family reconstitution', p. 87.
35 National Library of Scotland, MS 3045, diary of the Rev. James Murray.
36 Teitelbaum, *Fertility decline*, p. 175.

APPENDIX 1

SCOTLAND – *mainland and other islands*

Regions:
1. Lothians.
2. Fife.
3. Central Lowlands.
4. Western Highlands.
5. Eastern Highlands.
6. Aberdeenshire.
7. North-East.
8. Caithness.
9. Ayrshire.
10. South-West.

APPENDIX 2

Sample calculation of a regional figure, Central Lowlands, for the 1760s. Illegitimacy figures:

Muiravonside,	11 in 10 years, population 1,539
Logie,	11 in 8 years, population, 1,985.
Muthill,	11 in 7 years, population 2,902.
Fossoway,	20 in 10 years, population 1,765.

Total of illegitimate births, 53, for a base population of 69,234.
Seven parishes in the *Statistical account* give retrospective figures for the average annual number of births.
A median figure for these gives a birth rate of 31. Total births to be expected 2,146. Illegitimacy ratio 2.47.

APPENDIX 3

A List of the Parishes Used

LOTHIANS

Cramond	1661, 1665–73, 1676–87, 1690–1770
Dalkeith	1661–80, 1682–9, 1691–1708, 1723–46, 1761–80
Pencaitland	1663–9, 1691–1760
Spott	1664–88, 1693–1770
Torphichen	1681–8, 1694–1717, 1724–50, 1761–80

FIFE

Kingsbarns	1664–1780
Dysart	1663–96, 1698–1780
Wemyss	1661–80, 1693–1780
Kinglassie	1661–97, 1701–35, 1737, 1751–80

CENTRAL LOWLANDS

Dunbarney	1661–3, 1666–74, 1676–80, 1691–1710
Dunblane	1661–70
St Ninians	1661, 1663–73, 1676–90, 1694–1727, 1729–30
Falkirk	1661–70
Muiravonside	1671–86, 1688, 1701–10, 1731–80
Trinity Gask	1671–5, 1677–9
Longforgan	1681–2, 1685–6, 1689–96, 1711–20
Auchterarder	1681-90, 1701–10
Logie	1691–1700, 1751–8, 1762–9
Gargunnock	1701–40
Fossoway	1711–80
Muthill	1711–56, 1759–65, 1768–9
Forgandenny	1741–50, 1771–80
Fintry	1671–5, 1677, 1679–80

WESTERN HIGHLANDS

Kingarth	1671–5, 1677–86, 1691–1700
Kilmartin	1692–1700, 1725–36, 1739–62, 1767–70
Rothesay	1692–7, 1701–40, 1751–80
Kilmory	1703–20
Gleneray	1702–28, 1745–50
Inveraray	1701–8, 1712–20, 1745–50
Golspie	1731–4, 1738–50
Kilfinan	1743–4, 1746–9
Kilbrandon	1755–66
Lochgoilhead	1751–6, 1760–80
Durness	1765–70

EASTERN HIGHLANDS

Petty	1665–90, 1713–18, 1720–30, 1761–70, 1772–7
Croy	1663–6, 1669–89, 1721–40, 1751–70
Kilmadock	1661–7, 1669–71, 1673–80
Alvie	1714–20, 1731–7, 1740–4, 1746–9
Moulin	1711–18, 1720, 1741–80
Kenmore	1731–8, 1743–56, 1758–60
Blair Atholl	1741–80

ABERDEENSHIRE

Longside	1663–1710, 1733–80
Belhelvie	1661–96, 1699–1714, 1716–23, 1726–60
Kemnay	1662–1706, 1709–30, 1765–80
Ellon	1661–86, 1713–80
Foveran	1671–95, 1697–1710, 1721–73, 1775–80

NORTH-EAST

Grange	1661–70, 1681–88, 1711–33, 1735–59, 1761–6, 1768, 1770–4, 1776–80
Fordyce	1661–96, 1701–14, 1717–20, 1741–50
Forglen	1661–1755, 1760–80
Alves	1661–90, 1705–10, 1722–37, 1735–80
Drainie	1671–1731, 1735–80
Banff	1701–15, 1717–26, 1742–80

CAITHNESS

Thurso	1671–80, 1691–3, 1698, 1701–42, 1746–9
Wattin	1702–80
Olrig	1701–80
Canisbay	1711–38, 1751–80

AYRSHIRE

Ayr	1661–6, 1671–4, 1677–1707, 1712–7
Kilmarnock	1671–2, 1677–80, 1691–1730
Kilwinning	1671–80
Mauchline	1671–83, 1685–93, 1696–9, 1732–6, 1751–68, 1771–80
Dailly	1693–1700, 1711–58
Sorn	1693–1740, 1753–60
Kirkoswald	1701–30, 1761–80
Straiton	1733–40, 1742–8, 1761–80
Dundonald	1701–13, 1718–20, 1731–9, 1742–50
Dalrymple	1741-80
Kilbirnie	1741–80

SOUTH-WEST

Dumfries	1671–87, 1690–2, 1694–1730
Westerkirk	1694–1719, 1722–38, 1751–60

Applegarth	1695–1719, 1751–8, 1764–70
Kells	1694–1700
Penninghame	1701–40
Minnigaff	1701–9, 1721–50
Glencairn	1702–10, 1721–40
Wigtown	1702–28, 1731–40
Eskdalemuir	1731–70
Stranraer	1741–80
Colvend	1741–50
Troqueer	1745–80
New Abbey	1761–80

FOOTNOTE REFERENCES

Acts of Parliaments of Scotland (A.P.S.), 12 vols. (1844–75).

D. Campbell, *The Lairds of Glenlyon* (Perth, 1886).

A. Coale and P. Demeny, *Regional model life tables and stable populations* (Princeton N. J. 1966).

S. J. Davies, 'Law and order in Stirlingshire, 1637–1747' (unpublished Ph.D. thesis, University of St Andrews, 1984).

R. A. Dodgshon, *Land and society in early Scotland* (Oxford, 1981).

R. A. Dodgshon, 'Agricultural change and its social consequences in the southern uplands of Scotland, 1600–1779', in T. H. Devine and D. Dickson, eds. *Ireland and Scotland, 1600–1850 (Edinburgh,* 1983), pp. 46–59.

M. W. Flinn, ed. *Scottish population history* (Cambridge, 1977).

J. G. Kyd, ed. *Scottish population statistics* (Scottish History Society, Edinburgh, 1952).

P. Laslett, *Family life and illicit love in earlier generations (Cambridge,* 1977).

P. Laslett and K. Oosterveen, 'Long term trends in bastardy in England', *Population Studies,* 27 (1973), pp. 255–86.

P. Laslett, K. Oosterveen and R. M. Smith, eds. *Bastardy and its comparative history* (1980).

P. Laslett, 'The bastardy prone sub-society', in P. Laslett, K. Oosterveen and R. M. Smith, eds. *Bastardy and its comparative history* (1980), pp. 217–46.

D. Levine, *Family formation in an age of nascent capitalism* (1977).

D. Levine and K. Wrightson, 'The social context of illegitimacy in early modern England', in P. Laslett, K. Oosterveen and R. M. Smith, eds. *Bastardy and its comparative history* (1980), pp. 158–75.

V. Morgan, 'Agricultural wage rates in late eighteenth-century Scotland', *Economic History Review,* 2nd ser. XXIV (1971), pp. 181–201.

K. Oosterveen, R. M. Smith and S. Stewart, 'Family reconstitution and the study of bastardy: evidence from certain English parishes', in P. Laslett, K. Oosterveen and R. M. Smith, eds. *Bastardy and its comparative history* (1980), pp. 86–140.

R. I. Rotberg and T. K. Rabb, eds. *Marriage and fertility* (Princeton N.J., 1980).

R. S. Schofield, 'English marriage patterns revisited', *Journal of Family History*, 10 (1985), pp. 2–20.

E. Shorter, 'Illegitimacy, sexual revolution and social change in modern Europe', in I. Rotberg and T. K. Rabb, eds. *Marriage and fertility* (Princeton N.J., 1980), pp. 85–120.

Sir John Sinclair, ed. *The Statistical account of Scotland [O.S.A.]*, 21 vols. (Edinburgh, 1791/ 7).

T. C. Smout, 'Aspects of sexual behaviour in nineteenth-century Scotland', in A. A. MacLaren, ed. *Social class in Scotland* (Edinburgh, 1976), pp. 55–85.

T. C. Smout, 'Where had the Scottish economy got to by the third quarter of the eighteenth century?' in I. Hont and M. Ignatieff, eds. *Wealth and virtue* (Cambridge, 1983), pp. 45– 72.

M. S. Teitelbaum, *The British fertility decline* (Princeton N. J. 1984).

K. Wrightson, 'The nadir of English illegitimacy in the seventeenth century', in P. Laslett, K. Oosterveen and R. M. Smith, eds. *Bastardy and its comparative history* (1980), pp. 176– 91.

E. A. Wrigley, 'Marriage, fertility and population growth in eighteenth-century England', in R. B. Outhwaite, ed. *Marriage and society* (1982), pp. 137–85.

E. A. Wrigley, 'The fall of marital fertility in nineteenth-century France, part 1', *European Journal of Population*, I (1985), pp. 31–60.

E. A. Wrigley and R. S. Schofield, *The population history of England: a reconstruction, 1541– 1871* (1981).

Richard Arkwright and the Scottish cotton industry

A J Cooke 1979 in *Textile History* 10, 196–202.

In spite of the important role he played in the development of the factory system, our knowledge of Richard Arkwright (1732–92) is relatively limited. This is particularly true of his involvement in the development of the cotton industry in Scotland where his intervention was brief but important.[1] Arkwright's interest in Scotland was partly a reaction to his battles in the English courts over patent rights and partly a shrewd appreciation of the potential of Scottish water-power resources and of Scottish labour. Hence his claim that 'he would find a razor in Scotland to shave Manchester'.[2]

The key person in persuading Arkwright to take an interest in Scotland was George Dempster (1732–1815) who was MP for the Perth burghs from 1761 to 1790. Dempster had a small estate at Dunnichen in Angus and was active in agricultural improvement and in various schemes for Highland development, including the British Fisheries Society, and the abortive cotton-spinning project at Spinningdale on the Dornoch Firth.[3] Writing in 1800 to his friend Sir John Sinclair, Dempster claimed 'some concern in engaging Sir Richard Arkwright to instruct some of our countrymen in the art [of cotton spinning] and also to take a share in the great cotton mills of Lanark and Stanley'.[4] He went on to describe how on one of his journeys to and from Parliament he had stayed at Matlock for a few days and continued – 'In the course of a forenoon's ride I discovered in a romantic valley a palace of a most enormous size having at least a score of windows of a row and five or six stories in height. This was Sir Richard Arkwright's then Mr Arkwright's cotton mills'. Dempster and his party got permission to look round the mills, of which unfortunately, he gives no further description, and he then rode to Arkwright's house and introduced himself. Dempster describes how: 'Some business brought him soon after to London. He conceived I had been useful to him and offered to assist me in establishing a cotton mill in Scotland by holding a share of one and instructing the people. Private business carried him the following summer to Scotland where he visited Perth, Glasgow and Lanark and I believe Stanley for I was not then in Scotland. Mr Dale and I became partners in mills to be erected in Lanark. A company of five or six Perth gentlemen, he and I, entered into partnership in mills to be built at Stanley in Perthshire. Some misunderstanding happening between him and Mr Dale which they submitted to me, I met them both at Sir Richard's house at Cromford in December 1786. Each gentleman offering to take the whole concern and to take my share also, I awarded the whole to Mr Dale as being most convenient for him to manage. Mr Dale thinking I had made him a valuable gift of my share offered me £1,000 by way of equivalent for it. But I was too glad to be rid of so extensive a concern to accept of any compensation for it. Sir Richard instructed Mr Dale's artists and young children gratis, as he also did those sent from Stanley'.[5]

Arkwright's first visit to Scotland took place in October 1784, when he was made an honorary burgess and guild brother of Glasgow and given the freedom of the city of Perth. He returned to Scotland in March 1785.[6] Arkwright was impressed by the water-power potential of the Falls of Clyde, and claimed 'that Lanark would probably in time become the Manchester of Scotland',[7] but he and David Dale soon fell out, according to one account, after quarrelling over the siting of a bell-tower.[8]

New Lanark and Stanley were not the only Scottish cotton projects in which Arkwright was involved. On Donside, where Gordon, Barron & Co. began cotton-spinning in 1785, he had offered to train men at his works in Derbyshire and license them to use his patent.[9] He also introduced his millwright, Lowe of Nottingham to Dale and Alexander, who contracted for him to build the first four water wheels at Catrine.[10] Similarly, the Buchanans of Glasgow had links with Arkwright. They were his first agents in Scotland, and Archibald Buchanan, who later became manager at Deanston, was trained at the Cromford factory'.[11] Indeed the first cotton mill in Scotland, that at Penicuik, was said to have been founded by Arkwright's former workman John Hackett.[12] This formed part of a more general 'English invasion', for at least fourteen individuals active in the Scottish cotton industry between 1779 and 1795 'were associated directly or indirectly with English practice'.[13]

Of all his Scottish cotton-spinning projects, however, Arkwright's links with Stanley in Perthshire seem to have lasted longest and been most influential. As early as August 1784, before his first visit to Scotland, a letter of agreement had been drawn up between the Duke of Atholl on the one hand and George Dempster, Arkwright and a group of Perth merchants on the other, to feu 70 acres of land at Stanley to build a cotton mill.[14] The Duke had already received a memorandum entitled 'Considerations on the Cotton Manufacture' setting out Arkwright's achievements and arguing the case for the industry to be established in Scotland. The memorandum claimed that Arkwright owned or had a part interest in eleven different 'Engines', some consisting of 4,000 spindles, some working for twenty-three hours a day with an hour allowed for oiling and cleaning. Arkwright's sales were described as being not less than £12,000 to £15,000 a month and his annual profits were said to exceed £40,000 in some years. Some bought the privilege of using his patent at £7 per spindle, others contended it 'and foiled him at law'. However, the patent did not apply to Scotland and several 'Engines' had already been erected there. The author of the memorandum believed that linen manufacturers would find it impossible to compete with cotton, and argued the case for setting up a Scottish industry, adding 'the more quietly undertaken the better chance to success'.[15]

In February 1785, the Duke reported that he had sent Robert Graham of Fintry 'The length of Derbyshire' to see Arkwright's mills and persuade him to become involved. Arkwright was to visit the area in March, and Atholl would not enter into any agreement until then.[16] According to George Penny, his father, William Sandeman of Luncarty bleachfield, Atholl and Arkwright met in the Kings Arms Inn, Perth to discuss the Stanley project. Arkwright was delighted with the quality of the muslin that Penny produced and said they had the necessary skill to start the project. Building commenced and a number of boys and girls were sent up to Manchester [sic] to learn the spinning trade.'[17]

The Derby Mercury reported on the impact of these new arrivals in Cromford in May 1785:

> A few days since, between forty and fifty North Britons with bagpipes and other music playing, arrived at Cromford near Matlock – Bath, from Perth in Scotland. These industrious fellows left that place on account of the scarcity of work, were taken into the service of Richard Arkwright Esq, in his cotton mills and other extensive works, entered into present pay and provided with good quarters. They appeared highly pleased with the reception they met with and had a dance in the evening to congratulate each other on the performance of so long a journey. [18]

In the same month, an agreement was drawn up between the Duke of Atholl and the Stanley Company. Arkwright, who was one of the partners in the Company, had been appointed 'sole arbitor' to decide on such matters as the length of the lease, the annual rent and the expenses of the Duke who had 'the sole expense of building a house fit for the necessary machinery', housing the workers and enlarging the lade. On his advice it was agreed that the Company would pay £69 10s annual rent for the use of the existing corn-mill and water-rights, and that the Duke would grant a 21 year lease for thirty acres of ground to build a village. Atholl also agreed to spend £2,000 putting up buildings on which the Company would pay 7½ per cent interest.[19] James Stobie, who factored the Stanley area for the Duke, drew up a plan for the development of the village on a rectangular grid-iron plan which survives in its essentials down to the present day. Arkwright's contribution to the development of the village was acknowledged by naming the square after him.[20] It seems likely that Arkwright also had some influence on the design of the first cotton mill at Stanley, which is still known locally as the Arkwright mill. It is a handsome six-storey building, the two lower floors built of stone, the rest of brick with segmentally-arched sash windows, and bears a strong family resemblance to the early Derbyshire mills.[21]

At the beginning of 1787, the Company registered a provisional contract of co-partnership 'Betwixt Richard Arkwright Esq., and others for the purpose of carrying on the business of preparing and spinning cotton wool in this Country in the way and manner in which it is carried on by the said Richard Arkwright at Cromford.'[22] The seven partners were Richard Arkwright, George Dempster, Robert Graham of Fintry, William Sandeman of Luncarty bleachfield, Patrick Stewart and William Marshall 'Merchants in Perth' and Andrew Keay, another Perth merchant who became the first manager at Stanley after a spell at Cromford. The capital stock of the Company was fixed initially at £7,000 and it was agreed to open a cash account with the Perth United Bank for £3,000.[23] Each partner agreed to advance £1,000 towards the capital stock of the company and this share could only be sold to one of the other partners or with the consent of a majority of the partners. An exception was made for Arkwright that, 'whenever the spinning of cotton at the said mill shall so far succeed as to become a profitable concern' he should be at liberty to assign his share to George Dempster or, if Dempster declined, he could sell or assign his share 'in any manner he shall see fitt'. The contract also referred to 'sundry indentures with different persons to be sent to the said Richard Arkwright at Cromford aforesaid to be taught the constructing and making of the machinery used by him in preparing and spinning of the said wool (raw cotton) itself'.[24]

Arkwright soon exercised his right of withdrawal, for when the feu contract between the Duke of Atholl and the Stanley Company was drawn up in February 1787, he had been replaced as a partner by William Stewart, a Perth merchant.[25] Why Arkwright withdrew is unclear. He was at the height of his career having been made High Sheriff of Derbyshire and been knighted in 1786, but his health had never been good and he was not the easiest man to fit into a partnership. It is also unclear what benefits he hoped to get from his Scottish projects, as the evidence of the Contract of Co-Partnery suggests that from the start of the Stanley project, he intended to withdraw once the Company began making profits. Dempster claimed that Arkwright trained the Stanley and New Lanark workers free of charge, and nowhere in the Contract of Co-partnership is there any mention of licence fees going to Arkwright.[26] Dempster explained Arkwright's involvement as a return for services rendered, and this may have been in return for services in Parliament. Towards the end of 1785 and in the early months of 1786, Arkwright became involved in a scheme to secure a statutory monopoly of wool-spinning, in which he was helped by Sir Joseph Banks, then President of the Royal Society, who undertook to bring any proposals by Arkwright to the attention of his 'parliamentary friends'.[27] Dempster may well have been one of those friends, as he wrote a letter in the same year to the Earl of Buchan about the application of Arkwright's machinery to the spinning of wool.[28] Although this project fell through, Dempster and Banks feature prominently in an eyewitness account of Arkwright's knighthood when presenting a loyal address on George III's escape from assassination. They seem to have acted as sponsors for Arkwright, who appeared unsuitably dressed in 'a black wig, brown frock coat, worsted stockings and boots' and when challenged replied 'he was not afraid they were but men – and so was He'. He was persuaded to change and the assembled company were surprised 'to see little fatty appear a beau with smart powdered *bag* wig so tight that coming over his ears it made him deaf, a handsome striped sattin waistcoat and proper coat with a sword which he held in hand, all provided it is supposed by Mr Dempster . . . The little great man had no idea of kneeling, but crimpt himself up in a *very odd* posture which I suppose his Majesty took for *an easy one* so never took the trouble to bid him rise'.[29] New Lanark and Stanley were perhaps the result of George Dempster's contribution towards easing Arkwright into London society.[30]

Although the evidence remains scattered and incomplete, it seems clear that Richard Arkwright played a key role in establishing the factory system in the Scottish cotton industry. His motives remain less than clear. Despite his reported statements about using Scotland as a razor to the throats of his Lancashire competitors, the evidence of the Stanley Co-Partnery suggests that for Stanley at least, he never intended to become involved on a permanent basis.[31]

NOTES

1 See E. Baines, *History of the Cotton Manufacture* (1835), 147–96; G. M. Mitchell, 'The English and Scottish Cotton Industries', *S.H.R.*, XXII (1925), 101–14. P. Mantoux, *The Industrial Revolution in the Eighteenth Century* (1931 impression), pp. 225–39; R. S. Fitton and A. P. Wadsworth, *The Strutts and the Arkwrights 1758–1830* (1958), pp. 60–107; H. Hamilton, *The Industrial Revolution in Scotland* (1966 edition), pp. 124–28; S. D. Chapman, *The Early Factory Masters* (1967), pp. 62–76; and S. G. E. Lythe and J. Butt, *An Economic History of Scotland 1100–1939* (1975), pp. 185–86. For recent discussion on investment in the Scottish cotton industry see T. M. Devine, 'The Colonial Trades and

Industrial Investment in Scotland c1700–1815,' *EcH.R.*, 2nd series, XXIX (1976), 1–13, and J. Butt, 'The Scottish Cotton Industry during the Industrial Revolution 1780–1840', in L. M. Cullen and T. C. Smout (eds), *Comparative Aspects of Scottish and Irish Economic and Social History 1600–1900* (1977), pp. 116–28.

2 Baines, op. cit., p.193.

3 O.S.A., VIII, 382–83.

4 SRO, Sinclair of Ulbster MSS (microfilm) RH4 49/2, vol. 3, fos 266–68, Dempster to Sinclair, 21 January 1800. I am grateful to Dr Bradford Garniss of Rhode Island for drawing my attention to this reference. This letter is printed in full in *The Correspondence of Sir John Sinclair*, vol. 1 (1831), 360–63.

5 Ibid.

6 Fitton and Wadsworth, op. cit., p.85.

7 O.S.A., XV, 46.

8 R. D. Owen, *Threading My Way* (1874), p. 9.

9 H. Hamilton, op. cit., p. 128.

10 S. G. E. Lythe and J. Butt, op. cit., p. 185.

11 H. Hamilton, op. cit., p.127 and Anon., *James Finlay and Company 1750–1950* (1951), p. 60.

12 A. P. Wadsworth and Julia de L. Mann, *The Cotton Trade and Industrial Lancashire (1600–1780)* (reprinted 1965), p. 494.

13 S. G. E. Lythe and J. Butt, op.cit., p. 186.

14 Atholl MSS Charter Room, Blair Castle, Perthshire Box 25., Parcel IX, Letter of Agreement between the Duke of Atholl and the Stanley Company, 28 August 1784. For a fuller account of the development of Stanley see A. J. Cooke (ed.), *Stanley – Its History and Development* (1977), which is the product of an Extra-mural class.

15 Atholl MSS Box 25, Parcel IX, Considerations on the Cotton Manufacture, undated.

16 Atholl MSS Box 65/5/43, Atholl to General James Murray, 20 February 1785.

17 G. Penny, *Traditions of Perth* (1836), pp. 250–51.

18 Fitton and Wadsworth, op.cit., p. 105.

19 SRO, Sheriff Court of Perthshire Register of Deeds SC49/59/99 fos 307–22. Decreet Arbitral between the Duke of Atholl and the Stanley Company, 17 May 1785.

20 Stanley Mill, Perthshire, Copy Plan of 30 acres of ground let for building a cotton mill and a Town surveyed by James Stobie 1785, copied 1831. The name was later altered to Duke Square. Stobie also drew up a plan for a new mill-lade to replace the old tunnel, which was to be 776 feet long, with a fall of 1ft. 4in. Copies of this plan dated 1785 survive at Stanley Mill and Blair Castle.

21 The dimensions of this mill are approximately 90 ft x 33 ft. In 1832 the lade was enlarged and seven water-wheels generated 200 h.p. (Scottish Development Department, List of Buildings of Architectural or Historical Interest, and *New Statistical Account*, X (1845), 440).

22 SRO, SC49/59/104, fos 1–5 Contract of Co-Partnery, 1 January 1787. This was the date of registration – Arkwright had signed the document at Cromford on 2 December 1785 witnessed by David Dale.

23 This compares with a 1788 valuation of Stanley of £13,000 'in building houses and erecting the machinery of a cotton water-mill sufficient to work 3,200 spindles which employs 350 people' (PRO, BT6/140/fo.129). I am grateful to Dr Stanley Chapman for this information which forms part of his paper 'The Arkwright Mills – Evolution or Revolution?', delivered to the Seventh International Economic History Congress, Edinburgh, 1978.

24 SRO, SC49/59/104, fos 1–5, Contract of Co-Partnery, 1 January 1787.

25 SRO, SC49/59/104, fos 120–29. Feu contract between John Duke of Atholl and the Stanley Company, 13 February 1787.

26 Compare the claim that 'Arkwright succeeded very unaccountably in finding fresh partnerships, though former ones were dissolved in consequence of their not answering, and he always came richer from the misfortune, like Anteus, who in his falls gained strength from his mother earth'. Quoted in Mantoux, op. cit. p 238.

27 Fitton and Wadsworth, op. cit., pp. 87–90.

28 University of Edinburgh, Laing MSS II, 588/1 Dempster to Earl of Buchan, 16 December 1786. The letter described how a Mr Barber of Derby had 'long since' used Arkwright's machinery for spinning the coarser kinds of woollen yarn at mills in Cirencester and Glasgow and recommended the idea for Buchan's estates.

29 Atholl MSS Box 65/5/171 Mrs George Murray to Captain George Murray, 25 December 1786.

30 Compare S. D. Chapman, *The Early Factory Masters* (1967), p.63, 'The one characteristic of Arkwright which, above all others, emerges from the various accounts of him is his social vanity'.

31 I would like to thank His Grace, the Duke of Atholl for giving permission to examine the Atholl Manuscripts at Blair Castle, and Mr H. F. Stott of Sidlaw Industries for giving access to the records and mill buildings at Stanley.

The revolution in Scottish textiles: 'A New Invented Spinning Machine'

Extracted from I Donnachie and G Hewitt 1993 *Historic New Lanark*, Edinburgh (Edinburgh University Press), 1–16.

New Lanark, the former cotton spinning village in the valley of the River Clyde near the old town of Lanark, is of international importance as the locus of pioneering management, and social and educational experiments led by the reformer who made it famous, Robert Owen. But New Lanark is also an important industrial monument, thanks to its role as an early centre of mass production using state-of-the-art technology at the time of its construction in 1785. Built by David Dale, a resourceful textile entrepreneur and banker, New Lanark harnessed the power of the Falls of Clyde to drive its spinning machinery, and is thus identified with the early stages of the Industrial Revolution. But contrary to the impression of dramatic change suggested by the term, the transformation of production from workshop to factory was as much evolutionary as revolutionary. From the 1700s onwards technological change had begun to affect several vital industries, most notably, textiles.

In the mid-18th century the principal occupation of Scotland's population of around one and a quarter million was linen manufacturing. This industry, having survived a distinctly unstable period in the years after the Treaty of Union in 1707, began to expand steadily from the 1730s onwards. Unquestionably, credit for much of this revival must be given to the Board of Trustees of Fisheries and Manufactures. This body was formed in 1727 following repeated representations to the government by the Convention of Royal Burghs for some initiative to assist Scottish trade and industry. The Board, while also concerned with canal building, was initially closely linked with helping linen manufacturing. This was achieved by utilising the Equivalent, a sum of money set aside by the Treaty of Union in favour of certain Scottish interests, which was now to be invested in various schemes for economic improvement.

Thus, under the direction of the Trustees, Dutch and French craftsmen were brought over to this country to teach their skills in spinning and weaving. Improved flax scutching or cleaning mills of continental design – driven by water power – were introduced. Subsidies were made available in the hope of encouraging farmers to cultivate more native flax as well as to meet the cost of establishing new bleachfields at sites all over the Lowlands, such as around Loch Lomond, in the Vale of Leven, the Cart Valley in Renfrewshire and Luncarty among other places in Perthshire. Scientific research was encouraged so that by the 1750s it had been discovered that the use of sulphuric acid reduced the souring part of bleaching from several months to a few days. A system of quality control was obtained by the formation of a linen inspectorate, the stamp-masters, who affixed their seal of approval to the finished product. Finally, the government, on certain occasions, was persuaded to grant premiums for specific types of linen or to place embargoes on rival French imports.

As a result of these measures, and in conjunction with other contributory factors – such as the stimulus provided by the financial activities of the British Linen Company (later 'Bank') not to mention the fact that Scottish linen was very competitively priced compared with its main rivals – the industry continued its steady expansion during the second half of the 18th century. By the first stages of the classic Industrial Revolution it was widely dispersed; there were large areas of production in Angus, Fife and Perth making mainly coarse yarns and cloth; in counties like Ayr, Dumbarton, Lanark and Renfrew the speciality was fine threads and linen fabrics. At the centre of this activity was Glasgow, which by the 1770s was the leading linen manufacturing town in the United Kingdom.

Undoubtedly all these developments in the manufacture of linen had an important bearing on the rise of the Scottish cotton industry. For example, there was the mechanisation of the scutching process. Formerly, workers had cleaned the flax of impurities, but by 1722 there were 250 scutching, or lintmills, as they were frequently called, driven by water power, and 'scutching' the flax mechanically. Moreover, on account of the capital required for the building of such mills (each one cost around £80–£100 to erect) their construction encouraged the growth of what had been described as 'merchant capitalists'. Certainly this type of entrepreneur already existed, but there was an increase in the numbers of such businessmen, David Dale, for instance, being one of those who helped to swell their ranks. Indeed, it gradually became the case that virtually all the financial risks inherent in linen production were being assumed by such individuals. At the same time as greater quantities of flax became available, the workforce, especially the weavers, increasingly became full-time employees working in the various loom shops owned by the linen merchants. Lastly, there was the finishing sector of the industry controlled by a separate group of capitalists. It had initially been revitalised, as has been seen, by the use of sulphuric acid as a bleaching agent. Following the discovery in the 1770s that chlorine could be used instead, Charles Tennant's experiments ultimately resulted in the production of a bleaching powder although this was not in production at his St Rollox works in Glasgow until 1799. Simultaneously, there were important innovations in the printing side of the industry culminating by the 1780s with the vastly quicker cylinder printing process replacing the use of mainly wooden blocks.

In short, by the late 18th century there was a highly skilled and well organised linen industry flourishing in Scotland. However, although some sections of the finishing end had abandoned the domestic system and entered what historians now call the 'proto-industrial' stage, its main areas, spinning and weaving, were both still basically dependent on workers labouring in their own homes, mainly under an agency system operated by entrepreneurial middlemen. Admittedly, by 1787–8 a mechanical linen mill was operating at Brigton (Angus). But this was a decade after the earliest cotton factory and, because of various technical difficulties, was not followed by many other such mills. Consequently, linen manufacturing provided much of the organisational structure for the cotton industry but it was to be the latter which found itself in a position to take advantage of new developments which had been taking place in textile technology. In other words, these new inventions were quickly discovered to be more suitable for the production of cotton than either woollen or linen goods.

In 1764 James Hargreaves invented his spinning jenny, the earliest model consisting of a long wooden frame with a single large wheel and equipped with eight vertical spindles. Thus eight threads could be spun at once and by quite an unskilled person – even a child. Soon improvements made it possible to increase the number of spindles to a frame, but the frames grew larger, heavier and more costly. The biggest disadvantage was that jenny thread could only be used as weft (the short thread carried by the shuttle) on the weaver's loom because it was not strong enough to be used as warp (the thread stretched lengthwise on the loom). What was needed next was a machine to spin strong firm thread, a breakthrough made possible in 1769 when Richard Arkwright patented his water-frame. The first frame incorporated two sets of rollers, the second revolving faster than the first and so drawing out the carded fibre to the required thickness or 'count' before the twist was imparted. Ten years or so later, Samuel Crompton devised his mule, which, as the name suggests, combined the methods of the two previous inventions to give a yarn which was both finer and stronger than anything produced so far. As in Arkwright's frame, rollers were used to draw out the cotton rovings to greater length and to twist the thread. In common with Hargreaves' jenny, there was a moving carriage, but now it was the spindles which were mounted on the wheels. When the carriage moved away from the rollers it stretched and twisted the thread, and as it moved in again it wound the thread on to the spindles. Thus the rollers of the mule did not stretch the roving as much or as roughly as did Arkwright's frame. It was these machines, particularly the water-frame and the mule, which were soon found to be better at spinning cotton than either wool or flax. Thus, with the earlier processes of scutching and carding already mechanised, the stage was set for the import of this new technology and the 'take-off' period in the cotton industry in Scotland.

Initially this occurred in various parts of the country in locations as far apart as Galloway and Sutherland but very soon Glasgow and its neighbouring counties became the centre of the new industry. This was understandable since in the west of Scotland, like Derbyshire and Lancashire, were to be found the factors necessary for the expansion of cotton manufacturing. In the first place numerous fast-flowing rivers and streams, such as the Rivers Clyde, Cart and Ayr, could provide the water power which was an essential requirement before the advent of steam power. At the same time, raw cotton was readily available. This had been imported in considerable quantities, for combining with linen yarn in the weaving of fustian, since the mid-18th century and could be conveniently shipped from the West Indies or the plantations of the southern United States once trade links with the former colonial states were re-established. While a few of the former 'tobacco lords' seem to have transferred their assets into the cotton trade most of the capital which was required seems to have come from the existing linen industry. Thus, although there was a considerable involvement from gentlemen with landed interests such as Claud Alexander of Ballochmyle, George Dempster of Dunnichen or Sir William Douglas, it was linen manufacturing families like the Buchanans, the Findlays and the Monteiths who played a major role in developments. Pre-eminent among all these was David Dale who from the outset was in partnership with many of the other leading figures. This involvement of Dale and the rest was hardly surprising considering their earlier background in the linen industry particularly when we note Professor Slaven's observation in *The Development of the West of Scotland, 1750–1960* that 'cotton was based on imported technology and local skills employed within the framework of the linen trade'. Finally, when the growth in population in these years and the gradual progress in improving communications are taken into account, the preconditions for the rapid expansion of the cotton industry especially around Glasgow and its environs had largely been established.

All that remains is to identify the exact moment when cotton achieved its breakthrough. This is obviously a crucial point in the development of the industry and appears to have taken place between 1775 and 1780 through the combination of three separate factors. There was, firstly, the entry of Holland and France on the side of the American colonists in the War of Independence; there was also a serious depression in the Paisley silk gauze trade, apparently the result of changing fashions; and finally the impact of the Arkwright and Crompton inventions began to have a serious effect north of the Border.

Although the first cotton mill was actually built at Penicuik in Midlothian in 1778 and there were to be other important developments in east and central Scotland, the cotton industry, as has already been noted, gradually became concentrated around Glasgow. There had been a strong English presence at Penicuik which was designed for an Edinburgh partnership by John Hacket, a former employee of Arkwright's, and it was a similar story at Rothesay where the first mill in the west of Scotland was erected in 1779. Here, on the Isle of Bute, taking advantage of an abundant water supply from Loch Fad and utilising the labour supply available from the existing linen trade, John Kenyon, an English businessman, entered the cotton trade. Rothesay, besides, had other advantages, being close to Port Glasgow where the raw cotton was landed, as well as being fairly remote from Cromford, Derbyshire, where Arkwright had his headquarters. Consequently the latter's water-frame as well as some of his ex-workmen could be employed with comparative impunity on the island.

The Rothesay experiment was followed by a series of similar or more ambitious ventures over the next decade or so. The third mill to be built in Scotland was in 1780 beside the Levern Water, a tributary of the White Cart, at Neilston. It was to this building, in fact, that Sir John Sinclair, the prominent politician and improving landowner brought a party from the French Chamber of Commerce in 1789 to demonstrate how industry could be developed in rural surroundings. The next mill was at Johnstone in 1782 succeeded by others shortly afterwards at East Kilbride and North Woodside in Glasgow. By April 1785, as it happened, the first mill building was being constructed at New Lanark while by the following March spinning was underway on the site. Outwith the Glasgow area there were some other impressive developments especially in Ayrshire and Perthshire. In the former county a factory village was created at Catrine on the banks of the River Ayr; while in the east, Deanston and Stanley spinning mills were erected beside the rivers Teith and Tay respectively, both with impressive cotton mill villages attached to them. Finally, there was a modest off-shoot of the Lowland industry in the south-west of Scotland, where several spinning mills were built by local landowners in partnership with merchants from the north of England and Ulster. One was the mill at Newton Stewart, in which Dale played a role, another the complex in the planned village of Gatehouse-of-Fleet, both built on prime water power sites (and the latter is now an interesting social and industrial history museum).

By 1793 and the outbreak of the French Revolutionary Wars there were 39 spinning mills either in operation or being constructed in Scotland. Most of them were within a 25–mile radius of Glasgow although, as has been seen, there were some successful big units in other parts of the country as well. Simultaneously there was a switch from linen to cotton weaving throughout the textile centres of West of Scotland while imports of raw cotton rose in spectacular fashion in order to satisfy the increase in demand. Certainly the most significant feature of this expansion was the building of large mills with huge workforces in places like Blantyre, Catrine and New Lanark. However, it is worth recalling that scattered all over counties like Galloway, Ayrshire, Lanarkshire and Renfrewshire were numerous smaller factories, frequently converted from old corn mills or other buildings and employing smaller numbers of workers.

The role of David Dale in the first phase of the growth of the cotton industry was definitely a considerable one. Thus, apart from his activities at New Lanark itself, which will be discussed separately, he was involved in a variety of other projects during these early years. In 1787 for instance he established a factory at Blantyre, subsequently sold to James Monteith in 1792 and, today, the site of the David Livingstone Museum; in the same year he also went into partnership with Claud Alexander. The latter, possibly better known for being the brother of the 'Bonnie Lass o' Ballochmyle', immortalised in verse by Robert Burns, had been a paymaster in the East India Company. He had used the large fortune he had amassed overseas to purchase the Ballochmyle estates in south Ayrshire and proved to be an extremely suitable partner for Dale. They corresponded regularly with each other over the details of their investment and the cotton mill which they built at Catrine soon prospered.

Indeed, by 1793 there was an extensive factory complex with workers' houses, a school and a community with a population of 1,350. Meanwhile, in 1791 Dale entered into another partnership, on this occasion, with a group which included George Macintosh with whom he was already involved in a Turkey-red dyeworks at Dalmarnock. Others in this company were George Dempster of Dunnichen and William Gillespie. This body set up a small factory village producing cotton handkerchiefs at the unlikely location of Spinningdale on the Dornoch Firth with the intention of relieving unemployment in this part of the Highlands. In fact it never was a flourishing concern, as the mill was destroyed by fire in 1806 and it was never rebuilt. Around the same period in the 1790s Dale also had connections with a factory near Oban and with that at Newton Stewart (or Douglas) where another dynamic merchant-capitalist, Sir William Douglas, was one of his partners in the firm of Douglas, Dale and McCaul. Finally, in 1803, he became closely involved in the Stanley mills.

Originally he had been a member of a group of several investors including Dempster, Graham of Fintry and Sir Richard Arkwright. In 1795 the Perthshire works had been assessed as second only to New Lanark in value but a fire shortly afterwards and the adverse effects of the war with France saw the mills being put up for sale. Dale, in the last commercial undertaking of his long career now joined with a Glasgow businessman, James Craig, in what was to transpire to be a financially disastrous venture.

By the 1790s cotton manufacturing was well on the way to challenging its older rival, the linen industry, for industrial supremacy. The former, relying as has been noted, on the manufacturing base created by the latter was able to take advantage of the technological innovations which appeared in the second half of the 18th century. This enabled cotton to become the first large-scale factory industry in Scotland. At Blantyre, Catrine, Deanston and Stanley hundreds of workers were employed at the mills built on these sites. But the largest and most successful of these enterprises was New Lanark.[1]

NOTE

1 For the history of the linen industry see Durie, A. J., *The Scottish Linen Industry in the Eighteenth Century,* Edinburgh, 1979; and on the development of the Scottish cotton industry see Hamilton, H., *An Economic History of Scotland in the Eighteenth Century,* Oxford, 1963, chs. V and VI; Campbell, R.H., *Scotland since 1707. The Rise of an Industrial Society,* Oxford, 1975, ch. VI; Slaven, A., *The Development of the West of Scotland 1750–1960.* London, 1975, ch. 4; Donnachie, I., *The Industrial Archaeology of Galloway,* Newton Abbott, 1971, ch.3

The Small Town

Extracted from LJ Saunders 1950 *Scottish Democracy 1815–1840: The Social and Intellectual Background*, Edinburgh (Oliver and Boyd), 145–56.

I

Urban conditions and municipal activities have been hitherto illustrated from the four largest towns of Scotland. But expansion is a relative term, and while the great city largely initiates, concentrates and magnifies the social changes of the period, the development of the smaller towns deserves some attention. They show other aspects of a general situation and their particular social experiences were to find political expression in the complex reform movements of the thirties.

The urban variety of the country has already been noted and any classification is largely a matter of convenience. But the range can be suggested from its extremes. At one end of the scale was a group of active local capitals in historic sites that still attracted commerce and mixed industries, and were likewise convenient centres for the professional services and the political and cultural institutions of an extensive region. Such were towns like Perth, Ayr, Dumfries, Stirling, Inverness, Elgin and Haddington – their populations ranging in 1831 up to 20,000, their expansion marked but not unbalanced and their influence and interest sometimes much greater than their size would seem to warrant. By contrast, at the other end of the scale were the rapidly growing industrial centres, some carrying forward a long historic tradition, others relatively new: textile towns like Paisley, Kilmarnock, Dunfermline and Hawick, ports like Greenock and Alloa with an industrial concentration in or behind them, confluent coal and iron villages that helped to expand Falkirk and Hamilton and to create Coatbridge and Motherwell. In this group expansion was abrupt and rapid, the staple industries were exposed to economic rise and fall. The agencies of control and adjustment were often defective or lacking and the industrial town tended to lie unconformably on its countryside. Between these extremes were to be found the village burghs of Galloway, the market towns on the Highland margins, the fishing ports of Fife and Moray, the old coal and salt burghs on the Firth of Forth or the Ayrshire coast, the small spinning and weaving towns and villages along the base of the Grampians or the Ochils or in the Border valleys, inland spas like Peebles, Bridge of Allan and Strathpeffer, growing tourist resorts like Rothesay and Oban.

The pattern of expansion was most obvious in the case of the county towns. With improved communications and an expanding hinterland, business and shopping moved from the 'old town' near to the new highways. The artisans kept their traditional places longer but they too eventually followed their market, and new working-class quarters grew up as near the new centre as site values permitted. The old town with its High or Broad Street surrounded by high-packed tenements thus tended to become a slum area for casual and migratory labour and the broken and derelict of the countryside, and the townhouse and the cross, the town church and school, the guildhall and the trades' house, were either removed or left in an inconvenient historical position while the new institutions of the period were more centrally located. On the outskirts of the town were villas of business and professional men in a new and planned quarter; occasionally a weaving or nail-making hamlet was strung along the highway or a group of industries attracted to the cheap transport of a river formed with the houses of their workers a semi-detached industrial village. In the rural neighbourhood were the estates of the local magnates, often traditionally identified with the burgh, active in its politics and business and reaping the benefit of its expansion in rising land values.[1]

This type of expansion was associated with an active middle class, concerned for the progress and efficiency of the town, interested in local development projects and prepared to support the semi-public provision of light and water. There was often a local banking company to encourage them and an increasing number of branches of the competing Edinburgh banks made their appearance. Near the new town centre were the contemporary institutions of commerce and culture: the banks and insurance offices, their security and repute symbolised by their impressive frontages, the corn exchange, the subscription library and reading room, the museum and hall of the Literary and Antiquarian Society, the offices of the local weekly newspapers, the new churches and schools. All this activity now affected the old town indirectly. The historical revival of the period stimulated some restoration (often injudicious) of old buildings and the printing of local records and histories and this growing enthusiasm had its share in the revival of the municipal idea. But the economic and social interdependence of old and new was not so apparent. In the earlier years of the century the responsibility of the rich for the poor was usually expressed in terms of a benevolent voluntary action which refused to demoralise its recipients. The artisans were encouraged to invest in friendly society and savings bank; the usual philanthropic agencies were concerned with the

deserving poor, the care of orphans, the various educational needs of apprentices, young females and infants. At the opening of the century most towns had a
dispensary; by the thirties, a succession of epidemics had so emphasised the
common mortality that some towns were building a public hospital. But the foci
of congestion, intemperance and disease seemed to defy the application of the
best principles; the necessity of a more effective provision for the poor became
patent and the imposition of an assessment was as disturbing a symptom of
social change as the erection of a Catholic chapel.[2]

II

This small-town development fostered a bourgeois liberalism that was the
expression of successful enterprise, rising comfort and self-respect. The spirit
of improvement then passed from private and philanthropic business to concern
itself with the reform of municipal institutions that were still feudal in pattern,
or with their creation where they did not exist. There were in Scotland 67 royal
burghs of varying size each with its chartered constitution, and all associated in
what had been a medieval hansa, the Convention of Royal Burghs. There were
43 burghs of regality and barony; these had begun their existence under a grant
from a feudal superior, lay or ecclesiastical, and they represented various stages
on the way to municipal autonomy – 12 were now independent of the superior,
7 still had a superior but had their position and powers clarified by a charter, 24
were without elected magistrates. There were lastly populous urbanised areas
with very little organisation at all beyond a committee of feuars or the vague
rule of a superior's bailiff.[3]

The contrast between the success of business ability and virtue outside and
its limitation inside the inherited and fixed municipal order can be illustrated in
various specific situations. One important issue was finance. The royal burghs
were ruled by self-perpetuating councils on which were represented the
merchant and craft gilds recognised in the burgh 'sett' or charter. To the
enlightened business man outside these inner circles, the conduct of affairs
by this patriciate was often inefficient, occasionally corrupt and at all times
beyond effective criticism and therefore suspect. The council handled the
burghal revenue from various sources – feu duties and the rent of burgh
lands, mills, fisheries and church sittings, local imposts, dues from market
and harbour, coal and wood yards, lime shed and dung depot. This income was
paid out in salaries to the town minister, the town schoolmasters, the burgh
officials, in court and jail expenses, in the provision of police, in street lighting,
repairing and cleansing and in some kind of fire-fighting organisation and

apparatus. In addition there was usually a heavy annual charge for debt services. But there was no effective control of the management of burgh property or of its alienation or lease.[4] Often there was no inspection of accounts. Nor was the definition of legal responsibility easy. There was doubt as to whether or no a private burgess could sue a council for maladministration and difficulty in finding a court to entertain such an action. By a decision of 1820 in a suit against the magistrates of Inverurie, the Court of Session declared that questions concerning the management of the common good and the revenue of royal burghs or the contraction of debts by their magistrates were incompetent before it except as specifically conferred on it by a statute of 1693, and further, that burgesses had no title to complain of acts of mis-management on the part of magistrates unless they directly touched their private and patrimonial right.[5]

An act of 1822 was designed to clear up this situation; no debts were in future to be contracted except by an act of council; alienation and leases were to be made by auction after public notice; accounts were to be open to the inspection of burgesses and they were entitled to make complaint to the Court of Exchequer. But the act was a practical failure. The Municipal Commissioners reported in 1836 that six suits had been initiated under its provisions, and the complaining burgesses had been successful in only one of them. The Court of Exchequer demanded such technical proofs of burgess-ship as to nullify the right of appeal and to expose complainants to heavy costs. The municipal régime continued to be characterised by growing indebtedness often leading to bankruptcy and to be punctuated by occasional exposures of dubious and sometimes illegal transactions.[6]

But even a republican virtue might not have secured efficiency. New municipal needs created new expenses. The various items of income were traditionally earmarked for specific expenses. The income derived from the common good was a free one, but the progressive alienation of town property did more than make the control of its expansion difficult; it deprived the burgh of an income from the rising site values which its expansion helped to create. The new services were therefore neglected or met by an unpopular assessment passed under an expensive Police Act and limited by its terms to specific objects. An historical county town like Stirling exhibited the results of this civic position and the contrasting vitality of private enterprise. The population had risen from 5,000 to 8,500 between 1801 and 1831, yet at this later date and after, it still retained an unpaid nightly watch of citizens (who might provide substitutes at 1/-) and a reserve of 'high constables' composed of respectable shopkeepers and tradesmen who acted 'spontaneously' or on the call of the magistrates.[7] Street paving was poor; oil lamps were still used in street lighting; the water supply came from public wells only and in the picturesque upper town, which was now a noxious slum, there were open sewers that ceased to run in times of summer drought.[8] Yet in such a town, while the civic administration was complex, it was not necessarily corrupt, for a relatively effective system of auditing was practised and the burgh accounts were open to the public and had been correctly kept at least since 1793. But there was not much money available for improved services. Much of the common good had been alienated early in the 18th century and there was little free income from this source. As it was, the town debt had nearly tripled in 40 years but any resort to a Police Act and an assessment was opposed as unnecessary.[9] Yet the local middle class was active, benevolent and (in the strict sense of the word) patriotic. During the first quarter of the century a new business centre with Corn Exchange and Athenaeum, banks and hotels, developed on a by-pass of the great northern road and an impressive villa area of terraces and squares was planned in the direction of the King's Park. There was much philanthropy and some attempt to put the public relief of the town on a business basis, its economy all the more justified since the numerous charitable endowments of earlier centuries were criticised as training a large number of the inhabitants to a species of pauperism.[10] The town schools were not reorganised but some public assistance was given to private and charitable effort and at a higher level appeared a School of Arts and a Commercial Seminary. There was a growing interest in the historical monuments of the place and in the amenities of its dramatic situation and some restoration and improvement was carried out at public expense.[11] Yet here as in a miniature Edinburgh, an historic walled town had spread beyond a confined site into a series of sharply defined quarters and the old centre was left to accumulate a mass of poverty, disease and misery that was ignored, repressed or treated by institutions and methods derived from an earlier social experience.

III

In many of the burghs of regality and barony the local conditions provoked a radicalism that was sharper than the middle-class liberalism of a county town. Some of these burghs were, like Hawick, practically royal burghs without the status. In others a modified right of electing magistrates was vested in burgesses or feuars, subject however to the veto of the superior; this was the position of an important industrial town like Kilmarnock. In a number of towns of considerable importance such as Alloa, Dalkeith, Kelso, Kirriemuir and Fraserburgh, the superior appointed the magistrates and the burgh officials; in other places, the essential services were the concern of a committee of feuars with few powers and little money.[12] Necessity or use and wont might supplement the action of some of these constitutions, but their limitations require to be illustrated in some detail. In 1831, the Dumbartonshire town of Kirkintilloch had a population of over 4,000, largely engaged in weaving and characterised by an enthusiastically radical disposition. It was a burgh of barony with a burgess franchise confined to the proprietors of an arbitrary area in the bounds; these proprietors were 22 in number, and as residence was required as a qualification for magistracy, all but 2 of the resident burgesses were members of council.[13] Galashiels was a small woollen centre in an area that kept alive its feudal traditions. With the growing popularity of tweeds towards the end of the twenties, numerous small factories were erected in a narrow valley and by 1831 its total population was over 2,000. The town was partly in Selkirkshire, partly in Roxburgh. In the one shire it was open country; in the other it was a burgh of barony under two superiors. The bailie of the burgh was appointed by Pringle of Torwoodlea but no court of barony had been held for over a century: there was no court house, no jail, no regular police establishment and attempts made to light and drain the town by voluntary assessment met with only partial success. But trade and manufacture were in all respects free and unplanned expansion was rapid.[14]

Several of the smaller weaving towns in the West were under a similar régime. Strathaven had a population of 4,000 and a radical reputation. The Duke of Hamilton was superior but there was no resident baron bailie as the Duke's factor at Hamilton held the appointment.[15] In North Ayrshire, the introduction of carpet manufactures and worsted mills had raised the population of Stewarton, a village on the outskirts of Kilmarnock, to nearly 3,000. The superior and patron of the parish maintained a court house for the justices and a lock up at his own expense; he had the right to levy an impost on meal and to charge for stances at the fair, but these dues were now trifling in amount. There were no local taxes or assessments for local services.[16] In Renfrewshire, Johnstone was now a large manufacturing village of over 5,000 inhabitants 3 miles west of Paisley: there was no magistracy, no corporate organisation beyond a committee of feuars chosen annually who managed an assessment for the poor. And in the same area of industrial expansion, considerable centres of population like Barrhead (2,600), Lochwinnoch (2,600) and Beith (5,000) were similarly organised.[17]

In the North East, Lord Douglas was the superior of Kirriemuir which had a population of 4,000. The burgh had neither property nor revenue nor debt; there were no burgh taxes levied except the customs at fairs and markets by the superior. The streets were kept in repair from the statute labour money of the shire and lighted by private subscription. The only magistrate was the baron bailie who was not in the practice of exercising any jurisdiction, but a small debt court was held once a month by a justice and a resident procurator fiscal inquired into offences presentable before the sheriff of the county.[18] Two other local situations in this area may be cited. The Duke of Gordon was the superior of Huntly, a burgh of barony with a population of 2,500.[19] He appointed a bailie whose jurisdiction was limited to the feudal duties of clearing obstructions from streets and water-courses, settling boundary disputes between feuars and collecting customs from markets and shops to the extent of over £40 a year. There was no authority for assessing, and the cleaning, lighting and watching of the place were 'occasionally and partially effected by voluntary subscription'. There was no common good, and the townsfolk accused their superior of having filched certain privileges of pasture, fuel and stone from them some 60 years ago, but there was no evidence of any original grant as claimed. In the same region, the contiguous villages of Keith, Fife Keith and Newmills were under the superiorities of the Earls of Seafield and Fife.[20] The total population was nearly 3,000; there was neither magistracy nor police; the streets were not lighted nor was water supplied; there was no common good, no local taxation except an assessment for road money, and this was alleged to be spent on the main thoroughfares used by the gentry while the side streets and bye-lanes were so neglected as to be unwholesome. The court house was in need of repair, the lock-up insecure, and in the absence of a police force, the inhabitants were apprehensive of the crowds of vagabonds and thieves who flocked to the fairs held in the town.

Such local details help to explain the intense radicalism of some small Scottish towns where a skilled, intelligent and self-respecting working class was denied any effective control of the intimate conditions of life and livelihood by what seemed a decadent and irrational feudalism. After 1820 the position began to be recognised as indefensible and some towns were encouraged to secure expanded powers by private act. The process can be exemplified in the case of Bathgate, [21] a West Lothian town of 2,600 inhabitants and the centre of a developing mining area. With the concurrence of the superior, the town obtained a new Act in 1824 which provided for a magistracy and council to be elected by the burgesses and authorised an assessment for police purposes. But the details were open to criticism. The assessment could be levied on occupants of houses of £1 rent or upwards at a rate not higher than 1/- per £. The burgess-ship was open to proprietors, tenants paying at least £3 of rent and subscribers of £1 towards the expenses of the Act of Erection. Payment of assessment did not therefore carry voting rights and since the payments of admission to burgess-ship might be as high as £2 2s. 0d., the new council represented the propertied classes. There were 84 residents whose rents in property or tenancy amounted to £10 or over, and of these 48 became burgesses; there were 57 persons whose rents came to between £5 and £10, but only 9 thought it worth while to pay the dues that gave them a local vote. Municipal reform by private act was thus expensive, piecemeal and conservative; but, limited as they were, the powers granted to a few expanding burghs under this procedure marked the beginnings of any effective municipal action at all.[22]

IV

Burghal conditions seemed to many to call for a general and logical scheme of reconstruction to clear away the historical debris, but the problem was complicated by its affiliations. On the one side, the old municipal régime was tied to the recognised gilds and crafts of the town and on the other to an equally medieval scheme of parliamentary representation.

In the burghs the merchant gilds and incorporated trades still survived but far advanced in institutional decay. The law courts continued to uphold the letter of their monopolistic claims, but permitted them to be whittled away in detail.[23] Even in the ancient royalties, gild privileges were now penetrated by recognised exceptions and evasions. The acts opening any craft to returned soldiers and sailors were interpreted after 1815 to include militiamen and fencibles in their benefits and no specific length of military service nor any test of craft skill was required from these 'King's freemen'.[24] Disputes that arose concerning the demarcation of old and new processes, or production for local disposal or for export, or the manufacture of subsidiary articles were now usually decided by the courts with a bias towards a reasonable freedom.[25] Often the gilds themselves made some money by selling licences to manufacture and trade in their reserved areas and time made the exceptional concession the rule and a source of steady income. In these respects the gilds had lost their economic importance or only retained it sufficiently to trouble those who looked for reason and found injustice in traditional arrangements. There were indeed some towns of importance like Greenock, Port Glasgow and Falkirk which had neither burgesses nor gild-brethren nor incorporated trades and in others, such as Paisley, the incorporations claimed no exclusive privileges and had become convenient forms of friendly societies.[26]

But especially in the royal burghs the gilds retained a political and social importance and a recognised place in the municipal structure. They took part in the election of the town council; they had rights of tax and toll; they inherited property and had claims to the enjoyment of charitable and educational bequests. They became vested interests and centres of municipal power and influence.[27] In some cases entry fees were high, not to exclude strangers from participating in the craft but to protect its political importance and its accumulated funds and perquisites. In the older burghs illustrations of perversion were the more frequent. The famous Glovemakers of Perth had an income of over £1,000 a year; they charged the sons of freemen £1 entry money with no obligation to practise the craft, while strangers had to be operative and to pay £100 – a system which 'produced results very injurious to young tradesmen', and in fact in 1832 there was not a single operative glover resident in Perth who was a member of the corporation.[28] A more extreme case was that of the Fleshers of Stirling. Owing to extensive litigation they had little property left, but they did claim the twelve best stalls in the market rent fee and other rights which were estimated as worth £30 a year to each member. These had been reduced to eight, of whom only two were residents of the town. The sons of freemen paid £8 entry fee but for outsiders the amount required had been progressively raised from £25 to £100 and the applicant had in addition to possess £150 of free property.[29] These may have been extreme cases, but they illustrate a general tendency for the gilds to survive with a spurious vitality as protected property-holding corporations. They secured certain benefits from endowments and other assets to participants selected on no very rational principle; they retained the right of representation in the town council and so were convenient stances from which to influence the disposal of public contracts.[30]

But the most important obstacle to a comprehensive burgh reform has yet to be mentioned. The royal burghs were part of two central institutions of medieval origin. One of these, the Convention of Royal Burghs, was now decrepit. It had no proper legislative or judicial powers and for long its chief business had been to consider applications from the poorer burghs for aids or grants from the land tax which was largely paid by the richer burghs. As the vote of each burgh in these transactions was of equal value, the larger burghs had come to consider this 'a most unequal and unjust, if not an illegal mode of taxation' and were prepared to see the Convention abolished as without any public utility.[31] But the royal burghs as tenants-in-chief of the Crown were also represented in parliament, first at Edinburgh and then at Westminister.[32] The procedure of election might be here as traditional and as irrational as in the other parts of the political structure but the effect was to link up local burgh issues with national politics and to associate local cliques and interests with the national parties. Burgh and gild reform was thus resisted as a flank approach to parliamentary change and a parliamentary change became the condition of burgh reform. The electoral arrangements of the Scottish burghs exposed them to political management. Edinburgh was the only burgh which returned a separate member; the others were associated in groups of 4 or 5 to elect a common representative. The elections were made by the self-elected town councils who appointed electoral delegates. These met in each burgh of the group in rotation. Each burgh had equal voting value, regardless of its population or wealth, but the burgh in which the formal election was held had a casting vote for the occasion. The results of these arrangements were increasingly irrational as population and wealth increased and concentrated in new sites. Some 67 self-perpetuating town councils, averaging 20 persons in each, returning 15 members to parliament.[33] Glasgow with a population of 150,000 in 1821 was linked with 3 other burghs of which the total population was under 10,000; in an election its vote was exactly equal to that of Dumbarton or Renfew or Rutherglen. There was no representation of any but royal burghs so that Paisley with a population approaching 40,000 in 1821, Greenock with over 20,000 inhabitants and such considerable industrial towns as Kilmarnock and Falkirk, each with over 10,000 inhabitants went unrepresented, yet 5 small royal burghs on the Fifeshire coast with a total population of 6,000 returned 1 member and 4 royal burghs of Galloway with less than 8,000 inhabitants had the same privilege.[34]

At every point in this chain of delegated authority from gild and burgh to parliament the parties were concerned to apply influence and pressure. The result was not a complete political incompetence. The party oppositions, the family alliances and counter-alliances, the burghal and trade cliques generated much friction and some movement; there were conventions even of give and take and some response to general issues. The abilities which were needed for political management were sometimes associated with practical capacity and civic pride. But the result was to secure burghal office to professional politicians who might be inferior, irresponsible and active only in their own or their patron's interest. In the small burghs particularly, the critics of the régime accused them of being the creatures of local magnates or of forming 'a junta of self-elected bankrupts who live upon the revenues of the corporation and give their voice to the aspirant for parliamentary honours who pays them best and makes them most frequently drunk'.[35] The municipal situation was thus part of an elaborate structure of law, sentiment and interest, an *ancien régime* from which it could not easily be isolated. The movement for burgh reform certainly revived after 1815 and it tried to harass the civic powers into a sense of their responsibilities by the use of ingenious legal devices and by a series of investigations to awaken public opinion. But a general change could come only after 1832 and the postponement of the initial issue complicated the next step. In opposition to a static, irrational and obstructive institutional inheritance, the reformers acquired a distrust of institutional action at all; they emphasised rational and liberal principles derived from metaphysics or the standards of efficiency and integrity which they had found effective in individual business or craft.[36] But the newer forms of social disorder increased and this kind of reforming enthusiasm was to find itself in the thirties confronted with problems of municipal development that seemed both to evade its analysis and defy its technique.

NOTES

1 This description is generalised from a survey of such towns as Perth, Stirling, Ayr, Dumfries, Haddington, Montrose and Elgin. The sources are mainly the *New Statistical Account*, the *Municipal Corporation Report* (1835), the *Sanitary Inquiry* of 1842 and local histories, tours and guide-books.

2 Perth was probably as 'typical' a town as any in Scotland. In 1831 the population was 20,000. The burgh was proportionately the richest in Scotland; after deducting a debt of £28,000, its property was estimated at over £67,000; the revenue was £6,300 a year and there was an appreciable 'Common Good'. The Guildry of Merchant-Burgesses held real property valued at £28,000, with an average income of over £1,300. There were seven Incorporated Trades; one of these, the Glovers, had a yearly income of over £1,000 but there was not a single operative glover resident in Perth who was a member.

The list of public and semi-public institutions in the town suggests the line of civic development. Smeaton's bridge over the Tay was built in 1771 and the Barracks in 1793. In 1807 Burn designed the Academy and in 1812 the Military Prison provided accommodation for the French prisoners of war. After 1815 came a Masonic Hall (1818), County Buildings and Jail by Smirke (1819), a theatre in 1820, Gas Works in 1824 and Water Works in 1830.

A Literary and Antiquarian Society dated from 1784 and a Subscription Library from 1786. A weekly newspaper first appeared in 1807 and another *(The Constitutional)* in 1820; two others were launched after the Reform Act in 1835 and 1836. Among the semi-public philanthropic institutions were a Savings Bank (1815), a Dispensary (1819) and after the cholera, an Infirmary (1836).

In the Thirties, the town had two local and four branch banks.

N.S.A., *Perth, passim*; Municipal Corporations Report, 1836, v. 23. *Local Reports, Perth*, 298.

3 Municipal Corporations Report, 1835, v. 29. *General Report*, 98.

4 ibid 29. Edinburgh Review. *Burgh Reform*, 30 (1818), 512.

5 Municipal Corporations Report, 1835, v. 29. *General Report*, 29.

6 ibid 30.

7 N.S.A., *Stirling*, 413. Stirling manufactured 'tartans'; it was a tourist centre and still a small port so that the sails of Dutch vessels might be seen twisting about through the carselands.

8 N.S.A., *Stirling*, 413; W. H. Forrest, *Report on the Sanitary Condition of the Labouring*

Classes of the Town of Stirling. Sanitary Inquiry, 1842, 261.

9 Municipal Corporations Report, 1836, v. 23. *Local Reports,* Stirling, 404. N.S.A., *Stirling,* 413.

10 N.S.A., *Stirling,* 416.

11 The writer in the N.S.A. recorded the opening in 1817, after three-quarters of a century of disuse, of the historic West Kirk 'at an expense which might have been more beneficially employed in building a new fabric in another part of the town'. He found the church damp and the pillars inconvenient and heavy, but he was impressed by 'a splendid central gaselier'. N.S.A., *Stirling,* 424.

12 Municipal Corporations Report, 1835, v. 29. *General Report,* 98.

13 Municipal Corporations Report, 1836, v. 23. *Local Reports:* Burghs of Regality and Barony, 109.

14 ibid, 69.

15 ibid, 158.

16 ibid, 150.

17 ibid, 92.

18 ibid, 112.

19 ibid, 90.

20 ibid, 94. In Fraserburgh the Commissioners were surprised to find a boy of 14 acting as Town Clerk. *Local Reports:* Burghs of Regality and Barony, 59.

21 Municipal Corporations Report, 1836, v. 23. *Local Reports:* Burghs of Regality and Barony, 11.

22 In 1821 Airdrie was also created a free and independent burgh of barony by Act of Parliament. *Local Reports:* Burghs of Regality and Barony, 55.

23 Municipal Corporations Report, 1835, v. 29. *General Report,* 83.

24 ibid, 83.

25 ibid, 82, 84.

26 ibid, 88.

27 ibid, 87.

28 ibid, 87.

29 ibid, 87.

30 There was representation but not election. 'In those burghs which include a guildry and various trades, which is the case with the most considerable burghs, the heads of these societies, namely the Dean of Guild and the Deacons of the Trades, are generally constituent members, in whole or in part, of the Council. For this reason, these office bearers are not elected by their respective companies, but are chosen, indirectly indeed yet ultimately by the Town Council, in order to preserve inviolate the rule that the old Council should choose the new'. Edinburgh Review, *Burgh Reform,* 30 (1818), 509. Theodore Keith, *Municipal Elections in the Royal Burghs of Scotland from the Union to 1833.* Scottish Historical Review, 33, 206. And also John Galt's *The Provost* (1822).

31 For the Convention of Royal Burghs at this time see the Municipal Corporations Report, 1836, v. 23. *Representation from Glasgow,* 14, 44.

32 Anon, *The Political State of Scotland*, 1811. John Wilson, *The Political State of Scotland*, 1831.
33 Westminster Review, *Parliamentary Representation in Scotland*, 14 (1831), 137.
34 ibid, 141, 142.
35 ibid, 143.
36 For Radical criticisms of post-Reform political practice see Tait's Edinburgh Magazine: *Political State of the North of Scotland*, 1835, 620, and *The Scottish Elections*, 1837, 545. The logical conclusion indicated was the ballot.

New Towns by Land and Sea

Extracted from AM Smith 1982 *Jacobite Estates of the Forty-Five*, Edinburgh (John Donald), 143–62.

While the foundation of new towns was by no means a novel pastime for landowners, it was one of the passions of the improvers of the eighteenth century, and one from which the commissioners could hardly be expected to be immune, even without express directions in the Annexing Act and in the first instructions sent to the newly appointed Board in 1755. Individual landowners who embarked in town-building occasionally indulged in some self-glorification, as we can see from the names of some of the new towns, such as Colinsburgh, Archiestown and Grantown, but behind even these eponymous titles there were often sound economic reasons for choosing particular sites. There was a fairly confident assumption that manufacturing industry would prosper better in a town than in open country, for the town would provide both a labour supply and a market both for agricultural produce in the vicinity and for the goods manufactured in the town. Estate rentals were also expected to rise as the population increased and the greater potential of land was realised, particularly if the landowner had made use of the extra hands to reclaim waste land on his property. Such expectations were not always fully or even partially realised, for many of the builders, like Alexander Dirom, the founder of Bridekirk, can be criticised, as J. D. Wood comments, because they never asked themselves, or indeed thought of asking themselves, even in contemporary terms as opposed to twentieth-century planners' jargon, 'What were the threshold requirements of the functions essential to the prosperity of a sizeable place in a predominantly agricultural setting?'[1] Statistics and the 'dismal science' had not at that time become the controlling genii of planners.

The public aims, however, were envisaged as more than economic. Just how radical a change it was hoped the annexation would make can be gathered from the reference to town building in the parliamentary debates on the annexation, and from some of the suggestions in the manuscript already mentioned giving 'Hints' on managing the estates.[2] In the third section of this document, it is suggested that the Trustees should 'fix proper passes', build bridges there, then churches, workhouses, i.e. factories, schoolhouses and prisons, and stone houses, with glass windows. Into these new settlements, *all* (my italics) the present inhabitants were to be gradually received and allotted new houses in which they could see to work during the winter – on account of the glass windows – whereupon their 'present dark smoky cabins indisposed for industry and work' were *all* (again my italics) to be destroyed. When one remembers that the last inhabited black houses have only recently been evacuated, the grandeur of this vision becomes awe-inspiring. A truly authoritarian society was described by this author, in which the 'junction of the people together' would provide stewards, factors and masters of crafts with convenient opportunities to propagate the mechanical arts and, even more important, a spirit of industry amongst them, especially as they would be 'easily overlooked and deprived of their usual recesses for sauntering and slothfulness'. The document had, however, the considerable merit of being realistic about finance, for the writer suggested that £10,000 should be advanced for this purpose, from the Treasury, interest to be paid out of the profits of the estates.

As the government gave the Board explicit instructions to erect new settlements, the commissioners made an early appointment of a sub-committee of four to take particular charge of the 'enlargement or new erection' of towns and villages and, in 1757, four places were suggested as suitable – New Tarbat, Callander of Menteith, Kinloch Rannoch and Beauly. Prisons and schools were to be erected at each place. Only two of these, strictly speaking, would have been new foundations; Callander had been the creation of James Drummond, former owner of the Perth estate, about 1730, and 'Beaulie' is stated in *Origines Parochiales* as having been in existence in 1562, though the present settlement is not necessarily on the precise site of the first. Kinloch Rannoch had only eight tenants and the proposed site for New Tarbat was part of the policies of the house of the former Earl of Cromartie. Some time later Ullapool was proposed as preferable to New Tarbet but, in 1761, when the first signs of royal approval for these particular plans were shown, New Tarbat was the favoured spot – probably because someone in London had been looking up old reports, not at minute-books.[3] Only general approval was elicited for the 'ends and purposes' these settlements were calculated to promote. To enable the government to make 'distinct and precise' judgements about the probable benefits of these and any future proposals, in relation to their situation, expense, type of manufactures proposed, and populousness, the commissioners were asked to send more information, such as plans of the estates, taken upon actual surveys, copies of properly authenticated rentals, and abstracts of the factors' reports; in 1755, the factors had been asked to comment on suitable sites for villages among all the other information the Board wanted.

The planned villages of the eighteenth century have been classified as falling into four categories, comprising those associated with agriculture and estate interests, manufacturing villages, fishing and other settlements connected with the coastal trade, and finally, inland spas, tourist and residential centres.[4] Many foundations fell into several categories, as most landlords hoped to increase the wealth of their estates by encouraging manufacturing industry as well as by improving agricultural practice, a perfectly feasible ambition before the days of mass-production. The commissioners had to take into account the possible social consequences of any urban development they assisted, in addition to considering economic aspects. Even so, four of the first five sites they proposed were fairly conventional by the standards of the time and, if Kinloch Rannoch is not yet either a thriving market town, an industrial centre, or even an important spa, a largish village in the Rannoch area was not in the 1760s a wholly unreasonable suggestion as a possibly potent agent of social change. As it happened, before any positive steps had been taken to start any building, the change in Britain's international position when the Seven Years War ended resulted in another element affecting the Board's town-planning, an element that was to be almost wholly destructive. The provision of holdings and employment for disbanded members of the army and navy became inextricably intermingled with what were often referred to as 'colonies' on the annexed estates. What solution could have seemed neater than placing these returning heroes in new towns in the Scottish Highlands, particularly if they were natives who could be expected to have benefited from the experience of 'civilisation' in other parts of the world?

Some evidence points to a degree of concern, at least among the governing classes, at the prospect of demobilisation. An act was passed enabling officers, mariners and soldiers to exercise their trades anywhere in Great Britain, an unusual privilege which may well have been aimed at dispersing at least parts of regiments.[5] Some Scottish landlords besides the commissioners encouraged servicemen to settle in specific towns and villages on their estates, such as Portsoy and Macduff, by offering bounties.[6] This was not pure altruism, of course. It was assumed that these men would bring craftsmanship and discipline into the settlements. Also, the question of providing for disabled soldiers had been brought up by Campbell of Barcaldine, the factor on the Perth estate, some time before the end of the Seven Years War. Early in 1760, he wrote to the commissioners that several Perthshire men who had served in America in the Highland regiments had lately returned home wounded and unfit for further service. They had applied to him for small holdings for themselves and their families, and he thought them quite able to manage a small farm. One advantage he saw for himself in giving tenancies to such people was that their pensions would enable them to pay their rents punctually. The Board approved and he was ordered to divide the farm of Morell to take several soldiers. Barcaldine had declared himself 'pretty positive' that the soldiers would set an example of industry to their neighbours, but his idea was never proved. In January, 1763, he had to report failure. He had tried to make an equable division of a farm, Drumlaken, as, for a variety of reasons, Morell had turned out to be impractical, but when the Chelsea Pensioners, as he termed them, foregathered for this purpose and found one of their proposed co-tenants without an arm, another without a leg, and no doubt others with similar handicaps, they 'took such an aversion to being brought together', that he had to give up the scheme.[7]

The commissioners did not read the omens correctly, however, and the factor's idea took a firm hold of the Board. Their onslaught on the problem began in 1763, when, in their report to the king, they proposed spending £3,000 to provide houses, each costing £5, 'Necessaries' estimated at £3 for three hundred married soldiers and a cash bounty of £3 for two hundred unmarried. Each of the soldiers was to be allotted three acres of ground for spade cultivation, and the ground adjoining the houses was to be enclosed and laid down in grass for pasture for cows, allowing two acres for a cow. Houses were to be rent-free for life. Farm ground, also rent-free for the first three years, was thereafter to be let at 5/- per acre. The unmarried men's bounty of £3 was to be paid out in three annual instalments. It was also proposed that £5 should be lent to deserving and indigent soldiers to maintain them for the first year, and to help them stock their holdings. It may be noted that the policy of giving land to craftsmen (and to fishermen) soon aroused criticism on the grounds we have already seen expressed that only a kailyard and potato croft were necessary, and that any more land would drive men from their proper business, making for inefficiency in both agriculture and trade.[8]

By this scheme, it was expected that the population would be increased, and that there would be introduced upon the annexed estates a number of good workmen for the various types of improvements envisaged, who would, 'by raising the spirit of emulation among the present inhabitants', promote industry, 'hitherto at its lowest ebb'. The commissioners were in for a rude awakening. One early dissentient voice was that of James Small in Struan who, significantly, had been an ensign in the army before becoming factor. He reported in 1763 that he had no land for them in the current year and he was obviously well pleased that he could say this. He forecast that five-sixths of the soldiers would be the greatest blackguards, in no amenable to civil discipline, 'only the rod having kept them under control'. Further, he antici-pated that they would sell their whole possessions and squander their money on drink. His prophecy was largely borne out in the next few years and, when the new towns were still embryonic, he was able to tell the commissioners that already, on the strength of the 'great things to be done for them', returning warriors were borrowing money in every public house on the road to Struan – from twelve to fifteen miles. Captain Forbes also disapproved. He wrote in November 1763, 'I do not much admire the grand plan of sailors and sogers being persuaded it will not easily execute'.[9]

However, in 1763, there was little likelihood that these Cassandra-like voices would be listened to and the 'colonies' as they were called were begun. It was unfortunate that, with the benefit of hindsight, the Board could not have read the words of wisdom of James Wilson that 'It is probably much more difficult to plant people than potatoes',[10] but even allowing for initial over-optimism, a great many of their actions in connection with this plan were unnecessarily precipitate. The first step taken was to insert advertisements in the Edinburgh newspapers and in the *London Gazette*, in March 1763, intimating that such provision was to be made for demobilised soldiers. Any interested were asked to apply to the secretary in the Edinburgh office, or to any of the factors and, within a few days, by March 30, several had appeared at the office. But no definite plans had been made for their reception, no inquiries had been sent to commanding officers of regiments about to be 'broke' as to the likely response from those being disbanded, and all that could be done was to ask the agent, Mr. Alston, to make plans for their immediate settlement on the estates. Previous to this, all that had been done was to give removal notices to tenants whose farms were wanted for the proposed settlements.

This had roused protests not merely from the tenants. In May the factor on Lovat pointed out that it was impossible to find holdings for soldiers without distressing the present inhabitants. He also suggested that the improvable muirs should be used, as the present farms were so small that taking off a few acres would make them 'no farm at all'. On the tiny estate of Monaltrie most of the tenants refused to give up any part of their ground. In November, four months later, the factor therefore had to report that he still could not get land for the soldiers, as the tenants were holding on to their possessions, and he had only six houses built, although there were far more than that number of soldiers on the estate.[11]

At the beginning of 1764, the Monaltrie factor had to defend himself against complaints from the soldiers that they had had no wages, and that their houses had no doors or windows. He was able to clear himself on both counts; the wright responsible for the houses had fallen sick and no wages had been paid because the men were absent from work. Also some had taken payment in meal. After it had been shown that the whole estate of Monaltrie was only sixteen oxgates and that some poor people held only one quarter of an oxgate, which with any land taken off to accommodate soldiers would be quite insufficient, the Board began somewhat belatedly to realise that 'there seems to be a difficulty in providing for all the soldiers' settled upon Monaltrie and told the factor to give them the opportunity to remove to other estates. In character with their general behaviour, none of them would then move. By May, 1765, however, some had disappeared, but they had disposed of their furniture and locked up their houses behind them, so that no-one else could inhabit them. The factor was instructed to apply for a sheriff's warrant to break down the doors of the locked houses.[12] The following year saw another voluntary clearance from Monaltrie when the Board ordered that no more money was to be given to the soldiers as loans; they were to be paid just as other workmen were when employed in public works. This drove a number of them south to solicit the Board in person. On the larger estates, a similar picture emerges.

In the meantime, in Edinburgh, Henry Barclay, the secretary, was bearing the brunt of the onslaught of the demobilised. In the special minute book, kept from April, 1763 to March, 1765, solely for business referring to the settlement of soldiers and sailors, there is a copy of his long report on his activities during the Board's adjournment in 1763.[13] He had dispatched 242 married and 78 unmarried soldiers, to the various estates, and the applications were increasing daily. What he describes delicately as the 'general importunity for being received' showed there would be no difficulty in finding sufficient candidates. One qualification was that the best recommended soldiers should be accepted, but Barclay and such commissioners who looked in at the office – 'casually attended' was Barclay's phrase – soon realised that they could not operate on a first come first served basis, as this might exclude some regiments that had distinguished themselves in the war but had not yet been disbanded. They inserted a further advertisement therefore that only old-established corps would be received in the meantime.

The next difficulty arose from the factors' correspondence, which plainly showed that they were facing very considerable problems in getting suitable accommodation for such numbers of settlers, as they had not been allowed time to build houses. In 1764, John Forbes complained that soldiers and sailors with their wives and children came every day 'in shoals' to his house, sometimes late at night, starving, when he had to lodge them and feed them, at least for one night. It was obvious that to relieve the factors there must be some delay in accepting any more prospective settlers. Despite yet another advertisement in the newspapers and a letter sent to the commanding officer when Keith's battalion was dismissed, numbers came crowding to the office and, no doubt because of their 'importunity', the beleaguered secretary judged it expedient to satisfy them by giving them seventy-six billets, most of this regiment expressing a preference for Cromartie. Again the newspapers were to be used to let them know when they could apply to the factor, as places became available. Many of them were unfit for work; others had travelled a considerable distance and had exhausted their allowance for travelling home. As it was the hope of the bounty that had attracted them, it was thought only reasonable to give some a few shillings to help 'carry them home to their friends' and to recommend others to the infirmary.

Another mistake in the original concept was discovered when the cheapest estimate for houses on the Perth estate appeared to be £16 each, and on Lovat and Cromartie £12–£15, while the commissioners had calculated on £5 each house. Other landlords avoided such an outlay by leaving it to the settlers to build their own houses.[14] The secretary had to report further that on the Struan estate some soldiers had already proved disorderly, and two were dishonest, while further unexpected expense had arisen when the Crieff surgeon's services had had to be called on for the sick on the Perth estate. He also advised the Board to give pecuniary encouragement until houses could be provided; like the doctor's fees, such expenditure had not been provided for in the original estimates. The one bright spot in this lugubrious tale was that at Whiteley, a farm on the barony of Stobhall, the eastmost part of the Perth estates, in the parish of Cargill George Young of Coupar Angus, who had been employed to oversee the settlement proposed there, had arranged for houses to start being built. He had got contracts and, as there was a stone quarry near, costs could be kept down.

Ever-optimistic at this point in the history of the annexation, the Board reported in 1764 that the scheme for settling the soldiers had succeeded. 276 houses had been built and 249 men, married and unmarried, had been provided for. The commissioners' main worry was that they had spent over £2,000 more than had been originally authorised. The original estimate stood at £3,000 but the actual costs had risen to £5,214.0.9$\frac{5}{12}$, which included £1,042.4.1$\frac{11}{12}$ on travelling and subsistence, £2,619.16.7$\frac{6}{12}$ on houses, and £1,552.0.0 on bounties. The next year's report was less sanguine. The success in settling the soldiers did not now seem so assured, and this about-face from 1764 had to be explained. Many quite defensible excuses could be produced. Bounties had been planned for stocking small holdings but instead had been used by the settlers to buy necessary furniture and for subsistence. There was no work available, so there was no money to buy seeds and, in any case, many were unable to work as they were 'valetudinary'. As a result, the Board had had to employ the able-bodied in enclosing heath or moorish ground for plantations on the annexed estates, in making fences for their settlements and in other 'New Deal' activities. Forbes, on Lovat, was at his wits' ends to know what to do with soldiers in the winter. Invalids were given enough to keep them alive but not 'sufficient to indulge them in idleness'. Many colonists had needed additional money to buy cows or the tools of their trades. The sole benefits the Board could enumerate in 1765 were that they expected the rents of the houses to correspond in a few years to the interest on the sums laid out – they must have forgotten that they proposed initially that the soldiers would live rent-free – and that the population was increased. The soldiers had been encouraged to marry and there were 368 children 'who in all probability would have been lost to the kingdom' without these colonies. However, to prevent further expense, they had decided to bring in no more soldiers, but they asked for permission to spend £500 more to complete what was already begun.[15]

Though the commissioners may have been satisfied with the progress made in settling soldiers in 1764, it is doubtful if the factors were ever happy about the conditions of the colonies or colonists, or if the majority of the beneficiaries were ever particularly appreciative. Nor was this unreasonable. It must be clear from the preceding pages, and especially from the quotations from the secretary's reports, that the central handling of the scheme was not well thought out, if indeed it was thought out at all to its logical conclusion. It was inefficient from its initiation; soldiers and factors and, as we shall see below, sailors too, had all legitimate grounds for complaint.

One of the worst features of the arrangements made was the type of ground allocated to the new settlers. It was realised that all would need some ground for subsistence, but even experienced agriculturists would have had difficulty in dealing successfully with what faced them at Benniebeg, for example. In 1756, Barcaldine had described this farm as a 'small piece of bad meadow ground'. Though the rent had been brought down over the years from £20 to £13, the possessors still found themselves losers and had given up their tenancy. The soil was hard and gravelly and was eventually valued at £10. Other sites were not more promising. The area available at Kinloch Rannoch the Struan factor thought too small, and he suggested two hundred acres of 'muir ground very improveable', belonging to another proprietor on the south side of the loch. Borelandbog Park on the Perth estate was proposed as suitable because it would dispossess no-one but, though it had good soil, it was so interspersed with large stones that the factor thought they would have to be taken into account when the holdings were being measured. The Lovat factor had been given explicit instructions that he should settle soldiers without distressing the present inhabitants and he too suggested 'improveable muirs where the soil is good and may be turned to good account by ditching and trenching'. Later, in the history of the settlements, Menzies, the General Inspector, reported that those on the outskirts of Callander, who were local tenants' sons, had had trouble. He thought they were sober and industrious but because they 'had not been importunate and troubled the board with petitions' – unlike all the other colonists, it should be noted – they had been overlooked and their land was 'very difficult to improve'.[16]

The siting of the New Tarbat settlement was perhaps not so bad, though the farmer who was given notice to make room for soldiers and sailors had used it only for pasture. But the soldiers on Strathpeffer sent in a heart-rending petition to Lord Kames, describing their bad lots, stony and watery ground, and telling him they had been obliged to 'strip our backs to feed our bellies or els die for want, your lordships not fulfilling promises . . .' In 1768, some of those settled in the estates of Cromartie let the Board know that they had had to give up their ground on the Moss of Conon because it was 'entirely covered with water'. And these were men who had managed to improve other parts of their holdings. Skilled men, carefully supervised, might have been successful in these conditions but, by 1765, it was admitted in the minutes that on 'stony moorish, some swampy ground', the soldiers were not of themselves capable of improving without the help of the Board.[17] It is significant that the settlement which was most immediately successful was Strelitz. Named in honour of Charlotte of Mecklenburg-Strelitz, the wife of George III, it was built on reasonable ground, on the farm of Whiteley in Cargill parish and, from the beginning, George Young of Coupar Angus was engaged as supervisor. He kept a close watch on all the settlers' activities and by 1766 there were almost 300 inhabitants.

Neither were the houses as sound as the commissioners had hoped, for the haste with which factors had had to work to provide so many, with material and workmen not always at hand, had militated against that. Timber for building at Beauly and Conon had to be carried twenty-four miles over bad roads. On Coigach, the factor complained bitterly of the inefficient mason work and carpentry (wright work) on the soldiers' houses. Villages were not always laid out well, sometimes because the factors were not skilled town-planners – something they could hardly be blamed for. It took one of their servants to suggest to the commissioners that a surveyor should be employed for these purposes. Admittedly this suggestion was immediately agreed to but previously the Board had merely instructed the factor to set about designing and building a village. The results are not surprising. Borelandbog houses were in the 'upper part very ill-disposed running crooked and close . . . access to the houses very inconvenient not having space to make a sufficient broad road. Soldiers cannot let a chicken out of their houses but on their own or neighbours corn'. Some of the houses on the Perth estates had their slates set without sarking, the wood between the rafters and the slates, so that they would be uninhabitable in winter.[18]

The last essential element in the settlements was the human one, and it was no more satisfactory than the others. The only group of settlers who received any official or other commendation were those in Callander, and they may merely have shone by comparison with the original inhabitants, whose reputation was that, though they were usually at variance with one another, yet they joined in distressing any stranger settled amongst them. Previous knowledge of this trait of the Callander people may have been the reason for sending only locally born there in the first place, and of the first fourteen, none remained, as there were no houses built when they arrived. For the rest, there is almost universal condemnation, borne out it should be said by detailed descriptions of their conduct. In Strelitz, in 1765, George Young wrote that some had left and carried away their tools, officially government property, but they were 'troublesome, idle people'. He did add in some mitigation of their conduct, that they also had the worst lots; but, though he had promised them lime, they had lost patience and gone off to Dundee. The following year he reported that he had sold looms that he had recovered from some runaways[19] but, at least, these had remained for a couple of years. On Cromartie, by July, 1763, two had deserted and in 1764, in the sixty-nine houses built, only six sailors remained, while twenty left after receiving the bounty. The Monaltrie factor described them as a 'thankless pack', while Barcaldine explained his delay in sending his intromissions for the forfeited estate of Gask to the Barons of the Exchequer in 1763 by saying that 'ever since these plaguy soldiers came upon me, I could not get half an hour at a time free of some one or other of them'. He wrote even more feelingly in 1768, that he would not go through the same experience again for triple the sum, and he was surprised the Board would grudge an allowance for his trouble about those soldiers' settlements. He thought he was poorly paid for the effort it had cost him.[20] It is a welcome relief to hear of £20 being given to George Sinclair, 'an industrious soldier', a dyer at Ullapool, for a waulkmill, even though he was cheated by those he employed; and of another who on his own initiative opened a small store in Benniebeg. In 1766, the last year the soldiers were to be free of land-rent, those in Coigach had exhausted the money given them, had run into debt with the country people and would be unable to sow their acres if the Board did not assist them, but the factor added that 'such idle fellows are not worth countenancing'.[21]

By the spring of 1766, one can appreciate the commissioners' thorough disgust with the whole project. It had cost more than they had calculated – the wildest optimist could hardly have prophesied success by this time – and the Board was faced with asking once again for allowances to be made for their having spent more than had been authorised – £500 extra on this occasion. They decided to combine the plans for settling soldiers with that for establishing craftsmen and labourers and to call all soldiers in future merely King's Cottagers, using the fund appropriated for the latter type of tenant.

They were not so easily free of trouble from soldiers, however, and complaints and petitions carry on throughout the annexation and beyond. Even in the nineteenth century, the remaining inhabitants of Strelitz expressed dissatisfaction with the accommodation provided specially for them in the loft of Cargill church.[22] There was never enough produce from their lots to keep them. James Small had given warning of the dangers of over-small holdings, saying it was better that tenants should be employed on the roads rather than starve on their farms, but this had made no impression on the commissioners. They undoubtedly felt some moral obligation towards the colonists, however, and as they were ultimately responsible for the deficiencies of their holdings, they felt that work and wages must somehow be found. This involved the factors in laying out quite large sums, for wages mounted up at 4d per day; £204 was needed on Lovat and Cromartie alone between May and December, 1763.[23] One soldier at least went off to work in the Ayrshire mines, leaving his wife in possession, but he was killed. Millers complained that they could not obtain their thirlage from the settlements; in 1776, the inhabitants of Benniebeg were still applying for assistance in buying seed, while the villagers of Black Park were to be warned to remove in 1781, as they would neither pay additional rent nor work for it, and observed none of the regulations of the barony, and most went 'abegging through the country'.[24] Also they refused to do their statute labour.

This 'Utopian' scheme of the commissioners, as Pennant sneeringly described it, achieved very little in either the short or the long term. There were four planned villages on the Perth estate, Strelitz, Borelandbog Park, Benniebeg and Callander. When William Frend the Inspector visited the estate, he had to report that the soldiers' houses and land at Borelandbog were in general in very bad order. At Strelitz, a great number of the houses were ill-kept, the ditches were neglected, and the park land was flooded. There was much the same sort of comment on the soldiers' houses and ground at Callander with the additional disapproval of the dung being still kept before the doors of the houses. At Benniebeg, a rather odd situation had arisen, for James Glass, a linen manufacturer from Crieff, had by 1773 obtained the let of seven lots. Quite early on in the history of the village, one couple who had left had returned to find their house broken open, by order of course, their goods rouped, and Glass's looms installed instead. When Frend reported, he found that seven houses under the factor were reasonably kept, but Glass had begun to let or rather to sublet the houses he had, and they were very poor, with no thatch. The reason for this was discovered in 1783. Glass was charging a very heavy rent and would not allow the tenants to use the pasture.[25] Such a situation was hardly envisaged in the original plans.

Benniebeg, once all the inhabitants were dead or removed, was flooded by a Lady Perth, who presumably could no longer bear the sight of what must have been an unattractive lot of hovels on the avenue to Drummond Castle. When Pennant travelled that way in 1772, many of the houses were already empty.[26] Now the Pool of Drummond covers the site. Callander may be counted a reasonably profitable town in Highland terms, but the site was not chosen by the commissioners but by the titular Duke of Perth, about 1730. The Board added to it, the factor reporting in 1764 that he had marked out 45 acres, 2 roods and 3 falls on Murdieston and Ballanton to the north-west of the existing village. In 1800, Callander was described as having a 'neat, cheerful appearance', the writer pointing out the sudden change to the Gaelic tongue and Highland garb and, even worse, the bad and extravagant inn. The village of Boreland was occupied almost entirely by weavers by the time of the first Statistical Account.[27] As the original settlers left all the settlements, the factors were ordered to let their houses to the country people.

By the time Wight visited Strelitz, some of the inhabitants were unable to work, which was not surprising considering they had been there since 1763, and had been in the army before that. Others, he thought, were unwilling, but as a result they all had to hire labour, which kept their work behind as they had to wait until the labourers' own work was done. On the other hand, he gave a reasonably favourable description of the state of the village, especially of the nursery garden, which both Frend and he thought well-kept.[28] After the restoration of the estates to the heirs in 1784, Burrelton, a nearby village, grew and the name of Whiteley was apparently resumed locally,[29] though in the 1863 Ordnance Survey it is marked as Strelitz, and a farm of that name still exists.

According to Thomas Hunter, the soldiers here were notorious smugglers; and he also tells that they instituted an annual march to remind them of old campaigns, 'marching through the parish to the strains of martial music, the demonstrations generally ending in not a few bloody Fontenoys on a small scale'. This promenade gradually changed into a ploughman's festival and then merged into Burrelton Market and finally Burrelton Games. Unfortunately one's faith in this highly coloured story is somewhat lessened by his making the statement that the country people would not take the holdings the soldiers left, for Young seems to have had no difficulty in letting the houses, and Wight explicitly says that there were country people there in 1778. In 1810, soldiers were being moved off their holdings on the Perth estate and there was a certain amount of legal business, deciding whether the government could interfere between tenant and proprietor, or whether the soldiers did in fact have a right of tenure during their lifetime.[30] Tenacious as ever, some were still in possession in 1816. Eventually Strelitz was almost wholly hidden by plantations, the largest in the barony of Stobhall. Traces of Borelandbog, on the other hand, are very much in evidence. At least two of the soldiers' houses, extended and modernised, are inhabited, one very suitably by a noted Scottish historian. Another of the three left on the farm of Lower Borland stands in outline as it did in the mid-eighteenth century. In living memory, it was the home of farm workers and is now used by the local farmer for tools. And, while the upper part of Borland may have been badly laid out, the road through the sites of the lower rows of houses lies straight and not too narrow by the standards of the time, though the stoniness of the ground, complained of in 1763, is attested by its condition today. The fields behind the houses are also known by the names of some of their earlier cultivators.[31]

On Struan, there were three settlements, at Kinloch Rannoch, Georgetown, and Black Park. It will be remembered that Small, the Struan factor, refused to agree that he could find any land in 1763, but in 1764 he reported that the village was being built, as well as the bridge at Kinloch Rannoch.[32] Additional delay had arisen from the need to harvest the departing tenants' corn before beginning the new houses. Of the three, only Kinloch Rannoch has survived as a village. Black Park, by the burn Allt na Moire Buidhe, was shown as a few houses in the 1862 Ordnance Survey, and the foundations are still visible. Rannoch barracks occupied the site of Georgetown long before 1862.

Unless one accepts the title of New Tarbat, the areas chosen for colonies on the Cromartie estates were not given names. They figure only as 'stations' on the baronies of the estate. Like Benniebeg on Drummond Castle grounds, the houses built on the policies of New Tarbat house offended the eyes of the reinstated proprietor, and he seems to have begun to remove tenants from them immediately on his entry into his family estates. At New Tarbat in 1764 there had been thirty-two houses, and twelve spread around on Tullich and Kilmuir, the inhabitants including four weavers, two shoemakers and one tailor. On Strathpeffer, there were twenty-six King's Cottagers, four unmarried. These included two masons, one flax-dresser, three tailors, four weavers and two shoemakers. On the estate of Lovat, small numbers of soldiers were given holdings on various farms. In 1764, the factor could report that fifty-one soldiers and King's Cottagers had been provided for, including twenty on Barnyards, and ten on the Morass of Conon, which were the largest groups, with only two on Castle Downie, and one on Crochell, who happened to be a surveyor. None of these groups were apparently meant to develop into villages. In all, fifty-eight houses had been built, but two on Crochell were used as the school and schoolhouse, and two others had been given to a flax dresser and a spinning mistress as the factor considered these necessary. The Lovat factor encountered a difficulty with settlers regarding their houses. These had been well enough built but, as the colonists thought the commissioners were to keep the houses in order, they were making no attempt to do so and some were even 'inclined to hurt them'. They had to be informed that the Board would spend no more on them.

While the trades practised by the soldiers make it obvious that the scheme had been effective to a degree in helping to bring craftsmen into the areas at the end of the Seven Years War, the origins of these men give rise to the suspicion that many might have found their way back in any case. The majority came from the northern counties of Scotland. On Lovat, two hailed from Fermanagh and one from Inniskillen; on Cromartie, there were a few 'foreigners', one from Armagh, one from Devon, another from Renfrew, but the greater number gave the place of their birth as Ross, Sutherland, Caithness and Inverness-shire.[33]

Like other landlords who built villages, the commissioners were anticipating economic growth, but initially on the annexed estates there was a drop in rental. The Struan rentals show a decrease of £16.14.11$\frac{8}{12}$ in Kinloch Rannoch until 1767, because the cottagers did not pay rent until Martinmas that year. The old rent had been £19.14.8$\frac{8}{12}$. In 1775, Georgetown had only eight cottagers, paying a total of £6, while in Wester Finart, in 1767 considered part of Georgetown, there were six tenants paying £20. By 1775, too, there were eleven crofters in Kinloch Rannoch, assessed at £24.18.0; rents were raised that year for improvements.[34]

In its conception, the plan of providing for disbanded soldiers and sailors, increasing the population of the Highlands and Islands, importing necessary trades, and building houses of a higher standard than was usual, all in one step, was a splendid one. In its implementation, little can be said in its favour. Haste was perhaps necessary at the end of the Seven Years War, but haste without accompanying caution and care led to the situation described. This was yet another occasion when the commissioners paid far too little attention to the full implications of their brainwaves, and certainly too little to the practical details of management. Equally, in this case, the Treasury could perhaps have exercised more control more profitably than on some other occasions, but no doubt, to the government, it must have seemed the ideal answer to the problem of what to do with the demobilised forces, training in many cases only for fighting.

Though the commissioners fairly quickly gave up the idea of forming completely new towns, they continued the encouragement of settlement in towns that were already established, in Crieff and Callander particularly. When the Callander minister, Mr Robertson, wrote about Perthshire agriculture, he remarked that several people could at that time, 1794, remember the town when it contained four families. The attainted Earl of Perth had begun to enlarge it and the commissioners continued his work, both by helping to establish small factories in the town, by obtaining an allowance of £200 to place craftsmen in Callander and Crieff and, as we have seen, by placing soldiers there. This last step is in some quarters given the credit for starting Callander's prosperity.[35]

Crieff was even more important in the commissioners' eyes, and industry and craftsmen as well as the hotel trade were all assisted. In 1762, the inhabitants complained of loss of the droving trade and of the assistance the late owner of the Perth estate had been wont to give them, but the town was so well placed in an eighteenth-century context that it was bound to, and indeed did, begin to thrive again. In 1768, Mr. Swinton studied the feus granted by the Earl of Findlater and decided that the Board could use the same formula for feuing the land they owned in Crieff. It was believed that many people settled there because of the good reputation of the school. In 1771, the factor wrote that the increase in the size of Callander had increased the rents by £30 yearly in rent and feu duties, which no doubt pleased the Board, but the local heritors in Crieff viewed increased number of feus there with mixed feelings. By 1775, the factor wrote that the number of poor in the parish had multiplied by so much that an assessment had had to be made, something that most parishes considered a step to be avoided. The tax was not large, at 5/6 in £100 rent, but in 1776 it was pointed out that, as the Board for the Annexed Estates had been responsible for bringing such large numbers into Crieff, it was to be hoped that they would help care for the poor. The new houses built were so much better than most Highland dwellings that in almost all of them rooms were let, one to a whole family. As the work these incomers were looking for was not always available, they became dependent on poor relief from the parish.[36]

Despite the help that the Board could bring to each of these towns, neither could claim the quick success of Grantown-on-Spey, where building only began in 1765. By 1780 it was said to be in a 'very thriving condition'.[37] Certainly Grantown could alone attract much of the local business of Badenoch, Rothiemurchus, Strathaven and Glenlivet, in a way neither Crieff nor Callander could perhaps manage. Also, Grantown was the brainchild of one proprietor, while the lack of a resident landlord in the Perthshire towns may have been a disadvantage. Among the soldiers' settlements, too, the comparative success of Strelitz, under the watchful eye of George Young, provides some evidence of the benefits of that particular oversight which the factors were unable, or perhaps unwilling, to provide.

Moved as ever by contemporary trends, the commissioners, towards the end of the annexation but too late for any positive steps to be taken under their creaking administration, glanced at the possibility of a spa. The mineral well at Strathpeffer had attracted favourable attention, as the doctor at New Tarbet, Dr. Alex. McKenzie, had reported to the Royal Society that it was equal to that at 'Harrowgate'. According to him, it created an appetite and helped the digestion. John Baxter the architect was sent to have a look at it but, despite the factor's suggestion that some of the Board members should come up to experience its benefits themselves and the further pleasures of good hunting,[38] nothing more came of the suggestion under the commissioners' aegis. One cannot help feeling that this was just as well for Strathpeffer.

It will be remember that, in the parliamentary debates on the annexation, the foundation of coastal villages as well as inland towns was contemplated. The Lord Chancellor, too, suggested that fisheries established on the west coast would bring economic benefits to the while country and, further, would help provide skilled manpower for the navy. In 1763, it was a superfluity of manpower from the navy that posed problems, but the principle of encouraging the fishing industry was the same. Concurrently with their plans to settle demobilised soldiers, therefore, the commissioners decided to cope with three national problems at one blow, in a similar fashion.[39] They thought that fishermen who had been pressed into the navy had been greatly missed in several ways. Firstly, their landlords lost their share of the catch; secondly, neighbouring inhabitants had been deprived of fish in their diet; thirdly, there had been general national loss as there had been no surplus of fresh and dried cod, which had previously been exported. It was declared, on no apparent concrete statistical grounds, that 1,000 men were required to replace them, and the Board proposed that 500 discharged sailors should be encouraged to settle as fishermen on the annexed estates, and another 500 would be given support on those of other proprietors.

An expensive and rather grandiose plan was put to the Crown for approval, by which 124 boats were to be provided at £15 each, half on the annexed estates, half on those of private landlords, where houses were to be built, or at least made available at a rental of £1 per annum, to be paid by the Board. It was assumed that not all the sailors would be married, and on that calculation only 375 houses were to be rented but each was to receive a bounty of £3. Once established, houses, gardens and boats were to be the responsibility of the tenants, and crews were expected to furnish sails, nets, oars and any other fishing tackle needed. The landlords' share was to be one-fifth of the fish caught, or the equivalent in money as rent or 'boat-dale'. On the annexed estates, the Board proposed to build fishing villages near the mouth of the Cromarty Firth on the estate of Cromartie, on Barrisdale, and on the side of Lochbroom, thereby accommodating yet another 500 men. The same number of boats and houses was reckoned necessary as on private estates, but the bounty was to be only £2. The total cost was estimated at £6,610, and placed in conjunction with the Board's annual surplus of £4,500 in a good year, this might indicate a certain lack of realism among the commissioners. Admittedly, it was not the only one of their plans about which this accusation could be made but, in this case, they had some excuse, as the lack of expenditure on anything but fairly basic administration between 1755 and 1760 had left them a little in hand. Originally, too, they had some hope that private proprietors, who were to reap the benefit of the influx of fishermen, should provide the boats, and this would have cut down their capital outlay, but their final estimates include the price of all the boats required. At the end of three years the crews were to own the boats and to settle wherever they wished, while settlers on the annexed estates were to live in rent-free houses as long as they remained there. Difficulties immediately appeared in the spring of 1763 when the Lovat factor found that he could not procure boats for the sailors, but he was instructed to apply to the Banff boat-builders for such boats as were used on the Moray Firth or by Mr. Garden of Troup's crews.

The commissioners then went off on their usual summer adjournment, leaving the secretary to face what must have been in many respects for him a nightmare summer. Like the soldiers, the sailors appeared in considerable numbers at the Edinburgh office, where Mr. Barclay had to do something about them. The first group who applied were easy to deal with. Eleven Orcadians, fishermen bred, claimed the bounty, wanting to go home first, and then to settle near New Tarbat. There were neither houses, boats nor land ready, so Barclay gave them each £1 to travel home and then to New Tarbat by next Lammas. In fact, these men do not seem to have used the bounty in the way it was meant, as no natives of Orkney appear in the Cromartie factor's lists. Some other Orcadians also applied, but as they meant to live in Orkney they merely had their names recorded and were given instructions to apply for the bounty when they had settled. In an attempt to speed things up and at the same time to provide profitably for the sailors, he sent twenty-six more to New Tarbat, where as yet there had been no time to prepare for them, telling the factor to mark out the ground and then to set the sailors themselves to collecting material to build their houses, and also to throw up ditches round their portions of ground. They were to be paid the usual country rates, were to start collecting fuel for the winter and, whenever the houses were ready, the factor was to buy boats.

Fortunately it was realised that the idea of the Lochbroom settlement needed some further inquiries and Peter May, the surveyor, was sent there to make a proper survey, but, with an astonishing degree of insouciance, 117 sailors were sent off with a 'viaticum' and letter of introduction to some noblemen and gentlemen considered likely to welcome them, and to the magistrates of some seaside burghs, Campbeltown, Fort William, Aberdeen, Peterhead, Stonehaven and Montrose, and to those of the northern counties, Caithness, Orkney, Shetland and Cromarty. Two snags arose. Firstly, it was soon found that many of the sailors had never gone to the places assigned to them. The secretary stopped handing out travelling expenses at the office. If the wandering mariners arrived, the letters they carried told the addresses – factor, heritor or magistrates – how much to give them, promising repayment by the commissioners. Secondly, the secretary reported, in what would seem a slight understatement, that it had been found inconvenient to send off sailors, without the heritors having made any previous application for them, and he began to advertise for offers from landowners in the 'disarmed counties'. Some sailors who were already settled had applied, with certificates from 'Reputable persons', who asked the Board to forward the bounty.

The question of recommendations was one that also caused the secretary some worry. Sailors, unlike soldiers, did not get official discharges and none brought any references. He obviously felt the best thing was to get rid of them at once, but several never set off and others, who did reach their destination, refused to become fishermen. Another complication arose in Campbeltown where the boats went out only twice a year, in the spring for cod and in September for herring; the sailors had missed their opportunity there for immediate employment. Some of the group who arrived there must have been genuinely seeking work, for they travelled back to Edinburgh specially to report this, and those willing were sent to Lewis where Dr. John McKenzie had given houses and tackle for three boats. Because of his generosity the same bounty was allowed as on the annexed estates. Unfortunately, these models of virtue did not maintain such commendable behaviour, for, in January, 1765, Dr. McKenzie wrote asking for money to replace one of the boats which he had originally provided. The crew had deserted in the summer before, taking the boat with them. Earlier reports varied in their verdicts, a Mr. Silver being tolerably satisfied with the seven sailors and a marine whom he had settled at John-shaven and provided with hired boats, clothing and lodgings. Lord Fyfe on the other hand wrote in some disgruntlement that he had given three sailors a guinea each to bring their families to settle but only one returned. Having built boats in expectation of being supplied by men from the Board, he was left with only one possible crew member. He had to be repaid by the Lovat factor.

The picture emerging was not a cheerful one and, by 1764, the commissioners had to admit, contrary to their views on the solders' settlements, that the scheme was not succeeding. They had to report that 154 of the 205 who accepted the bounty had deserted. Travelling charges had amounted to £124.14.2, house and boat-building to £429.19.73$^3/_{12}$, with the bounty, the total was £758.13.9$^3/_{12}$. Many sailors had applied, not realising that they must confine themselves to being fishermen, and withdrew their applications when the conditions were explained to them. However, the Board persisted with the scheme in outline. In 1764, they had expressed a hope that they might still establish fisheries for either discharged sailors or natives of the annexed estates, at Lochbroom near the Cromartie estates, or at Inverie on the estate of Barrisdale, and had suggested that £1,000 be allocated for this purpose. In 1765, they paid out bounty money to eighty-eight sailors settled on the coasts of the Highlands and paid their house rents for a year. They also paid £27 in bounty money on Barrisdale, built houses there, and provided three boats and tackle worth £60.10.0, a total for the year of £264.10.0.[40] Originally, tackle had been intended to be the crew's responsibility, but, by August, 1763, the factor on Lovat, Captain Forbes, had written that the sailors demanded nets before they could make a living. A week later, the Board accepted this, allowing £5–£6 for nets, similar to those used in the Moray Firth, and for bladders and ropes.

Assistance to the fishing industry did not end with the failure of the original plans for settling sailors. Many of the optimistic economic theorists of the time considered the underdevelopment of the fishing industry by those living in or near the coasts in the north and west most reprehensible. Further, such neglect was totally incomprehensible, for it was considered that the potential food supply should have been an irresistible attraction to a population existing at subsistence level. It was beyond the understanding of writers and travellers like James Wilson that the people in most parts of Scotland would fish 'only on compulsion' whereas, by regular exploitation of the sea's harvest, they could 'add most materially to the comfort of their family'. What Wilson and many of his contemporaries did not see on a superficial survey of the situation, but what modern historians have illustrated only too well, was that the capital outlay on efficient equipment was beyond the means of most aspiring fishermen, while loans made from whatever source gave rise to interest charges that absorbed any financial gains. This was especially so where the landlord was the lender and had also a legal right to a sizeable share of the proceeds. Land in Shetland was let on condition that fish be delivered to the proprietor in exchange for goods at set prices.[41] Something else that received no sympathy at all, and was not wholly understood, was the innate distrust of the sea displayed by the landsmen, added to unfamiliarity with the skills needed for successful fishing on a commercial basis in deeper waters.

The sin of lack of comprehension cannot of course be laid at all doors, and can certainly not be attributed to the factors on the coastal estates. The writer of *The Highlands in 1750* pointed out that the country people had neither the ability nor the skill to fit out proper vessels to catch the plentiful herring in Loch Broom, while the gentlemen did not concern themselves with the trade. It is interesting to note in light of their energy in road-building activities ... that the gentlemen of Argyllshire were among the few who had made quite a profit out of fishing in the year he was writing.[42] This was a harbinger of things to come when several of the landed gentry in the Highlands asked for assistance from the funds of the annexed estates to forward their fishery schemes. Pennant was another who realised the potentialities of fishing cod and ling near Canna, but he also understood that the inhabitants were too poor to be able to take full advantage of this wealth.[43]

Ninian Jeffrey and Henry Butter, both factors on remote estates with sea-coasts, Coigach and Barrisdale, realised the need for capital expenditure, if the inhabitants' poverty was not to be an unconquerable obstacle. Jeffrey, when asked to prepare a plan for organising the fishing in his area, emphasised that experienced fishermen would be essential immigrants if any fishing was to succeed, as the natives were not used to such activity on a commercial scale. He had noted, in 1766, when there had been some herring shoals nearby, that ships subsidised by the bounty had caught fish when the local boats did not. His enquiries as to the reason for this had elicited the answer that the latter used inferior nets with too few ropes, and he suggested that the Board could help by supplying better nets. A few years later, in 1772, nothing had been done and, as a result, though the fishing generally had been good, the Coigach people had been unable to take any advantage because the shoals had not come north of Gairloch, and their equipment was only of use locally. He pointed out that fishing in Coigach must always be 'a precarious rent' as long as it depended on so many poor people unable to afford the better gear, which in the long run was so much more profitable. He and Butter, separately, also proposed schemes by which the Board could usefully give assistance in overcoming yet another impediment to profitable fishing in remote areas. This was the lack of a convenient supply of salt for the curing of the fish, and barrels for storage and transport. Jeffrey suggested that a storehouse should be provided and a cooper's business subsidised at a cost of about £500, while Butter, who must also be given credit for the idea of settling fishermen at Inverie, thought a cooper should be employed. In addition the latter was prepared to purchase salt and casks to deposit at suitable centres along the coast, where he would sell them to the local fishermen at cost price.[44]

As the commissioners had been receiving applications for similar help from several gentlemen with estates on the west coast, such as John Stewart of

Fasnacloich, Daniel Campbell of Shawfield, and Donald Campbell of Mingary, they were disposed to listen to the factors, particularly to such a notion as Butter's which promised some immediate return on their outlay, and he was given permission to spend £500, rather less than the sums of £700 and £1,000 he had wanted for Barrisdale alone. Unfortunately, as the herring with their usual fickleness did not appear in such profusion during the following seasons, Butter came to rue his earlier enthusiasm. In February, 1767, the minutes record his report that the herring fishery had disappointed everyone concerned and that the salt and casks would have to wait until the following year to be used. He had been provided with £648.11.8 of supplies, and in his accounts for 1768 showed he had sold only £104.18.1 worth. He had also discovered that managing debenture salt at a distance was no sinecure, and said quite bluntly that had he realised all the inconveniences he would not have been very willing to engage in the business. One of his suppliers who had sold him casks had to write to the Board for payment of over £300, a year after the goods had been provided. As he said, it was 'a great hardship for a person in trade to lye out of his money'. The remaining casks were to be sold by public roup to retain some of the capital.[45] As a result, this experiment was not repeated.

Various proposals thereafter reached the commissioners from would-be entrepreneurs, such as John Woodhouse, a Liverpool merchant who wanted to smoke herring 'in the Yarmouth way' on Island Martin. Colin Mackenzie, the kelp merchant in Lochbroom, asked for a lease of a Coigach farm where he could follow not only the fishing but the kelp, rope and net-making industries. However, there were only two more large grants towards the fishing. One was to Daniel Campbell of Shawfield who wanted to build a boat, costing £200, and quays in Islay, where what he described as the ignorance of the people, the rapidity of the tides, and inadequate vessels prevented any advantage being taken of the rich banks of fish near the island.[46] The other was the sum of £250 towards the exotic cairban fishing.

The cairban is the sailfish or the basking shark, which was hunted only for its liver oil. About six to eight barrels of a pure sweet oil could be extracted from each one caught and this was bought by the tanners for up to £3 a barrel. Inspector Menzies described the oil as being reckoned superior to any other for 'currying leather'; it was also approved of by clothiers and he thought something might be made of this type of catch. Many of these somewhat sluggish fish were to be seen between June and October, sometimes in pairs, sometimes in shoals, and he thought their slow speed ensured that they could be easily harpooned. The adventurer who eventually benefited from the Board's largesse was Donald M'Leod, a tacksman on Canna, whose name was brought before them by Dr. Walker.[47] M'Leod was too young to be able to afford a boat large enough to stand up to the strength of the cairban or to follow it far enough. A wherry of fifteen to twenty tons was needed. £250 was duly spent on the project, which does not seem to have brought long-lasting benefits to either M'Leod or to the country. He 'tryd the kerban', catching seven in 1767 and eight in 1768, but his letters show that he was not happy with the arrangement. He complained that the vessel given him was too unwieldy for either cairban or cod and, at the end of 1768, he wished he had never had any connection with cairban, 'at least in a public way'. On the other hand, Pennant thought that 'the person they (the commissioners) confided in shamefully abused their goodness' and, when he visited the area, only private adventurers were 'trying the kerban'. The Board too instructed their inspector to make sure the boat was being properly used. Whether cairban fishing is in fact very practical seems doubtful. M'Leod claimed that it could not succeed without subsidies, and at least one twentieth-century attempt was unprofitable, as Gavin Maxwell described.[48]

All things considered, it may plausibly be argued that the greatest contribution the commissioners made to the fishing industry in the west was an indirect one. Leasing land to the Liverpool merchant, Woodhouse, for a lengthy period provided a market for local catches, and the appointment, jointly with the Board of Trustees, of justiciary bailies to maintain order in the fishing season must have been a boon to the local inhabitants at least. The fishing fleet was not the most peaceful of groups and the need for some sort of policing was perennial. In 1755, orders were sent to Lord Beauclerk, the Commander-in-Chief in Scotland, to send a party to Lochbroom and Coigach to prevent 'the usual abuses committed by the herring fishers'. The mutual misunderstandings of the crofters and the fishermen are illustrated by the description of the inconveniences suffered by the farmers of Lee and Skiarree, the only safe harbour in Loch Hourn, where the herring fishermen cured and salted their fish on the verge of the grassland and also walked over the fields in bodies, thus spoiling the grass for the cattle. They also cut wood indiscriminately, but they were not alone in that. In 1756, the baron bailie of Coigach was appointed a sheriff substitute to try to control the 'many disorders' resulting from the number of boats and people in Lochbroom during the season, and this was an annual problem the inhabitants had to face. In 1773, Archibald MacDonnell asked for powers to supervise the area between Loch Broom and Mull, as this area was rather far from the nearest official in Stornoway and Lewis. He claimed that the greatest herring fishery was in this area and in 1779 his son Coll joined him as a justiciary bailie. The bailies' performance did not always satisfy the Board and, indeed, on occasion there were suggestions that their salaries should be withheld or cut, but their presence in the area must have provided a useful tangible proof of the existence of authority and the information they sent was clearly of use; the Board of Trustees borrowed John McIver's report in 1764.[49]

One final point may be made that not everyone was enthusiastic about the results of a thriving fishing industry. One can understand the hostility roused among farmers by the sort of behaviour they faced in Skiarree; those who thought the hope of the Highlands was the introduction of manufacturing industry found much to complain about in the seasonal attractions of the fishing. Mr. Robertson, the minister of Lochbroom, wrote to Captain Forbes protesting that industry would never thrive as long as a man and maidservant could be released from service to go to the fishing, 'he to fish and she to gut'. No servants could be got to work for any hire, 'no not a herd or little girl', because of this practice. He foretold the impoverishment of the tenants and the loss of cattle through lack of labour. Worse in his eyes, perhaps, when the fishing ended, the potential servant had become accustomed to drinking and idleness and, when the herring forsook the loch, they became beggars. Robertson, however, was swimming against a tide which was to flow strongly until the early twentieth century and which, it may be, brought more capital and comfort to the west than any of the abortive industrial schemes dreamed up by the eighteenth-century entrepreneurs.

It is unlikely that the members of the Board, any more than later landowners who transported their tenants to the coasts, had any idea of the magnitude of the financial and educational programme that would have been needed to produce, from a race imbued with attachment to the land, a community that was prepared to settle for a house and garden in a fishing town. Coming events cast their shadows before, however, in Jeffrey's plans for cod, ling and herring fisheries at Coigach; he proposed that families with too small farms, whom he castigated as 'just a nuisance upon every Highland estate' because they could not support their families, should be employed by the Board at 5/- to 20/- a year, provided with boat and tackle free, and lodged in a fishing town. This was the classic clearance programme, one the Board could not adopt, not on any moral or emotional grounds, but because of financial stringency. They would probably have considered the financial benefits expected to accrue to the tenants apology enough, and consistent with the philosophy of the annexation. But even had they been inclined to follow such a plan in its entirety, it is unlikely that government consent would have been won so soon after the fiasco of their recent foray into a similar field, the settlements for discharged soldiers and sailors.

NOTES

Abbreviations

NLS   National Library of Scotland
E   Exchequer – Prefaces all references to the current cataloguing of the
       Forfeited Estates Papers, 1745, lodged in the Scottish Record Office
NSA   New Statistical Account of Scotland
OSA   First (Old) Statistical Account of Scotland
SRO   Scottish Record Office

1 T. C. Smout, 'The Landowner and the Planned Village in Scotland', in *Scotland in the Age of Improvement*, ed. N. Phillipson and R. Mitchison (Edinburgh, 1970), 73–106; J. D. Wood, 'Regulating the Settler and Establishing Industry in Planning Intentions for a Nineteenth Century Scottish Estate Village', *Scottish Studies*, 15, part 1, 50.
2 NLS. Adv. Ms. 19.1.35.
3 E723/1, p.46; E721/2, p.19; E725/2, p.9; Cosmo Innes, *Origines Parochiales*, Bannatyne Club (Edinburgh 1851), ii, part 2, 5–7.
4 J. M. Houston, 'Village Planning in Scotland', in *Advancement of Science*, v, 18, 1948–9,130.
5 3 George III c.8.
6 D. G. Lockhart, The Evolution of the Planned Villages in North-east Scotland, Unpublished Ph.D. thesis, University of Dundee, 1974, Vol. 2, 130–131.
7 E721/4; E777/84/66.
8 E721/7, p.138; E746/75/22; E723/2, pp.46ff.
9 Quoted by William MacGill, *Old Ross-shire and Scotland* (Inverness, 1909), 214, 215.
10 James Wilson, *A Voyage round the Coasts of Scotland* (Edinburgh, 1842), i, 311. Hereafter Wilson, *Voyage*.
11 E721/4, p.76; E721/7, p.106; E721/14, p.38.
12 E721/8, p.194; E721/14, pp.52,77,88.
13 E721/14, pp.6ff.
14 Lockhart, i, 226.
15 E721/7, p.145; E723/2, pp.53, 74, 75.
16 E777/84/15, 16; E721/7, pp.31, 59; E721/14, p.25; E729/8, p.58.
17 E721/14, pp.34, 115; E721/10, p.187.
18 E746/75/3; E721/7, pp.218; E729/8, P.38; E721/14, p.74.
19 E729/8, p.55; E721/9, p.92; E721/8, p.190; E777/119.
20 NLS. Adv. Ms.28.1.6 Vol.2, p.58; E777/84/238.
21 E746/75/11(1), 18; E721/14, pp.45, 56.
22 E702/4; E777/32/8,14.
23 E783/58/23; E721/8, p. 156.

24 E721/14, p.86; E721/24, p.8; E721/15, p.116; E721/27, p.62.

25 E777/305/1, pp.4–5, 67, 78, 85; E723/2, insert between pp. 46–47; E777/128, 252.

26 T. Pennant, *Tour in Scotland and Voyage to the Hebrides in 1772* (London, 1776), ii, 91. Hereafter Pennant, *Tour*; *NSA*, x, 314.

27 RHP. 3477; E721/8, p.16; NLS. Ms. 213. George Douglas, Advocate, *Tour to the Hebrides*, in his autograph; *O.S.A.*, iv, 43.

28 Andrew Wight, *Present state of husbandry in Scotland* (Edinburgh, 1778–1784), i,17,118;E777/252. Hereafter Wight, *Husbandry*.

29 *NSA*. x, p.1171; William Marshall, *Historic Scenes in Perthshire*, (Edinburgh, 1880), 245.

30 T.Hunter, *Woods, Forests and Estates of Perthshire* (Perth, 1883), 351; Wight, *Husbandry*, 1, 114; E777/32.

31 I have to thank Mrs Kirk of Lower Borland Farm for this information. Note the modern spelling.

32 E721/8, p.22.

33 Sir William Fraser, *The Earls of Cromartie* (Edinburgh, 1876), 1, cclviii; E787/28/1–5, E721/14, p.8.

34 E783/42, 43.

35 James Robertson, *General View of the Agriculture of the Southern Districts of the County of Perth*, (London, 1794), 65; Francis Groome, *Ordnance Gazetteer of Scotland*, (Edinburgh, 1882), i, 222.

36 E721/6, p.175; E721/11, p.23; E729/8, p.84; E777/301; E777/87/86, 87.

37 SRO.GD.248/25/2/8.

38 E746/106; E746/110/6.

39 E723/2, p.39ff.

40 E723/2, pp. 52, 53, 86.

41 Wilson, *Voyage*, i, 198, 199; M. Gray, 'Crofting and Fishing in the North-West Highlands 1890–1914', in *Northern Scotland*, i, No. 1, 89–114; *Caledonian Mercury*, 25 August, 1784.

42 A.Lang, *The Highlands of Scotland in 1750*, (Edinburgh and London, 1898), 34, 45; see Chapter 9.

43 E721/14, p.36; E727/60/1; E728/13/2; Pennant, *Tour*, i, 313.

44 E721/7, p.27; E741/38/2; E746/75/4,20; E786/22/2.

45 E721/9,p.145; E721/10, p.33.2.2.1767; E786/51; E721/17, pp.2, 6.

46 E727/60/1; E723/2, 1777; E746/127.

47 J.Knox, *A Tour through the Highlands of Scotland and the Hebrides Islands in 1786*, (London, 1787), 36–38; E729/9; E721/8, p.74.

48 E727/16; E721/17, p.1; E728/13/4; Pennant, *Tour*, ii, 194; Gavin Maxwell, *Harpoon at a Venture*, (London, 1964).

49 NLS. Ms. 305–130; E729/1, 70; E746/93/2; E702/2, p.228; E727/18, 19; E728/14/1 (1,2).

The character of protest

Extracted from S Nenadic 1990 'Political Reform and the Ordering of Middle-Class Protest', *in* TM Devine (ed), *Conflict and Stability in Scottish Society, 1700–1850*, Edinburgh (John Donald), 68–76.

Some of the forms of protest that were employed by elements of the middle class in the mid-eighteenth century, and in certain situations even at a later stage, had much in common with the protests of the working population. Male middle-class participation in riot and disorder was not unusual. Parliamentary elections in rural constituencies and the smaller towns were, for instance, notorious for their explosive combination of drunken entertainment and violent conflict, in which members of the local middle class inevitably played a part.[1] Even the 'polite' élites of Edinburgh occasionally indulged in riots, albeit of a genteel variety.[2] In addition to a willingness to take part in such protests, elements of the middle class, including those in positions of authority and power, were often suspected of having promoted mass community disturbances in order to demonstrate the strength of public opinion on controversial issues. In Scotland a series of notable instances of this type of action was associated with the anti-Catholic emancipation riots in Edinburgh and Glasgow in 1779, which, like the Gordon Riots in London in the following year, appear to have been manipulated by those in authority, and were successful in convincing national government of the unpopularity of proposed legislation.[3] Forms of non-physical protest – such as the petition and pamphlet – were widely used by the early middle classes, but physical protests and participation in mass disorder were acceptable in many circumstances, and remained a feature of middle-class behaviour, though much diminished in scale and acceptability, well into the nineteenth century.

From the 1770s, though with earlier antecedents, rapid changes can be observed in the patterns of protest, associated initially with demands by the higher middle class of merchants and professionals, for reform in the system of burgh government and greater representation in national political affairs. The first and most striking development was the emerging primacy of the printed form of protest, in particular those printed forms whose purpose was to sustain a rationally argued case for change on the basis of factual information and statistical data. Now, it is clear that middle-class protests had taken printed forms for a long time. Pamphlets arguing for or against a particular issue had been published since the seventeenth century, probably before, especially where the issue addressed had implications that went beyond the locality and the protest was articulated within a non-local arena; the 1707 Act of Union, a cause of nation-wide debate, is a good illustration.[4] By the mid-eighteenth century the publication and distribution of pamphlets was both cheap and easy. The main cause of protest, political reform, was inherently non-local and the developing sense of middle-class community was such as to defy geographical boundaries. One might expect the net result of these trends to have been a greater reliance on printed protests. But the change was greater than this alone. Written protests of the late eighteenth century were not only more common than in earlier periods, they were different in both character and purpose.

First and foremost the language of protest had changed and this says something of the thinking that went behind the language.[5] In the late seventeenth and early eighteenth centuries the use of a language of 'declaration' and 'defence' was usual. These terms commonly appeared in the titles of political pamphlets and suggested that the purpose of the written protest was to state or defend a specific position. By the later eighteenth century the language was different; the following terms are most often employed – 'observations on . . .', 'an inquiry into . . .', 'an examination of . . .', 'facts on . . .', 'an explanation of . . .', 'statistics on . . .' These suggest a new way of articulating protest and imply a perceived need to present facts, statistics and information as evidence and part of a rational analysis of the object of protests, as in *An Examination of the Conduct of the Town Council* (published in Edinburgh in 1776); *Facts and Observations Concerning Voters for Members of Parliament in Scotland* (Edinburgh 1789); *Facts, Reflections and Queries submitted to the Consideration of the Associated Friends of the People* (Edinburgh 1792); or *Documents Connected with the Question of Reform in the Burghs of Scotland* (Edinburgh 1817).[6] Even when a protest was against a specifically local abuse, or where the cause of the protest imposed on an individual rather than a group, the printed form with similar language was used. Consider the case of James Fennel, the manager of an Edinburgh theatre, who became embroiled in a dispute with some of his élite patrons in 1788. The dispute resulted in a threat to remove his licence (and therefore his livelihood) and led to his publication of *A Statement of Facts Relative to the Late Disturbance at the Theatre Royal*, a personal pamphlet in support of his own case.[7]

It was not just the titles, of course, but the contents of these pamphlets that were new in style and form. Numerical tables and itemised facts abounded; the statistical appendix was now a common feature. In the agitations in favour of political reform, the gathering and presentation of empirical evidence had become the basis of a rational and ordered challenge to the status quo. The Convention of Delegates of Burgesses from Royal Burghs, meeting in Edinburgh in 1783, furnishes one of the earliest British examples of systematic information-gathering and dissemination as an aspect of protest.[8] The purpose of this body of 'decent and respectable' citizens was to organise and set in motion a Scotland-wide campaign in favour of burgh reform. One of the first resolutions was to gather information on the nature of the abuses against which they protested – information on the value and uses of burgh-owned property, on the want of facilities in specific towns, the character of the people who formed the town councils, and the number and wealth of those who favoured change.[9] In a similar fashion one of the first proposals to the inaugural convention of Delegates of the Societies of the Friends of the People, held in Edinburgh in 1792 to call for changes in the national franchise, was to gather information for the support of a rationally argued case for a wider franchise. A Mr Fowler moved 'that a committee be appointed to inquire into the state of the country – its population, commerce, taxation, revenue, exports and imports etc', but this was declared unnecessary, since, due to the 'exertions of the patriotic baronet, Sir John Sinclair' such information, in the form of the *Statistical Account of Scotland* was in the process of being published.[10] In the 1820s middle-class protesters were still calling for reform, and in the capital, as elsewhere, were enumerating in considerable detail the financial interests of those who were excluded from the political process. In 1824, following a series of lengthy calculations, the 33 town councillors of Edinburgh, who were also the electors, were shown to be the owners of property valued at a mere £2,788 annual rental, while the 104,706 non-electors had property valued at over £395,000.[11]

In the development of this aspect of protest there were obvious links with the eighteenth-century enlightenment pursuit of rational knowledge and progress through empirical inquiry. Throughout Britain there was an interest in 'Constitutional Information and Knowledge' as a means of reform and for the protection of liberty.[12] The year 1780 had seen the foundation in London of the Society for Constitutional Information – a body that sought a range of political changes, such as the repeal of legislative restrictions on the activities of non-Anglicans, and attracted wide support among the middle classes.[13] The influence of enlightened inquiry and belief in the role of constitutional knowledge were present from the early days of reform protest in Scotland. There is evidence to this effect in the letters of an Edinburgh merchant by the name of Thomas McGrugar – published in the press under the pseudonym 'Zeno' – which launched the burgh reform movement in the Scottish capital in 1783. McGrugar declared:

At this advanced stage of society, when refinement and civilisation, the effects of an enlightened period, have so universally improved our manners and expanded our conceptions, it is really astonishing that local systems of polity, the offspring of barbarous and tyrannical ages, should still be established among us . . . surely men of superior learning and abilities cannot more beneficially employ their talents than in diffusing among their fellow citizens a knowledge of the great principles of Constitutional Freedom: For let it be remembered that nothing is more important to society, and more essential to the preservation of public liberty than that the body of the people should know and understand their constitutional rights.[14]

In a similar vein the reformer, Robert Gourlay, son of a Fifeshire landowner and advocate of the ideas of Malthus and Bentham, was to write:

In all things . . . we can trace the workings and operation of increasing knowledge. For assuredly it is fated in the end to undermine the guilt of governments and . . . overtake systems of polity the most damnable.[15]

In addition to the link with rational knowledge and constitutional information, the forms of written protest that were increasingly employed by the middle classes were influenced by the development of systematic practice in commerce and business, and the evolution of a free market in commercial information.[16] There were links also with the practices of government and the emerging concern among bureaucrats and professionals to use information as the basis of effective policy. The latter was an especially notable aspect of post-1745 economic management in Scotland. According to Sir John Sinclair – a notable collector and disseminator of information, and involved in the early activities of the Society for Constitutional Information – Webster's population survey of 1755 had been partly intended 'for the information and service of government'.[17] The decennial census was introduced in 1801 for similar reasons. Party agents and quasi-official bodies collected vast quantities of political and economic data, and the government in London committed significant resources to the development of information-gathering systems and spy networks.[18] Based on the belief that knowledge equalled power, the purpose of such activities was to promote and protect the interests of government. The reforming middle classes were motivated by similar beliefs and objectives. Through their voluntary societies and organisations they created the mechanisms for generating information, and were assiduous in the pursuit of those types of information that were only available through closed bodies such as the town councils. Indeed, much of the acrimony of the early burgh reform conflicts was linked to the denial of access to official information on the economic affairs of burghs.[19]

The connection between the new forms of written middle-class protest and enlightenment thinking, modern commercial practice and the methods of bureaucratic government, is striking but not especially surprising. The groups who first engaged in this type of protest, and were dominant in the early movements for political reform, were also those who were active in these other areas. Their number incorporated professionals, especially lawyers whose role in government and in the societies for enlightened debate and enquiry was considerable. There were those who were involved in the 'information industries', such as newspaper proprietors and publishers; some of these were also lawyers. Finally, and in the greatest numbers, there were the merchants and financiers – groups of businessmen who were especially representative of a modernising commerce and industry-based urban economy.[20] Collectively they favoured changes that represented an ideal of progress and efficiency, but were also of a character that would secure their own interests. This is shown especially well in the issue of burgh reform. Their primary aim was the removal of corruption and mismanagement through the abolition of the practice of self-election to town councils – a practice that had developed several centuries before, and in many towns had secured the interests of the lesser urban trades, but excluded from power those who in the late eighteenth century were of the highest rank and wealth, that is, merchants and professionals.[21] In removing corruption a clear objective was to establish a 'democratic' system that favoured men of wealth and knowledge such as themselves.

The significance of factual or statistical information in support of protest lies in the stress on rational and ordered forms of argument based on empirical evidence. As rationality and order developed in importance, emotional arguments came to be regarded as inappropriate to the process of 'legitimate' protest. It is significant that those groups who opposed the burgh and franchise reform campaigns, though they commonly employed information techniques in counter-argument, relied heavily on emotive statements to sustain their case. The counter-protesters in the Scottish burghs – by the 1790s these were joined by London-directed loyalists organisations – emphasised tradition and patriotism in support of the existing polity. In the rhetoric of counter-protest, political reform in all its forms was linked to overt images of disorder, violence and the collapse of economic and political institutions. One of the most forceful articulations of this perspective came from the pen of Sir Walter Scott in 1819 in a series of letters to the *Edinburgh Weekly Journal* - under the pseudonym 'Somnambulus', and later published as a pamphlet entitled *The Visionary* - in which he presents his visions of the scenes of anarchy that must follow upon reform.[22] This influential statement played on fears and emotions; reform and all its implications, far from being in the cause of enlightened progress, is shown as a nightmare founded in collective madness.

Given the types of emotive images that were commonly used to undermine reform aspirations and the commitment to ordered and rational argument within the reform movements, it is not surprising that one of the characteristics of middle-class protest that developed from the 1780s, was a conscious dissociation from popular forms of emotional and physical protest (such as riot) and many deliberate statements of disapproval of disorder as a method of protest. These were most evident during periods when the incidence or threat of disorder was high. In 1792 the first Edinburgh Convention of Friends of the People resolved and published that:

> The members of this convention will, to the utmost of their power concur in aiding and strengthening the hands of the civil magistrates throughout this kingdom to repress riot and tumult, and all attempts whatsoever to disturb the tranquillity, happiness and good order of society.[23]

Members of the convention who were proven to be have acted 'illegally, tumultuously, or in any way to the disturbance of the public peace' were to be expelled from the association. There was also a suggestion, though this was not accepted, that association members be 'properly provided with arms' for the purpose of suppressing all riots and tumults.[23] Similarly, in the years from 1815 to the early 1820s the emphasis was on the peaceful and well-ordered character of the reform movement. An 1819 account of the origins and progress of the calls for burgh reform stressed that from the foundation of the movement in 1782 to the post-Napoleonic War revival, protesters had acted in an 'open, manly and constitutional manner. They were not persons who desired to create disturbance to the state, but . . . the steady friends of tranquillity and liberty.[24]

A conscious desire among middle-class reformers to distance their activities from the more traditional forms of mass physical protest through a stress on 'orderliness' was paralleled by a tension between collective and individual action. Collective action was fundamental to success, but closely associated with notions of 'the mob'. In order that it be both acceptable and legitimate, collective action had to conform to certain orderly and open forms, where the role of the individual was affirmed. This partly accounts for the significance of the 'petition'. In the legal sense the petition was representative of individuals alone. Democratic procedures which stressed the role of the individual were central to the activities of middle-class protesters. Moreover, the limits on what constituted a particular collective were usually stressed in the furtherance of legitimacy. It was important, for instance, that all actions of collective protests be attributed to named individuals. From an early stage there was a wide rejection of anonymous action; in part, and as an element in the process of distancing, this was due to the anonymity of much disorderly protest.[25] But it was also to demonstrate, through the nature of the action, one of the ideals of openness that was the object or reform and was clearly not in evidence among the unelected power brokers and self-selected councillors who held control in local affairs.[26] In support of the notion of the individual within the collective, it was usual to publish the names of members of the collective group – the president, the committees, the delegates to meetings and the proposers of particular courses of action. Petition lists were published and pamphlets or letters were increasingly to include the real names of the author as well as those of the organisation and printer (the latter required by law). As one author stated with regard to the authorship of political pamphlets – 'To stab may be necessary, but to stab in the dark must ever testify crime'.[27]

The collective protests of the early middle classes were usually undertaken in a manner that was open and business-like, and on the basis of organisations or associations for the specific purpose of protest. Here the urban middle classes were building on an established pattern of formally organised sociability and debate.[28] Local organisations would frequently co-ordinate their protests with those of similar bodies elsewhere. Co-ordination meant that activities could be both local and national. Nation-wide co-ordinating committees came into existence, usually with representatives based in London where media-based publicity was most available and effective and policy was made. The Convention of Delegates from Royal Burghs was a Scottish body seeking changes in a specifically Scottish system of burgh politics. Yet considerable efforts were expended by members of the convention in establishing links with English reform groups like the Yorkshire Association, and in generating supporters in London.[29] As an aspect of the process of generating order and openness, the purpose and the actions of protest organisations were usually publicised in advance, and the procedures and resolutions of specific meetings were made available afterwards, through the publication of minutes or newspaper reports. The late eighteenth century saw significant developments in the use of the press as a vehicle of protest. Advertisements appeared in the newspapers of the area where an organisation was active; they were published in the national press and in the provincial press in those parts of the country where an organisation believed it might find support. All middle-class protests followed this pattern. Merchant groups who lobbied in favour of commercial reforms were especially successful in exploiting press advertising.[30]

Middle-class collective protest was undertaken in public and firmly associated with the public press. It is also noteworthy that protest activities developed links with symbolically important public spaces. Legal access to specific public spaces, or the denial of access by town councils and magistrates, was a cause of conflict and became a feature of the process of protest. Perhaps the most dramatic case of the denial of a public space to middle-class protesters was seen in Glasgow in 1816, when reformers sought a large area to hold a public meeting 'respecting the distress of the country'.[31] The initial intention was to meet on the Green, the traditional heart of the old city, but city magistrates refused to permit the use of this and other publicly-owned spaces. The council and magistrates also put pressure on the owners of private spaces – such as large inns or courts – to prevent the use of any other facility within the city boundaries. The meeting, one of the largest to be seen in Scotland, was eventually held on the outskirts of Glasgow, in a field at Thrushgrove, the estate of a sympathetic merchant landowner. As with the Green in Glasgow, the right of legal access to public spaces such as the Pantheon in Edinburgh or the Magdalen Green in Dundee, were important to the reforming citizens of those towns.[32]

With openness, formality and a sense of order, the use of the public media and a location where possible in legitimately sanctioned public places, even at times of repression and anxiety – as during the years of the Napoleonic Wars when restrictive legislation and threats of invasion undermined the scale of protests – certain types of activity could still be employed to good effect. A good illustration is provided by the widely publicised and popular 'Fox celebratory dinners' that were held by middle-class Whigs throughout Britain on an annual basis following the death of Charles James Fox in 1806.[33] In Glasgow, the first Fox dinner took place in January 1810. Nearly one hundred 'gentlemen', who termed themselves the 'Friends of Constitutional Principles in Glasgow', dined at the 'Black Bull' on the occasion of Fox's birthday. They sang 'national and patriotic airs', and made numerous toasts in which themes of reform were linked to expressions of loyalty: 'The House of Hanover! And may they never forget the principles which seated them on the Throne', and: 'Lord Grenville! And may the Kingdom soon be really united by his liberal policy to the Catholics', are but two examples.[34]

A final characteristic of middle-class protest that is worthy of note since it reflects a broader aspect of the 'ordering' of middle-class community, concerns the lack of female participation. In all activities, organisations and movements, women were absent, even though in some respects the abuses that were the object of protests – the chicanery of local councillors or the mismanagement of burgh revenues and property – imposed equally on those women who were householders and ratepayers as on men. There are several reasons for this non-participation that go beyond the simple fact that women were not part of the formal political process. From the 1780s the developing notion of 'separate spheres' had conspired to undermine the public role of middle-class women. The legitimate sphere of women's activity was perceived to be the home, the private and domestic environment, while the public sphere of politics and work became exclusive to men. In parallel with the concept of separate spheres, the later eighteenth century had witnessed the development of the popular view that women were blessed with sensibility and emotion and that these were attributes of nature to be actively cultivated through upbringing and education in the interests of society.[35] The domestic and emotional qualities that were held to exemplify women were simply inconsistent with forms of protest that gained their legitimacy through being public, business-like and rationally argued. Since the 'disorderly' community protests of the rural and labouring populations frequently included women, the interests of legitimacy were further served by the non-participation of middle-class women.[36] Finally, it is worth restating the point that middle-class protest, by adhering to certain ordered forms, sought to exemplify a model of acceptable and reformed political behaviour, to be set in contrast to that which then prevailed. In respect of women this was important, for in unreformed politics they had played a significant role through their place in the family, and the role of the family, and family connections in patterns of voting and in political patronage. This is shown to a striking degree in the private report of a Scottish political agent who advised his London masters in 1788 on the best ways of securing votes by reference to the 'political opinions, family connections or personal circumstances' of the county voters. Two random quotations can serve by way of illustration.

> Sir William Erskine of Torry. Opulent. Can make several votes. His daughter married to Colonel Wemyss, which detaches him from the Erskines. A connection of General Sir William Howe. Has sons.

> Alexander Bayne of Rires. Small estate. Unmarried. A connection of Sir John Halkett in the County. His mother married to Dr Menzies at Dura in Fife. She has a family by the Doctor whom he will wish to provide for.[37]

NOTES

1 Contemporary condemnations of disorderly elections and burgh politics in general were legion, as shown in J. Sinclair, (ed.), *The Statistical Account of Scotland*, 21 vols (Edinburgh, 1791–1799). A fair illustration is given in the account of Cupar in Fife – 'burgh politics have ever operated here as a fatal check to industry. A succession of

contested elections have introduced, and it is to be feared, confirmed, among the members of the incorporations, habits of idleness, dissipation and vice'. (vol. 17, 45).

2 See the report of one of the Edinburgh 'theatre riots' contained as in *A letter from a Gentleman in Edinburgh to his Friend in the country occasioned by the late theatrical disturbance* (Edinburgh, 1766).

3 Two differing perspectives on the anti-Catholic riots in Edinburgh are given in *A Memorial to the Public in Behalf of the Roman Catholics of Edinburgh and Glasgow* (London, 1779), and *A Narrative of the Late Riots at Edinburgh and a Vindication of its Magistracy against the Charges advanced in the Memorials for the Papists in Scotland* (Edinburgh, 1779).

4 P.H. Scott, *1707. The Union of Scotland and England in Contemporary Documents with a Commentary* (Edinburgh, 1979).

5 On the relationship between language and social relationships and perceptions see P. Giglioli (ed.), *Language and Social Context* (1972), especially B. Bernstein, 'Social Class, Language and Socialisation', Also P. Burke and R. Porter (eds), *The Social History of Language* (Cambridge, 1987) 1–20.

6 These titles are taken from an extensive manuscript list of eighteenth-century Scottish political pamphlets in the Signet Library, Edinburgh. The collection as listed – which formed the basis of Meikle's study of 1919, *Scotland and the French Revolution* - is no longer extant.

7 The dispute that gave rise to Fennel's statement of defence arose out of unpopular changes to advertised programmes. This led to a riot and eventually a petition against Fennel.

8 The authors of the pro-Catholic memorial of 1779 (see note 3) had also presented statistical data in support of their arguments.

9 A. Fletcher, *Memoir Concerning the Origin and Progress of the Reform proposed in the Internal Government of the Royal Burghs of Scotland* (Edinburgh, 1819), p. 25.

10 'The minutes of the proceedings of the first General Convention of the Delegates from the Societies of the Friends of the People throughout Scotland . . . as contained in the Spy's Reports', reproduced in Meikle, *Scotland and the French Revolution*, Appendix A, p. 260.

11 See *Considerations submitted to the householders of Edinburgh on the State of their representation in Parliament* (Edinburgh, 1823), p.10.

12 J.V. Smith, 'Reason, Revelation and Reform: Thomas Dick of Methven and the Improvement of Society by the Diffusion of Knowledge', *History of Education* (1983), 255–70.

13 An outline of this movement is given in E.C. Black, *The Association: British Extraparliamentary Political Organization, 1769 to 1793* (Harvard, 1963), Chapter 5.

14 *The letters of 'Zeno' addressed to the citizens of Edinburgh on Parliamentary representation: a new edition with considerable enlargements by the author, published and distributed gratis by the Committee of Citizens* (Edinburgh, 1783), v.

15 R. Gourlay, *A specific plan for organising the people and for obtaining reform independent of parliament addressed to the People of Fife* (London, 1809), 21.

16 See S. Pollard, *The Genesis of Modern Management* (1965), Chapter 6.

17 Sinclair, *Statistical Account*, vol. 2, vi.

18 C. Emsley, 'The Home Office and its Sources of Information and Investigation, 1793–1801', *English Historical Review*, 94 (1979), 532–561; J. Brewer, *The Sinews of Power* (1989), Chapter 8.

19 E. Gauldie, *One Artful and Ambitious Individual, Alexander Riddoch (1745–1822) Provost of Dundee (1787–1819)* (Dundee, Abertay Historical Society Publication, No. 28, 1989), gives a valuable account of the burgh reform conflicts in Dundee, which included disputes arising out of the question of access to official information.

20 The delegates to the first convention for burgh reform in 1784 were described as 'wealthy and respectable burgesses', mainly merchants. There were also a number of smaller landowners with property close to towns and 'professional men of legal and constitutional knowledge'. Fletcher, *Memoir*, p. 15. One of John Galt's contemporary fictional accounts of reform activities refers to 'Mr Absolom the writer [lawyer] – a man no overly reverential in his opinion of the law and Lords . . . and some three or four young and inexperienced lads, that were wont to read essays, and debate the kittle points of divinity, and other hidden knowledge in the Cross Keys monthly, denying the existence of the soul of man . . . till they were deprived of all rationality by foreign and British spirits'. J. Galt, *The Provost* (Oxford, 1982; first published 1822), 121–2.

21 See Gauldie, *Alexander Riddoch*, Chapter 4; also A. Murdoch, 'The Importance of being Edinburgh', *Scottish Historical Review* (1983). One of the criticisms levelled against town councillors by wealthy merchants and professionals concerned their relatively low status. In Dumfries, for instance, they were described as being of 'obscure station and little knowledge': Fletcher, *Memoir*, 24.

22 W. Scott, *The Visionary* (Cardiff 1984, first published 1819), edited with an Introduction by P. Garside. This is mainly an attack on working-class radical reform.

23 'Friends of the People' in H.W. Meikle, *Scotland and the French Revolution*, (Glasgow, 1912, reprinted New York 1969), 260.

24 Fletcher, *Memoir*, 128.

25 One of the most dangerous riots of the 1790s – the King's Birthday riot in Edinburgh in 1792 – was preceded by anonymous notices of action. W.H. Fraser, 'Patterns of Protest' in T.M. Devine and R. Mitchison (eds), *People and Society in Scotland, I, 1760–1830* (Edinburgh, 1988), 270, illustrates one of the handbills. There is a detailed account of the riot in *The Book of the Old Edinburgh Club*, vol. 26 (Edinburgh, 1948), 7–10.

26 Further discussion of this point is made in S. Nenadic, 'The Structure, Values and Influence of the Scottish Urban Middle Class: Glasgow 1800 to 1870' (Unpublished PhD Thesis, University of Glasgow 1986), Chapter 4.

27 Gourlay, *Plan for Organising the People*, 3.

28 See D. McElroy, *Scotland's Age of Improvement: A Survey of Eighteenth Century Literary Clubs and Societies* (Washington, 1969); N. Phillipson, 'Adam Smith as Civic Moralist', in I. Hont and M. Ignatieff (eds.), *Wealth and Virtue: The Shaping of Political Economy in the Scottish Enlightenment* (Cambridge, 1983), 198–9.

29 Fletcher, *Memoirs*; Black, *The Association*, Chapters 2, 3.

30 Glasgow merchants in the East India trades had close links with similar groups in Liverpool and co-ordinated their lobbying in London – *Report of the Glasgow Committee*

to the Subscribers for the Object of obtaining a Free Trade to India and China (Glasgow, 1813). See also A.G. Olson, 'The Virginia Merchants of London: A Study in Eighteenth Century Interest-Group Politics', *William and Mary Quarterly*, 40 (1983) 363–88.

31 *Account of the Proceedings of the Public Meeting of the Burgesses and Inhabitants of the City of Glasgow held on the 29 October 1816 respecting the Distress of the Country* (Glasgow 1816)

32 *Considerations submitted to the householders of Edinburgh*, 10; Gauldie , Alexander Riddoch, 52.

33 N.B. Penny, 'The Whig Cult of Fox in early Nineteenth Century Sculpture', *Past and Present* 70 (1976), 94–105. Fox was popular in Scotland as he (with Sherridan) had championed the cause of Scottish burgh reform in parliament in the 1780s.

34 *Glasgow Herald*, January 26 1810.

35 J. Dwyer, *Virtuous Discourse: Sensibility and Community in Late Eighteenth-century Scotland* (Edinburgh, 1987), especially Chapter 5; L. Davidoff and C. Hall, *Family Fortunes: Men and Women of the English Middle Class 1780–1850* (1987).

36 J. Bohstedt, 'Gender, Household and Community Politics: Women in English Riots 1790–1810', *Past and Present*, 120 (1988), 88–122. By the early nineteenth century urban working-class protest had adopted some of the forms that typified the middle class. But the frequent involvement or presence of women and children was not viewed in a favourable light. This is indicated in an account of a Chartist meeting published in the *Glasgow Herald* on 24 January 1840: 'A meeting of the Chartist sisterhood was held last night in the Lyceum . . . the assemblage was rather a thin one, consisting of a few rows of young lasses in their Sunday bonnets in the middle of the room, an old matron in front and an infant in the rear, whose voice was heard pretty frequently during the evening; but it was difficult to tell whether its sympathies were Chartist or not'.

37 *View of the Political State of Scotland in the Last Century, a Confidential Report on the Political Opinions, Family Connections or Personal Circumstances of the 2662 County Votes in 1788*, edited by C.E. Adam (Edinburgh, 1887) pp. 135, 138.

Class formation and class fractions: The Aberdeen bourgeoisie 1830–1850

Extracted from AA MacLaren 1983, *in* G Gordon and B Dicks (eds), *Scottish Urban History*, Aberdeen (Aberdeen University Press), 114–9 and 126–7.

Elders were elected for life by cooption of the existing session. Although deposition was possible it was extremely rare and was usually confined to cases of fornication or business insolvency. It was the duty of existing members of the kirk sessions to ensure that those coopted were unlikely to be guilty of such offences and it followed that the kirk session members recruited men known to themselves whose morality and business integrity were highly regarded. The office carried considerable administrative and financial obligations. Elders were expected to perform various quasi-legal functions as well as to investigate the social and moral behaviour of individual members of the congregation and the inhabitants of the parish. They were also expected to make considerably greater financial contributions to the running of the church. Morality, by itself, therefore, was not a sufficient qualification for office – the need for men of suitable socio-economic standing was of equal importance to the successful running of church affairs. It followed that those 'set apart' as elders were usually men who had pursued a successful business or professional career – this in itself being regarded as a visible sign of worth in the eyes of God. Failures did not become elders. Membership of the kirk session carried considerable prestige. It not only reflected an individual's undoubted social respectability, it was both a recognition and warranty of his financial integrity. Kirk session elders therefore, were not simply an 'ecclesiastical elite' within the Church of Scotland. Certainly they were responsible for the government of the Church but in many respects their authority rested on the secular attributes which they undoubtedly possessed. As a body they were drawn from a cross-section of the most 'successful' elements in middle-class society and accordingly each member individually contributed to the collective power of the kirk session by bringing with him the authority he possessed in the wider society.

The relationship between the eldership and class formation is a complex one and requires closer examination. The kirk sessions were overwhelmingly middle class in composition, and the authority vested in the sessions was upheld by that class. Institutionally the eldership operated as instruments of social control on behalf of the middle class and were expected by their own individual behaviour to provide a social model for the wider society. Consequently they could be regarded as an institutional vanguard of the middle class in that they interpreted class interests and provided a 'moral' leadership. In a sense, therefore, although in no way divorced from the class formation in terms of power, their peculiar combination of divine and secular attributes allowed a degree of flexibility in interpreting its usage. On the other hand this flexibility would result from the internal operation of the kirk sessions albeit that each elder is a member of the wider bourgeois society.

However, given the social composition of the eldership and the method of recruitment by cooption, they would seem to fit loosely Gidden's definition of what he terms a 'uniform elite' – 'one which shares the attributes of having a restricted pattern of recruitment and forming a tightly-knit unity'.[1] This is not to imply that the eldership were in any sense an independent elite and it is clear from the above discussion that they were rooted in the middle-class social formation. However, although ultimately dependent on class power it is of some importance to examine the internal cohesiveness of the eldership in order to gain some insight into the interaction between the institutional vanguard and the class formation. Accordingly Giddens's characteristics of a 'uniform elite' are used only to probe the internal workings of the kirk sessions.

Finally it is important to note that although the eldership may share certain characteristics of a 'uniform elite', as a body they cannot be defined as such; nor indeed can they be seen as a specific class fraction which was bound by the overall needs of the class but yet retained a measure of specificity on the basis of occupational similarities or segmented economic interests. It might be possible to argue however that the eldership derived their support from certain dominant class fractions and the data would appear to support such a proposition. This is not to say that the eldership themselves comprised such a class fraction. Indeed the 'Ten Years' Conflict' was to demonstrate a divergence of fractional interests within the eldership. This divergence also illustrates one of the fundamental weaknesses of Giddens's typology in that his definition of a 'uniform elite' is essentially static and cannot incorporate dynamic social change. It follows that, whilst the definition may 'fit' certain of the characteristics of the eldership in 1830 in that the kirk sessions did have a 'restricted pattern of recruitment' and by their nature possessed a 'tightly-knit unity', it rapidly ceased to 'fit' in the face of structural changes in the class formation which are reflected within the kirk sessions. Nonetheless Gidden's definition does provide a useful starting point . . .

INTEGRATION WITHIN THE ELDERSHIP

Given the nature of the spiritual and secular qualifications one would predict that the eldership would be characterised by a high degree of social integration. This integration would be assisted by selective recruitment, followed perhaps by coherent and effective socialisation. Giddens distinguishes between what he calls 'social' and 'moral' integration. The former is concerned with 'the frequency and nature of the social contacts and relationships', and the latter – 'moral' integration – refers to the sharing of 'common ideas and a common moral ethos, and to the recognition of an 'overall solidarity'.[2] A third factor assisting integration would be numerical size. The problem would increase in relation to the number of members. Therefore a small body would be better able to retain an overall solidarity.

Prior to the Disruption the kirk sessions were made up of about 120 elders. These elders controlled all six city parishes in Aberdeen and comprised 15 congregations. There are strong indicators of a high degree of social and moral integration amongst senior elders ordained before the issue of patronage assumed importance. A persistent feature of the core of senior elders was both their business and residential propinquity. Despite the continuous and accelerating expansion of the city westwards after 1830 these families continued to occupy houses and business premises in the older residential districts in the east central area of the city. Their refusal to be attracted to the new and superior west-end housing may have been related to practical considerations such as the need to maintain business and commercial concerns which might have been put at risk by such a move. At a more ideological level it is clear that resistance to moving westwards was stiffened by a dislike and disapproval of those social elements which were in the forefront of the residential expansion. Increasingly those occupying these new town houses included among their number some of the most bitter critics of the prevailing order in the Church of Scotland. The fact that the Evangelicals were in the forefront of this urban expansion may well have associated the physical phenomenon in some way with men who were regarded as insolent social upstarts; men who exhibited a total lack of concern for existing social order and the property rights of patrons. Indeed more than two generations after the Disruption certain neighbourhoods continued to be associated with support for 'Moderatism'.[3] This reluctance to participate in the westward expansion of the city was not the consequence of financial constraints. A significant number of these families possessed substantial county properties which they had inherited or purchased over the previous three generations. Others had close family ties with the landed gentry. Indeed many of the families living in the east central area of the city were part of a much wider social network extending by both kin and commercial association into the landed families of the rural hinterland. This association had paid handsome dividends in the immediate past for it was from this association that much of the capital had been found for the rapid industrialisation of the city in the late eighteenth and early nineteenth centuries.[4]

Not unexpectedly, by far the largest occupational group represented in the eldership were the large merchants and manufacturers.[5] This single group made up about 38 per cent of the total number. Lawyers, professionals, and retired gentlemen together comprised 22 per cent and of the remainder only the small shopkeepers (12 per cent) were of any numerical importance. The large merchants and manufacturers, and the professional families – particularly the lawyers, tended to be closely linked by partnership and marriage. It was customary for younger members of one family to be apprenticed to another family business in order to learn the trade. It followed that a host of interlocking partnerships bound the major families to one another and one suspects that an economic consequence of this situation was a fairly restrained level of competition. These families dominated every major economic and political institution in the city and even after the passing of the Burgh Reform Act in 1833 they continued to occupy all the important municipal offices. In the interstices of the social network there existed a number of less prominent family connections sharing in its prosperity and contributing to its continuing stability.[6]

At the commencement of the decade which led to the Disruption the eldership exhibited a high degree of social and moral integration. This integration manifested itself in shared business enterprises and residential propinquity, as well as the domination of every major city institution. The relatively small number of elders assisted social integration as did the fact that they were derived from specific class fraction within the city. It should also be noted, however, that many of the elders were also part of a much wider social network extending into the landed families of the rural hinterland from whom in the past they had drawn considerable investment support.

POWER AND THE INSTITUTIONAL VANGUARD

If we view the eldership as an institutional vanguard of the middle class the expectation would be that the power conferred on the kirk sessions would be constrained within dictates broadly determined by class interest. These dictates would apply less to the running of the church as an organisation and would be concerned particularly with the other main sphere of kirk session activity as an instrument of social control. Thus predictably the eldership sought to preserve and advance bourgeois values by enforcing a generally accepted code of 'respectable' behaviour. It followed that the full weight of this power was brought to bear on the working class concerning a fairly wide range of social activities although particular attention was given to sexual immorality and alcoholic intemperance.[7] Apart from the most overt and scandalous cases the middle class escaped the scrutiny of the kirk sessions regarding this area of conduct. However, it would be mistaken to regard the power of the kirk sessions simply in terms of the authority vested in them as guardians of individual morality. Power was not only the capacity of the kirk session to impose its will; it was also related to the capacity of the eldership to prevent individuals doing what otherwise they might have done. Thus it could be argued that fear of exposure conditioned behaviour as much as kirk session activity. This fear itself was not derived solely from the capacity of the kirk session to warn of the possible hellfire consequences of deviant behaviour. As we shall see the more practical possibilities could not be ignored.

In terms of the analysis of social integration in the previous sections clearly it would be a mistake to attempt an assessment of the power base of the eldership in terms of spiritual characteristics alone. Whilst it might be argued that a man acting his role of elder was not effectively the same man acting as a cotton manufacturer, or as a city magistrate, such a concept – if useful in the contemporary situation – had no place in nineteenth-century society. Indeed to attempt to do so would be to misconstrue the nature of the office of elder and would run counter to the very basis of election to eldership. Calvinistic presbyterianism did not concede the possibility of separate roles. Anyone who failed to meet his debts in the business world had to cease forthwith from practising as an elder and a church member would be denied communion until he had satisfied those to whom he was indebted. Even a hint of financial insolvency could lead to investigation by the session and the practical consequences of an unconfirmed 'scandal' could be serious.

The power of the kirk sessions therefore, rested not simply on the spiritual aspects of eldership. The secular prerequisites were of equal importance in ensuring compliance. For the businessman, fallen by the economic wayside, appearance before the session amounted to investigation by one's peers. For all others it meant trial by a body of employers claiming the right to do so on the basis of the spiritual characteristics of their office. Moreover whilst it would be mistaken to see the office of elder as somehow independent from that of employer, it would be mistaken equally to attempt to view the other functions performed by the eldership as being divorced from the overall basis of kirk session power. The eldership had complete control over the distribution of poor relief and even after the passing of a new Scottish Poor Law in 1845 much of the power continued to lie in their hands. The kirk sessions also performed

numerous quasi-legal functions such as issuing certificates of poverty in order
that legal aid might be obtained, and supplying references as to the morality of
individual parishioners seeking admission to infirmaries for medical treatment.
The kirk session appointed the parish schoolmaster, tested his scriptural
knowledge, and had the power to raise or lower his salary. As custodians of
parish morality the elders undertook the 'purging' from the communion roll of
all those whose spiritual condition or social behaviour were thought to be
wanting.

Elders also attended meetings of the presbytery. Although this body dealt
with the more scandalous offences referred from the sessions, its scope was
wider and it could act on what were regarded as threats to public morality. Thus
considerable pressure could be brought to bear on local magistrates – generally
elders themselves and certainly always church members. In this way the
presbytery would act to ensure the removal of nuisances such as low thea-
tres, sabbath drinking-shops, brothels, and other distractions.

To conclude the eldership possessed a high degree of social integration and
were deeply entrenched in a wide-ranging power base. This power extended
from the institutional and quasi-legal functions carried out by the sessions, to
the coercive powers of the magistracy, and the economic powers shared by a
network of prominent families whose presence on the kirk sessions was
regarded as an indicator of the social respectability and financial integrity of
the eldership at large. Finally their position was further strengthened by the
power vested in the eldership to coopt new members to the kirk sessions. . .

IN CONCLUSION

Several factors emerge from this study which may have a general relevance to
the analysis of social class formations in other cities. Firstly, dominant class
fractions possessing a high degree of social integration and controlling an
'institutional vanguard' such as the eldership which has a relatively low level
of recruitment, are most secure in their power when the middle class 'reservoir'
remains comparatively stable in numerical terms. This would be particularly
true of dominant fractions whose power rested on a fairly narrow economic
resource base in the sense of being closely interlocked.

On the other hand the numerical size of the 'reservoir' is not in itself the
crucial element in determining the relationship with the dominant fractions. As
important is the general level of deference and acceptance of their overall
leadership. However, it is mistaken to assume that a continued acceptance of the
political leadership of the dominant fractions implies that such recognition
extends to all aspects of leadership. One must distinguish between levels of

deference. It follows that challenges to leadership may be related only to specific functions. For example a refusal to defer towards leadership in matters of religion may nevertheless be accompanied by a continuing deference in terms of political leadership.

However, it is possible that dominant class fractions exhibiting a high degree of social integration may be less able to sustain an attack on one area of their leadership simply because the power possessed is also so closely-knit as to be indivisible. Thus a specific challenge to one area of leadership would tend to become generalised although this was not the initial intention of the challenging fractions. It is possible that this particular case study has over-estimated the scale of this problem given that control over the kirk sessions was determined by the close association between the socio-economic and spiritual characteristics of eldership. In such a case a challenge to religious leadership would almost inevitably spill over into other areas of activity. Nevertheless it seems likely that a high degree of social integration limits ability to resist general involvement.

Finally there is the factor concerned with the social homogeneity of the urban population. Whilst one suspects this to be important it is likely that its importance rests on the presence or absence of other variables. Thus where deference and general acceptance of the existing dominant fraction remains high, shared social and geographical origins would further contribute to the overall stability. On the other hand these same features would assist the undermining of the authority of the dominant fractions where levels of deference were low or in decline. Certainly in the case of Aberdeen this peculiar aspect of the urban population would appear to have exacerbated the crisis.

NOTES

1 A Giddens, 'Elites in the British class structure', P. Stanworth and A Giddens (eds.), *Elites and Power in British Society* (Cambridge 1974), p. 5.

2 op. cit.

3 J Martin *Eminent Divines in Aberdeen and the North* (Aberdeen 1888), pp. 194–5, fancied that in certain streets 'the very air is laden with the breath of old 'moderate' times'.

4 A Keith, *The North of Scotland Bank Limited* (Aberdeen 1936), p. 6.

5 These figures and those following are derived from MacLaren, op. cit. pp. 216–55.

6 For example members of the Blaikie family held the office of Lord Provost for 11 of the 14 years between 1833–46. Ross, op. cit. See also the careers of the Cadenhead, Simpson, and Whyte families in MacLaren, op. cit. pp. 228, 248, 255.

7 For details and case studies of this process see A A MacLaren, 'Presbyterianism and the working class in a mid-nineteenth century city', *Scottish Historical Review*, 46, 2, no. 142 (October 1967).

Chartism in Aberdeen

Extracted from S McCalman 1970 *Journal of Scottish Labour History Society* 2, 5–7.

Historians of working-class history, especially those of the so-called 'left', have of late become absorbed by a desire to get to the guts of history. This is amply suggested by the work of Mr. E. P. Thompson who seeks to establish an 'illegal revolutionary tradition' among those whom previous historians have neglected: 'the poor stockinger, the Luddite workers, the obsolete hand-loom weavers, the utopian artisan'.[1] Similarly it can be seen in Hobsbawm and Rude's *Captain Swing*, which expresses with great academic thoroughness and detail the brutalities of rising capitalism as experienced by the rural labourers. However, whereas Thompson seeks to raise the defensive 'protesting' attitudes of that period when they were progressive to eternal virtues of the working class, still viable today, Hobsbawm and Rude refuse to draw any conclusions and simply implicitly encourage a typically English radical sympathy for the plight of the depressed and downtrodden.[2]

A second and equally idealistic approach to working-class history is that which, while the authors are not as openly partisan as those already mentioned, looks for the essence of history in the 'conflict': here such cases as those of Mary McShaffery,[3] the violence of the railway labourers, the meal mobs and so on become the guts of history. It is a twin to the method of Thompson and others in that it retains a mystical approach to class, which 'is not this or that part of the machine, but 'the way the machine works' once it is set in motion – not this or that interest, but the friction of interests – the movement itself, the heat, the thundering noise.'[4]

The only difference between the two methods is that the exponents of the former bow before the radicalism of the working class of this period, the latter bow before its violence, its staying power, its continual struggle. Both methods merely contemplate the working class in an essentially subjective manner.

One of the main flaws of E. P. Thompson's method is that he sees the working class spontaneously developing its own consciousness as a class – culturally and politically. Being enamoured by the greater, more extreme, radicalism of the 'poor stockinger' and so on of the North and Midlands, he overlooks the ideological link between these sections and the radicalism of the committees of middle-class reformers and self-educated artisans in London.

In a sense Mr. Thompson's view is only the reverse side of the coin to that of L.C. Wright in *Scottish Chartism*, who is concerned with the reformist character of the Chartist movement in Scotland. For him this is somehow an attribute of the 'moderate', 'sensible' Scottish working class. Both see working-class ideology, whether radical or reformist, as autonomous products of the working-class. Neither uncovers the way in which both strains are primarily creations of the middle class, of bourgeois ideology.

In the case of Aberdeen the links with the middle class are very close in that a number of Chartist leaders participated in common crusades with middle-class reformers, especially against the evils of alcohol.[5] Moreover, this participation was not restricted to the town artisans but found support among the displaced craftsmen also, those in whom Mr. Thompson seeks a more revolutionary strain of radicalism. Aberdeen had been going through a period of industrialisation. Growth in shipbuilding and woollens was attracting workers from the surrounding countryside. Depressed handloom weavers and flax dressers displaced by machinery were drifting into the town from the rural hinterland.[6] Two of these flax dressers who reached prominence in politics and reform were Archibald McDonald and Alexander Duncan, and their careers show clearly the dominance of middle-class ideology in the labour movement. One was a lifelong activist in the temperance movement and, as would be expected, he was in complete opposition to the rise of the Permissive Bill Association, because it supplanted the great crusade to raise the moral standards from below by pressure-group techniques geared to procuring legislation to enforce certain restrictions on the opportunities to sin.[7]

The available evidence suggests that many of this type, from the 1830s onwards, moved towards the Chartist movement as the vehicle of 'social redemption', where temperance, with varying importance, registered as a part of their philosophy. Of this type, Archibald McDonald was the one who reached greatest prominence in the Chartist movement in Aberdeen. By the late 1830s, the long decline in his trade of flax-dressing, 'which forced him to seek work where he could find it' was further exacerbated by the efforts of the local factor to push through enclosures.[8]

However, despite the numerous hardships he suffered from the advance of capitalism, industrially and in agriculture, and despite his unmitigated vocal opposition to the committees dominated by the middle class, the philosophy which he formulated was basically anti-aristocratic and anti-privilege. By the extremism of his language and his 'uncompromising' opposition to the movement led by Joseph Sturge,[9] he was generally accepted as a militant, and seems to have been popular as a speaker at meetings. Yet, he was totally incapable of breaking from the middle class ideologically.[10]

Moreover, the terms in which he posed his criticisms of society were not peculiar to the displaced craftsmen, the 'casualties' of early capitalism. These formed the basis of much of the propaganda of the town artisans. In fact, it pervades the whole work of John Mitchell, leader of the moral force section, and the only Aberdeen Chartist to have published anything above pamphlet literature.[11] Indeed, Mitchell's whole effort in the Chartist movement was geared to 'Unmask the titled locust band' – by moral force and propaganda.[12]

The important point, here, however, is that both these types, despite different backgrounds (Mitchell being a shoemaker), used the same basis for their criticisms of society. Both centred their attacks on aristocracy, on privilege, on sinecures. Clearly it was not a standpoint of their own making, but that of the various sections of the rising middle class and industrialists who had used these premises in their campaigns for Parliamentary Reform in the 1830s, and for the repeal of the Corn Laws, and which took a specifically Scottish form in the Disruption of 1843. It is this more than anything else which accounts for what later commentators on Aberdeen found 'curious':

> Among the prominent chartists in Aberdeen were several men who
> afterwards rose to a good position in the town, and it was curious to note
> how circumstances alter the case for in nearly every such case, when the
> individual came to be possessed of capital and had, so to speak, a stake in
> the country, his political views veered round to conservatism.[13]

NOTES

1 E.P. Thompson *The Making of the English Working Class* (Pelican, 1968) 13, 541.

2 J. Foster in a review of *Captain Swing* in the *Morning Star* 6 Feb. 1969: the book 'shows that it was precisely in the village that the most bitter price was paid for England's industrialisation'. Perhaps the towns were not so bad after all?

   See also E.L. Jones' review in the *Economic History Review* XXII, 2 (1969): 'It will be read with pleasure and sympathy by many who would have shied at a more ideological or (understandably) angry book.'

3 Mary McShaffery was the victim of a vitriol attack in 1833. She was attacked – perhaps as a result of mistaken identity – for being a blackleg.

4 Thompson *op.cit.* 939.

5 A.S. Cook *Pen Sketches and Reminiscences of Sixty Years* (Aberdeen 1906) 23. Cook remarks on the eclectic nature of Temperance radicalism, attributing the collapse of the first enthusiasm in the 1840s to its breaking into its component parts – Non-intrusion, Chartism, abolition of the Corn Laws, and better management of the poor 'which were promoted chiefly by those engaged in temperance reform'.

6 *Aberdeen Herald* 9 April, 21 May 1842.

7 Cook *op.cit.* 74. Duncan was forced to admit ruefully that by the 1840s events moved faster than the good word and he confessed that one of his main regrets was that there were no longer people 'accustomed to manual labour' on the Temperance Committee or active in the movement at large, and that in the 'early days of temperance these were not lacking'.

8 Archibald McDonald *The Poor Unprotected by Law; or the Existing Administration of Law Contrasted with the Principles of the British Constitution* (Aberdeen 1850) 11.

9 *Aberdeen Herald* 16 April 1842.

10 McDonald *op.cit.* 16, 19. The practical implications of his ideological position can be seen in that in 1843–4 he 'depended in a great measure for a living on making several chemical preparations and selling them', i.e. he always hoped to be able to be a small businessman, even if only a quack dispenser. Similarly, in 1848–9 he took to manufacturing 'spruce and ginger beer'.

11 John Mitchell *Poems, Radical Rhymes, Tales &c* (1840), The Wreath of Temperance (lyrics) (1842). He also began a short-lived radical paper in 1843, the *Aberdeen Review*.

12 Mitchell *Poems* 9.

13 W. Robbie *Aberdeen: Its Traditions and History* (Aberdeen 1893) 400.

Bogs and people since 1600

TC Smout 1997, *in* L Parkyn, RE Stoneman and HAP Ingram (eds), *Conserving Peatlands*, Oxford (Wallingford), 162–7.

When the first detailed geographical accounts of Scotland began to be written, generally in the years between 1630 and 1730, the reputation of bogs stood high as a useful resource. Thus at Fetteresso in Kincardineshire the parish was said to be supplied with 'inexhaustible mosses, wherein are digged the best of peats, very little if anything inferior to coals', from which the inhabitants supplied not only themselves and the neighbouring communities of Dunnottar, Inverbervie and Stonehaven, but also Aberdeen some 15 miles away (Mitchell 1906, I, 248). At Cortachy in Angus 'the hills and glens of this county abound with excellent moss and muir for feuell, with wild fowl of different kinds, and sometimes with deer and roe' (*Ibid.*, I, 284). A description of Aberdeen and Banff by Robert Gordon of Straloch, probably of the 1630s, says that 'there is no occasion here for stoves; the hearths are well supplied with peat, which is dug out of the ground, and is black and bituminous, not light and spongy, but heavy and firm' (*Ibid.*, II, 268). A parish with 'moss ground' was blessed, like Keith: it had 'great plenty of fir under ground, which the people thereabouts dig up some two fathoms deep, and by this they are served with winter light and timber for their houses. In this hill is a large peat bank about six or seven foot deep and near two miles long' (*Ibid.*, I, 89). A parish without such resources was cursed: of Cushnie it was said 'it is a poor countrey both for corn and pasture, and exceeding scarce of Fewel' (*Ibid.*, I, 31). Of the lower ground of Morayshire near the coast it was observed that 'they suffer from scarcity of peats for fuel, which is the only inconvenience felt by this highly favoured region, but even that in few places, and they remedy it by hard drinking in company, for this also must be admitted' (*Ibid.*, II, 457). The implication seems to have been that if you could not warm yourself with peat you needed to warm yourself with whisky.

This generally cheerful and positive attitude towards bogs may be contrasted with the attitudes that came to rule in the following century, the age of the agricultural improvers, when the old assumption that natural resources were a given, changed to one where they were regarded as capable of betterment. To the late eighteenth and early nineteenth century improvers, peat bogs cried out for money and effort to transform them from waste into arable land, even though locally in parts of the countryside the exhaustion of peat supplies was already said in the 1790s to be leading to depopulation.

Reclamation of mossland was not itself new: as early as 1724 it was observed that parts of Flanders Moss 'by casting, pareing and burning' had been in some places 'cut quite thorow and made arable ground' (*Ibid.*, I, 341). The great scheme to drain Blairdrummond Moss nearby, by the notable improver Lord Kames, was hailed as a national benefit, greater even than that conveyed by David Dale in founding his famous cotton manufactory at New Lanark. Both had employed displaced Highlanders, wrote William Aiton in 1811, but whereas at Blair Drummond 'the moss colony remain healthy and happy, delighting in their situations, warmly attached to their patron, and to the Government, daily increasing in wealth, and rearing a numerous offspring, ready to extend their brawny arms, in the cultivation of the dreary wastes, or to repel their country's foes', those in the cotton mill 'became discontented with their situation, and soon abandoned it'. That 'several hundreds of ignorant and indolent Highlanders' went on Aiton, were 'converted into active, industrious, and virtuous cultivators, and many hundreds of acres of the least possible value rendered equal to the best land in Scotland are matters of the highest national interest, to which I can discover no parallel in the cotton mill colony' (Aiton 1811, 341–2).

These tones were quite characteristic of early nineteenth century commentators. Thus the Rev. Robert Rennie of Kilsyth, a pioneer in the systematic study of bog formation, wrote in 1807 that 'innumerable millions of acres lie as a useless waste, nay, a nuisance to these nations. The benefits that might accrue to Europe by a slight attention to this subject, are above all calculation. It is impossible for numbers to express, or the imagination to conceive, correctly, the extent of these' (Rennie 1807, 6; see also Rennie 1810). Aiton himself believed that 'the intrusion of Moss earth has been attended with two evils of great magnitude; first, the loss, or at least the reduction, of the value of an immense extent of soil, and secondly, its pernicious effects on the atmosphere' (Aiton 1811). He estimated the amount of ground under bog in Scotland at over 14,000,000 acres, and believed that the accumulation of moss over so much of the original soil since (he thought) the time of the Roman invasion, had led to a decline in the temperature. Andrew Steele, in 1826, in the opening chapter to his treatise on peat moss, spoke of the bogs as 'immense deserts . . . a blot upon the beauty, and a derision to the agriculture of the British Isles'. He also commented that 'the only animals found on these grounds are a few grouse, lizards, and serpents' (Steele 1826, 38–40).

The agricultural experts received general support in their view of bogs as dreary incumbrances from the ever-growing band of Romantic tourists, who came to Scotland to view the glens and to obtain a frisson of excitement from the 'picturesque', 'the sublime' or the 'terrific', but who found nothing attractive in bogs as they floundered through them. Thus John MacCulloch, Walter Scott's friend, had a memorable diatribe against the Moor of Rannoch:

> 'hideous, interminable . . . a huge and dreary Serbonian bog, a desert of blackness and vacuity and solitude and death . . . an ocean of blackness and bogs, a world before chaos; not so good as chaos . . . even the crow shunned it . . . if there was a blade of grass anywhere it was concealed by the dark stems of the black, black muddy sedges, and by the yellow melancholy rush of the bogs' (MacCulloch 1824, I, 317–20).

When, however, the train replaced the pony as a way of crossing the bog, the traveller could view them more dispassionately and in greater comfort. The first thoroughly appreciative description of the aesthetics of the Moor of Rannoch came from the anonymous author of a public relations book for the new line. The moor becomes in winter 'a study in sepia', in summer 'one colossal Turkey carpet, so rich and oriental'. Even: 'to see a sunset on Rannoch Moor is as essential as to see Loch Lomond by moonlight' (Anon. 1894).

Nevertheless, until far into the second half of the twentieth century, the idea that the peat bog was a desert that needed reclamation, or at least was a wasted resource that could legitimately be used up for some economically productive purpose, ruled most thinking on the matter. Economic and political changes helped to reinforce the view. Following the great expansion of coal mining in the eighteenth and nineteenth centuries, and the transport revolution enabling coal to be more readily moved, the rôle of the local peat bog as a fuel resource declined to extinction except in parts of the northern and western Highlands. The coming of the national grid, and Thomas Johnston's insistence, as head of the first Hydro Board after 1945, that it should reach the remotest areas, further emancipated even the crofting population from absolute slavery to the peat spade. Meanwhile in the twentieth century the rise of the agricultural subsidy encouraged the transformation of many peatlands into farmed pasture, the coming of new ploughs and tractors made it possible to get conifers after 1945 into the hillsides and flows, materially assisted by tax concessions, and the rise of the garden centre gave further encouragement to cut out the bogs. If we were spared the depredations of the Irish peat-fired power stations, we were not spared much else. In the immediate post-war period there was even a prototype peat-fired power station set up in Caithness, but the experiment was not successful.

The ecological movement itself, with its talk of wet deserts, was not friendly to the notion of peatlands. In 1973, H.A. Maxwell, writing in highly favourable terms about modern forestry plantations, quoted a personal communication from Frank Fraser Darling: 'The Sitka spruce has been a godsend in re-afforestation of Scottish hill ground of peaty character . . . To recreate a forest biome after a long period of soil degradation is inevitably a slow process (I think myself in terms of one or two centuries) . . . as ground and shelter conditions ameliorate we can confidently expect improved appearance of the plantations gradually becoming forest' (Tivy, ed., 1973, 182).

In the post-war decades the call to reclaim marginal land of all descriptions reached a peak of frenetic zeal quite analogous to that of the early nineteenth-century improvers. The Scottish Peat and Land Development Association, around 1962, in a pamphlet entitled *Reclamation!* called for a Land Development Board to encourage the transformation of the waste: 'we can no longer afford to have so much marginal land put to so little use, or deteriorating through misuse'. Among its proposals were to establish experimental farms on bogs, and to initiate reclamation and improvement by concentrating drainage machines in groups 'in an area that forms a natural entity – e.g. the whole of a glen or a major bog'. J.M. Bannerman, the well-known Liberal, called for 'widespread arterial drainage schemes', especially in Strathspey 'where the land to be reclaimed runs into scores of thousands of acres'. He also proposed lowering Loch Lomond by four feet by removing the silted sandbanks at the outflow. Others called for an onslaught on the 4 million acres of partially productive land by 'chemical ploughing' – i.e. by massive application of herbicide. These people were visionaries but were not cranks: apart from Bannerman, they contained respected MPs like Tom Fraser and the future Conservative Secretary of State for Scotland, Michael Noble (SPLD ca.1962). The most useful outcome of these years was a national survey of peat-bogs begun by the Scottish Office after 1947 and taken over by the Macaulay Institute. Although intended as the basis for commercial exploitation of the resource, its greatest utility in the long run has been to aid nature conservation in accurate assessment of the bogs.

Changes within the last ten years have, ultimately, been towards much greater appreciation of the nature conservation value of all kinds of bogland, and towards a reluctance by government to allow public money to be spent on subsidising drainage ventures that made little sense in the realities of the world economy of the late twentieth century. The crunch came in the late 1980s, when the controversy over the Flow Country between forestry interests and con-servationists, in which the conservationists were enthusiastically supported by the *Daily Telegraph*, led to a reduction in tax concessions to the foresters' rich backers in Nigel Lawson's budget. If the threats to the bog are still numerous, its friends have never been so numerous either.

So far in this paper, we have considered how outsiders and largely self-defined 'experts' regarded bogs. This concluding section touches briefly upon the rather more obscure topic of how those who had bogs upon their land actually managed them on a day-to-day basis. Peatlands and bogs were, of course, of many kinds: for practical use the most important variation was the spectrum from wet to dry. Most occupiers, however, saw them as a source for two things – fodder, and extracted material for building, fertiliser and (above all) fuel. The previous speaker has already spoken about grazing and bogs, but I would here emphasise two aspects: bogs as sources of hay, and of spring bite. These have to be seen in the context of earlier grazing régimes, where the main constraint on stocking levels was the ability to keep animals alive between November and May without artificial feedstuffs, turnips, or silage. 'Until well into the last century', writes John Mitchell, 'cattle being over-wintered were fed almost exclusively on 'bog-hay', a mixture of wet meadowland plants scythed from undrained land': it could yield between 100 and 150 stone of hay per acre, and some of the bog hay meadows were of great extent. What was said to be the largest in Scotland was the Carron Bog, four miles long and a minimum of one mile wide: it almost all now lies beneath the Carron Reservoir, but in its heyday in the late eighteenth century was described by the local minister as adding 'great liveliness and beauty to the general face of the country. The scene it exhibits during the months of July and August, of twenty or thirty different groups of people employed in haymaking, is certainly very cheerful'. You may still see bog hay cut today in Co. Donegal and Sligo, and no doubt elsewhere. The Aber Bogs on Loch Lomondside (not themselves in the least peaty) were last so cut in 1952, but the practice must now be unfamiliar at least in mainland Scotland (Mitchell 1984). On the other hand, most upland farmers still know of the value of bogs for spring bite, when the emerging sprouts of bog cotton and other plants provide a richness of early protein that is still welcome for animals coming out of winter quarters.

The use of the peat bog for opencast extraction by the occupier was obviously important, but it is significant that in some societies – Ireland, Denmark – the generic term 'turf' (qualified in different ways) is used for anything cut from the ground. The Danes distinguish between 'grass-turf', 'heather-turf', 'bog-turf' (or peat) and 'sand-turf' (peat under sand) (Hove 1983). The point is that all were obtained by skinning the ground, and the difference to the farmer was in degree rather than kind. They were all suitable for cutting sods for burning, and subsequent use as fertiliser, a practice that in

Scotland was viewed sometimes with favour, and sometimes with hostility by experts, but at least until the middle of the nineteenth century widely practised by farmers. Turf, or 'grass-turf' to the Danes, was also used as a building material, for 'feall dykes' (the Scottish term) and for 'divots', or scale-shaped roofing turves (Fenton 1970). Peat, no doubt depending on its fibrous qualities, could also be used for building, but it would have a much shorter life, particularly in frost: it would therefore be avoided except for buildings that were essentially temporary, like shieling huts. The most significant use of peat, however, was for fuel, though in districts where peat was scarce – as in parts of Perthshire – turf was used in its place: the disadvantage of 'grassturf' was that it burnt too fast. Even good quality peat was needed in very large quantities. Fraser Darling reckoned that a family of four in the Western Highlands needed to cut 15,000 peats a year for cooking and warmth: a good man could cut 1000 a day, but a month's work for the family was involved in winning peats, drying and carrying them (Darling 1945, 6).

It was therefore very important to the farmer and crofter that cutting peat (and indeed 'grass-turf') should be as simple and quick as possible, and the best way to ensure that was to burn off the overburden of vegetation. Since this was often also likely to improve grazing, burning on moors and peat bogs was a regular event: presumably this, along with direct grazing itself, was what kept the drier ones from instantly regenerating with birch and other trees as so many are doing today. Because it was convenient, the burning itself often took place at unlawful seasons when the bog was driest, in late spring or summer, with attendant risks: a fact that perhaps accounts for much of the Scottish legislation limiting muirburn from the fifteenth century onwards.

For the farmer peat-cutter, convenience was more important than the law. This was how a cutter in Co. Antrim described his experiences around 1932: 'I had to get a winter's firing for myself, and having been used to watching my father when I was a young fellow, and seeing what he had done, I followed his footsteps. He always picked out a nice spot in the bog where he would start and cut. So I burned a nice wee bit first. That was to make the turf easier cut with the spade. Burning was against the law. I was even caught by the police myself one time and it cost me £3–10–0.' He went on to explain how a friend who worked alongside was determined not to be caught by the police in the same way, and always lit the moss before he went to dinner, so that he could pretend it was an accident if the police came and he was not there: 'one day when he got back and the moss was burning he saw Mr. Wilton [the policeman] watching and he ran as fast as he could and he got his shovel and he started beating out the fire and throwing water on it from the drain . . . . Wilton got over and demanded what he was doing and he said, 'Well you might ask. This was all right when I went for my dinner and look at it now – and even some of my turf has been burned.' He had the presence of mind to bluff Wilton that somebody else had lit the moss on him and Wilton just threw off his tunic and fell to and helped him to put it out and said nothing' (Smyth 1991, 10–11). No doubt the village constabulary in Scotland had many equally trying experiences when people's treatment of the bog did not quite keep within the law.

ACKNOWLEDGEMENTS

I am most grateful to Dr. Hugh Ingram and Professor Alexander Fenton for drawing my attention to several important texts.

REFERENCES

Aiton, W. (1811) *A Treatise on the Origin, Qualities and Cultivation of Moss-Earth, with Directions for Converting it into Manure.* Ayr.

Anon. (1894) *Mountain, Moor and Loch, Illustrated by Pen and Pencil on the Route of the West Highland Railway.* London.

Darling, F.F. (1945) *Crofting Agriculture: its Practice in the West Highlands and Islands.* Edinburgh.

Fenton, A. 'Paring and burning', in A. Fenton & A. Gailey eds. (1970) *The Spade in Northern and Atlantic Europe,* 155–93. Belfast.

Hove, Th. Th. (1983) *Tørvegravning i Danmark.* Poul Kristensens Forlag, Herning.

MacCulloch, J. (1824) *The Highlands and Western Isles of Scotland.* London.

Mitchell, A. ed. (1906) *Geographical Collections Relating to Scotland made by Walter Macfarlane.* Scottish History Society, Edinburgh.

Mitchell, J. (1984) 'A Scottish Bog-hay Meadow'. *Scottish Wildlife,* 20, 15–17.

Rennie, R. (1807) *Essays on the Natural History and Origin of Peat Moss.* Edinburgh.

Rennie, R. (1810) *Essays on the Natural History and Origin of Peat Moss.* Edinburgh.

Smyth, P. (1991) *Osier Culture and Basket-Making: A study of the basket-making craft in South West County Antrim.* Lurgan, Co. Armagh.

SPLD = Scottish Peat and Land Development Association (ca. 1962) *Reclamation!* n.p., n.d. Consulted in the Bodlean Library, Oxford.

Steele, A. (1826) *The Natural and Agricultural History of Peat-moss or Turf-bog.* Edinburgh.

Tivy, J. ed. (1973) *The Organic Resources of Scotland: Their Nature and Evaluation.* Edinburgh.

Budgeting for survival: Nutrient flow and traditional Highland farming

RA Dodgshon 1994, in S Foster and TC Smout (eds), *The History of Soils and Field Systems*, Aberdeen (Scottish Cultural Press), 83–93.

Traditional farming systems are a well-worked theme, but there has been surprisingly little debate over what they involved in terms of nutrient flow. I suspect this silence stems from the problem of specification. Because so much has to be guessed rather than calculated, there is a danger of producing very speculative analyses. In reply, I would argue that despite these problems of specification, just being aware of the questions involved can still contribute to our understanding of traditional farming systems.

The problems and possibilities are well shown if we try to reconstruct the nutrient flow that underpinned farming in the western Highlands and Islands before crofting and the clearances. Traditional farming systems everywhere were caught within a nutrient flow trap, but I want to argue that those to be found in the western Highlands and Islands before crofting and the clearances were caught within a particular kind of nutrient flow trap, one that typified other mountain or marginal areas in north-west Europe.

Not surprisingly, the key to understanding this flow trap lies in appreciating how local environmental conditions affected the problem. In a stimulating paper written back in 1980, the historian Chorley argued that for traditional farming systems in northern Europe, the key nutrient was nitrogen. Whilst such systems re-cycled nutrients via straw and feed, and added to the cycle by transferring nutrients from grassland and meadow, they were crucially dependent on the nitrogen available from within soils via biological fixation (Chorley 1981, 80–1). Furthermore, even for a nutrient like phosphorus, Chorley suggests that the amount available within the soil through mineralisation was sufficient to meet the needs of traditional farming without the need for extra inputs (ibid, 88). Such conclusions are highly significant for the Highlands and Islands because factors like heavy rainfall, leaching, waterlogging, acidity – all common problems in the region – inhibited processes like biological fixation and mineralisation and, together, form the main reason why soils across the region have an 'inherent poor fertility' (Bibby et al 1982, 127). In other words, townships across the region would have had significantly less nitrogen from biological fixation and phosphorus from mineralisation than Chorley had in mind. In addition to such problems, townships in the region also faced the still more basic problem of having only limited amounts of land physically capable of being cultivated. Estate surveys compiled in the years on either side of 1800 suggest that less than ten percent was classed as arable (Dodgshon 1992, 174). Much of the land available to townships comprised ground that was high, exposed, steep, broken by rock outcrops, waterlogged or peaty. Though townships made great efforts to cultivate this sort of land, by far the greater proportion of it lay beyond the physical and climatic limits of cultivation.

These constraints on cultivation – the low levels of key nutrients provided through processes like biological fixation and mineralisation and the high percentage of land that was physically unsuited to cultivation – undoubtedly affected the way in which traditional communities set about maintaining nutrient flow on their arable. In the circumstances, the logical response for Highland communities was to counter the low nutrient status of their soils by recycling as much nutrient as possible via straw-feed and by adding as much extra to the cycle by transfering nutrients from their meadow and extensive pastures via animal dung.

These, of course, were strategies adopted by traditional farming communities everywhere (cf. Olsson 1991, 300–5). As solutions though, they had limitations. They did not allow arable or output to be expanded indefinitely. A relationship existed between the amount of arable that could be maintained and the amount of manure available, the latter, in turn, being constrained by the amount of straw feed, pasture and meadow available. How these constraints operated varied between different environments. In particular, we need to draw a distinction between how they affected communities in Lowland Britain and how they affected those in upland or marginal regions like the Highlands and Islands. In the former, far more of the total land available to communities could be cultivated. This meant that under pressure of population growth, it was possible to have an extension of arable to the point at which pasture reserves were reduced below those needed to support arable. The result was a reduction in the flow of nutrients from pasture to arable and a decline in yields. In a recent review of the problem, the agronomist R Shiel has suggested that for optimum yields, traditional communities needed to keep no more than between 15–20 percent of the land under arable (Shiel 1992, 71–2). As the proportion of arable increases, yields fall away significantly (see Fig. 1). The economic historian, M

Postan, argued that such a fall took place in southern England over the late thirteenth and early fourteenth century. Rapidly increasing population was seen as precipitating a state of land pressure, with an over-expansion of arable leading to soil exhaustion as the flow of nutrients from grassland became depleted (Postan 1974, 23–5; 57–71). Detailed analyses by H S A Fox have confirmed that some communities in southern England were cropping as much

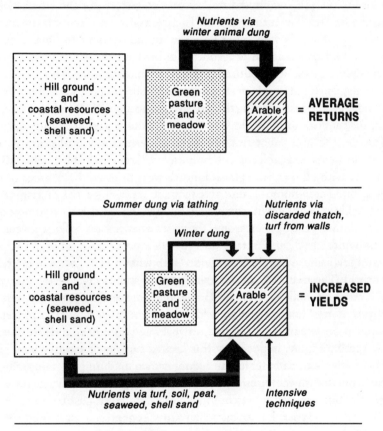

Figure 1 – Effect of increases in arable on levels of nutrient flow from non-arable sources. In upper part of the diagram, balance between arable (15–20%) and green pasture/meadow (80–85%) enables substantial flows of nutrient via stock manure and hay so that yields on arable are at least average or above average. As arable is extended, levels of nutrient flow from green pasture/meadow fall away progressively. In the lower part of the diagram, though, areas with extensive acreages of non-cultivable land (i.e. hill or marginal ground) can offset this decline with strategies that make use of summer manure, the nutrients locked into resources like turf, peat, seaweed and shell sand, and more labour intensive techniques of preparing the soil. If exploited to the full, these strategies could lead to an increase in yields.

as 50 percent of their land by the late thirteenth century (Fox 1984, 119–59). As Shiel's figures make clear, this would have greatly reduced the transfer of nutrients from pasture.

It could be argued that given the vast reserves of non-arable resource, traditional communities in the Highland and Islands were unlikely to have faced the spectre of a Postan-type crisis. After all, even around 1800, when population was close to a peak, arable did not exceed ten percent of the land available. Seeing the balance between arable and pasture in simple gross terms though, glosses the problem. If we look at how traditional communities manured their arable, we find the standard procedure – in lowland as well as upland areas – was to apply the manure produced during the winter months. This required the close management of stock over winter, with some being kept indoors over night and, in some cases, during the day so as to accumulate their manure. Come spring, the manure so collected was then added to a part of arable.

This need to accumulate manure over winter has a critical bearing on the flow of nutrients available to communities in areas like the Highlands and Islands. As with all upland regions in north-west Europe, the number of stock which farming communities were able to keep over winter was determined not by the total amount of grazing available, but by their more restricted supplies of sheltered winter grazings, including the grass growing on balks between rigs, plus the winter feed supplement offered by hay meadows and straw. Some Highland townships were, in fact, divided into what they called 'winter ground' and outfield. These supplies of wintering ground and hay meadow had to come out of a very tight budget of 'better' land and to compete directly with arable for use of this 'better' land. When we add population growth and the consequent pressure for an expansion of arable, townships would have quickly come up against the limitations imposed by this limited budget of suitable land. Some surveys of Highland and Hebridean estates drawn up during the late eighteenth and early nineteenth centuries draw the distinction not just between arable and non-arable, but between what could be classed as green pasture and meadow and what was hill ground. If we take their supplies of green pasture and meadow as representing what was available to maintain stock over winter and compare it with arable, it soon becomes apparent that the arable-pasture ratios of Highland and Hebridean townships may have been far more adverse that what would be suggested by a simple reading of the overall balance between arable and non-arable (Fig. 1). In some cases, we are dealing with between 50–75 percent of 'better' land under arable and between 25–50 percent under wintering ground and meadow. Seen in these terms, the case for seeing traditional communities in the Highland and Islands as facing a Postan-type crisis by the late eighteenth and early nineteenth centuries becomes a little more persuasive. I should add that the poor straw value of Highland and Hebridean grains and the practice of graddaning, or separating out the grain by setting fire to the husk and straw, would not have helped nutrient recycling via straw feed. In short, if manure alone was used, population growth may have led Highland townships – like their counterparts in Lowland Britain – into a nutrient flow trap. Indeed, given the problems affecting the biological fixation of nitrogen and the mineralisation of phosphorus and the strong possibility that many Highland townships had less resources of winter pasture and feed, there is a case for arguing that potentially this nutrient flow trap was deeper than that facing their Lowland counterparts.

We can enlarge on the nature of this flow trap by looking at actual case-studies. A few years ago, I carried out a joint project with an ecologist, Dr. Gunilla Olsson, using data from four township clusters in the central and western Highlands (Dodgshon & Olsson 1988, 39–51). Using techniques developed by the Ystad project in southern Sweden (Olsson 1988, 123–37; Olsson 1991, 293–314), the study attempted to analyse the flows of nitrogen and phosphorus provided by animal and human waste. The study was based on calculations about the movement of stock between different sectors, on their stocking density, on weight/feed intake, the length of time manure was kept in storage, the loss of nutrients whilst in storage, and so on, in townships from four sample areas: North and South Lochtayside, Barrisdale and Ardnamurchan. As Figure 2 shows, different types of stock produced different quantities. Obviously, faced with this pattern of flow, a township cannot solve its problems by switching to stock that produce more manure for what matters is the constraint introduced by the total feed available. The souming system acknowledges this point. Souming was based on a weighted equalization of different stock (one soum = one horse = two cows = 5 sheep = 10 goats). Switching between stock does not alter the total amount of manure produced by the total number of soums available. What mattered was the total winter feed available and the total number of weighted or soumed stock this would support, or the number which a township could soum and roum in winter. One further point: as townships came up against the limits imposed by winterings and meadow, the simple fact of more people would have meant more nutrients, although the proportion of nutrients derived from human waste at Barrisdale involved very small acreages (Fig 2). Systems with much larger acreages derived much less from this source. When we consider what the flows from all sources meant in absolute terms, they confirm that some townships might have faced a Postan-type crisis if they relied on the nutrients provided by animal manure alone, whether by recycling straw or by transfers from pasture and meadow. In actual fact, maintaining nutrient levels by conserving winter manure was only one of a number of strategies

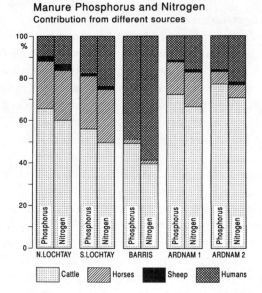

Figure 2 – Inputs of nitrogen and phosphorus derived from different sources of manure (based on Dodgshon & Olsson 1988: 46).

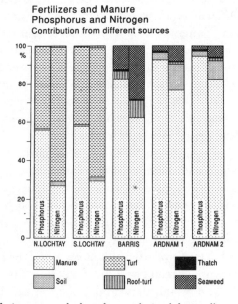

Figure 3 – Inputs of nitrogen and phosphorus derived from all sources of manure (based on Dodgshon & Olsson 1988: 47).

available to Highland and Hebridean communities. Though their nutrient flow trap was potentially a deeper trap than that of lowland townships, they had – like other upland or marginal areas in north-west Europe – escape routes. These escape routes depended on the simple fact that upland or marginal areas had large amounts of non-arable resource. This non-arable resource constituted a huge nutrient store, provided communities were prepared to explore new strategies for transferring it to arable. Three possibilities can be mentioned (see Fig. 1). First, there was outfield cropping. What distinguished outfield cropping was the simple fact that it depended on the use of summer manure, applied by a system of tathing. This meant that townships acquired a system based on the all-year-round use of manure. It directly addressed what contemporaries saw as the weakness of traditional systems: the neglect of summer manure. Because it was summer manure, the quantities involved would have been good but not when set against the manurial cycle or frequency (one in 6–9 years) with which outfield systems were manured.

Second, it was possible for townships to exploit the vast resources of their non-arable sector in a more direct way. A range of possibilities existed: shell sand, seaweed, peat, peaty soil, turf and heather via thatch. As inputs, these different transfers have varying significance for nutrient flow. Shell sand was used only in coastal townships and then only where calcium rich sand was available. Its main impact was in altering soil acidity, thereby increasing the availability of key nutrients. Seaweed was also a transfer used heavily in coastal and Hebridean areas (Fenton 1986, 48–82). As a source of nutrients, it tended to release nutrients quickly. Indeed, contemporaries were in no doubt that seaweed was essentially a quick-fix, one that could not sustain cropping for as long as animal manure. Significantly, it appears to have been associated with areas which practised a grass-arable rather than an infield-outfield system (Dodghson 1993, 637–8). It did not do much for phosphorus levels but it has as much nitrogen as similar quantities of manure.

The organic transfers provided by the hill or waste ground of townships – peat, peaty soil and turf – form an interesting group. For inland townships, such as those on either side of Lochtayside, these may have provided a more important source of nutrients than animal manure. An indication of how much nitrogen and phosphorus these different types of nutrient transfer may have contributed is provided by Figure 3 which uses the same sample of townships as Figure 2. As can be seen, on the basis of the amounts assumed to have been used, turf may have accounted for as much as 70 percent of the inputs of nitrogen and just under 45 percent of the inputs of phosphorus. Clearly, these are significant amounts. Indeed, for Lochtayside, turf may have provided more significant transfers of these vital nutrients than livestock manure. A word of warning though, of all the figures that went into these calculations, those for the amount of turf transferred were the most difficult to derive in the analysis. It was used as a major source of nutrient transfer in various ways. First, it was a foundation for roof thatch. In this form, we find it re-cycled on a regular basis. Second, it was widely used for building temporary enclosures for outfield tathfolds. Third, it was as a manurial transfer in a direct way. Eighteenth-century sources for the southern Highlands suggests that the aggregate amount of turf cut for these various uses was considerable. What is more, from bylaws enacted, it is clear that some townships faced acute problems because tenants cut turf on good or green pasture not just on hill ground. An act of 1685 prohibited the cutting of turf in parts of the eastern Highlands (APS, viii. 494–5). Indeed, one local farmer argued that the turf spade had done more damage than the Act of Union! (Cameron 1873, 298). In the Hebrides, one or two estates (eg. Seaforth estate) issued regulations against the cutting of turf on good land but the most telling indication of the potential damage done by the cutting of turf and peat is provided by the extent of skinned land. The damage done on Lewis was mapped for the West Highland Survey (Darling 1955, 272–8). As an input, the transfer of turf and peat clearly had an effect on soil nutrient status, but worked slowly. Turf especially, releases nutrients much more slowly than manure. Indeed, there is an ecological point in having turf locked into walls and dykes for some years, before composting it. Furthermore, its application in quantity leads to the gradual build up of organic matter or humus.

To judge from the figures available on yields, a third way in which nutrient flow could be favourably altered was by switching to more labour-intensive forms of cultivation. Using the spade and caschrom instead of the plough gave you a yield bonus. This was recognised by early commentators on the western Highlands and Islands. The spade gave an increase over the plough of about one-quarter and the caschrom an increase of one-third (Dodgshon 1992, 183). Where figures for returns on seed are available, they bear this out. Systematic data available for returns on seed in all the townships of Tiree during the mid-1760s, for instance, shows returns of 2.2 for oats and 3.5 for barley. By comparison, figures for Barrisdale – a far more marginal environment – suggest townships there had higher returns, about 5 (Dodgshon, 1993, 688–92). These differences can be explained partly by the fact that townships in the former mostly used ploughs whilst those in the latter – with only one exception – used the spade and caschrom. In fact, if the amount of nutrient inputted by manurial transfers and seed is set against that extracted as part of the harvested crop, it suggests that spade-based systems may have been the more efficient (Fig 4).

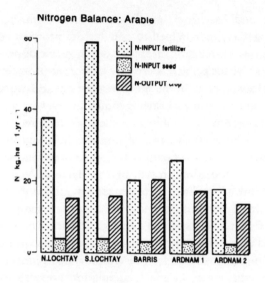

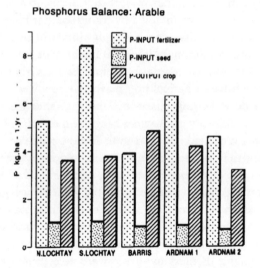

Figure 4 – Nitrogen and phosphorus balance (based on Dodgshon & Olsson 1988: 48).

My own view is that to see the use of hand tools as producing a more efficient mobilisation of nutrients is to see only part of the problem, since the spade and caschrom were labour intensive. So also was the transfer of manurial resources like peat, turf, seaweed and shell sand. I am inclined to see the problem in terms of a general strategy based on labour abundance, one that made use of both the spade and caschrom coupled with heavy transfers of manurial supplements. Together, they helped to counter the prospect of a Postan-type crisis in nutrient flow, turning the threat of a decline in yields per acre into one of increase. Of course, yields per acre were only part of the problem. There is a case for arguing that looked at from the point of view of subsistence as opposed to nutrient flow, Highland and Hebridean communities were in a no-win situation. Throwing labour at the problem on the scale required by the spade and caschrom, and by the extensive use of non-arable resources to supplement nutrient flow, probably led to a fall in yields per head so that when faced with a period of sustained population growth like the late eighteenth century, communities would probably have experienced greater not less pressure on subsistence. However, by raising yields per acre in a marginal way and by enabling cultivation to be extended out over difficult or marginal ground, including ground that could not be ploughed or cropped without considerable preparation, labour intensive techniques would have significantly dampened this pressure on subsistence. In effect, population pressure contained – to a degree – part of its own solution.

Once we see the problem in this way, then it opens up a further dimension. The sort of nutrient budget maintained by traditional farming would not have been a constant affair. Its character probably fluxed in step with population growth or decline and conditions of labour abundance or scarcity. When labour was scarce, we can expect standard manure-based systems, which, when coupled with plough-based agriculture, may have involved relatively modest levels of nutrient flow. During phases of labour abundance, though, we can expect two kinds of adjustment. A wider range of manures might be exploited and greater use might be made of hand-tools like the spade and caschrom. This would have meant that the flow of nutrients would have been increased and, arguably, the amount of nutrients extracted, or nutrient use efficiency, might have been increased, though probably at the expense of greater levels of environmental disturbance and, arguably, long-term sustainability. Clearly, this sort of fluxing runs counter to the Postan thesis. Instead of a nutrient flow trap that led communities into declining yields per acre, it supposes that communities in upland or marginal areas were able to adopt strategies that could lead to increased yields per acre in a Boserupian-like way (Boserup 1965). Indeed, it is now recognised that in parts of lowland Britain, some communities also worked to counter a Postan-type crisis over the late thirteenth and early fourteenth centuries by making use of new or more intensive strategies (Campbell 1983, 26–46).

It does not follow, though, that all areas found their way out of this nutrient flow trap. Even in the Highland and Islands, it is possible to find areas where a case for declining yields per acre might be made. For instance, Duncan Forbes of Culloden's report on Tiree (1737) made out a strong case for soil exhaustion and reduced yields on the island (Forbes of Culloden 1737). Certainly, when we look at the figures available, the yields on Tiree were low. In fact, they are comparable with the figures which Titow produced for southern England during the late thirteenth and early fourteenth centuries, when pressure on land is also thought to have produced a decline in yields (Titow 1972). In the context of the Highlands and Islands, though, Tiree was exceptional. It faced a dilemma which no other Hebridean or Highland area faced. The proportion of land cropped by 1768 was very high, that is, 50 percent or 8240 acres. If Tiree did face problems of poor yields caused by an insufficient flow of nutrients, then it was perhaps simply because too much land was suitable for cropping. This might have led it into a much deeper nutrient flow trap than other areas. The Duke may have complained about the supernumeries on the island (Cregeen 1964, vol. 1:1) but with so much arable, numbers may still not have been enough to intensify nutrient flows or techniques of cultivation in the way they were being intensified elsewhere in the Highlands by the mid-eighteenth century. But as the exception, Tiree may help prove the rule.

BIBLIOGRAPHY

APS. 1814–74. *Acts of Parliament of Scotland*, 12 volumes. Edinburgh

Bibby J S, Hudson G, Henderson D J. 1982. *Soil and Land Capability for Agriculture: Western Scotland*. Soil Survey of Scotland, Macaulay Institute for Soil Research, Aberdeen

Boserup E. 1965 *The Conditions of Agricultural Growth. The Economics of Agrarian Change under Population Growth*. Allen and Unwin, London

Cameron A C. 1873. On ancient farming customs in Scotland. *Trans. Highland and Agricultural Soc. Scotland*, 4th series, vol. V: 296–9

Campbell B M S. 1983 Agricultural progress in medieval England: some evidence from eastern Norfolk. *Economic History Rev.*, 2nd series, XXXV: 26–46

Chorley G P H. 1981. The agricultural revolution in northern Europe, 1750–1880: nitrogen, legumes and crop productivity *Economic History Review*, 34: 71–93

Cregeen E (ed.) 1964. *Argyll Estate Instructions (Mull, Morvern and Tiree) 1771–1805*, 2 vols. Scottish History Society, 4th series, Edinburgh

Darling F Fraser (ed.) 1955. *West Highland Survey. An Essay in Human Ecology*. Oxford University Press, Oxford

Dodgshon, R A. 1992. Farming practice in the western Highlands and Islands before crofting: a study in cultural inertia or opportunity costs? *Rural History* 3: 173–89

Dodgshon R A. 1993. Strategies of farming in the western Highlands and Islands prior to crofting and the clearances. *Economic History Review*, XLVI: 679–701

Dodgshon R A, Olsson E G. 1988. Productivity and nutrient use in eighteenth-century Scotland highland townships. *Geografiska Annaler,* 70B: 39–51

Fenton, A: 1986. *The Shape of the Past 2: Essays in Scottish Ethnology* J. Donald, Edinburgh

Forbes of Culloden D. 1884. Letter concerning the Duke of Argyll's Estates in Tiree, Morvern and Mull, 24th Sept, 1737. Reprinted 1884 in: *Report of the Commission of Inquiry in the Condition of the Crofters and Cottars in the Highlands and Islands* XXXII-XXXVI, appendix A: 389–92

Fox H S A. 1984. Some ecological dimensions of medieval field systems. In: Biddick K (ed.). *Archaeological Approaches to Medieval Europe.* Studies in Medieval Culture, XVIII. Medieval Institute, Western Michigan University, Kalamazoo: 119–58

Olsson, E G. 1988. Nutrient use and productivity for different cropping systems in South Sweden during the 18th Century. In: Birks H H, Birks J J B, Kaland P E, Moe D (eds.). *The Cultural Landscape: Past, Present and Future.* Cambridge University Press: Cambridge

Olsson E G A. 1991. Agro-ecosystems from the Neolithic time to the present. In: Berglund B (ed.). *The Cultural Landscape during 6000 years in Southern Sweden – the Ystad Project,* Ecological Bulletins no. 41, Munksgaard, Copenhagen

Postan M. 1972. *The Medieval Economy and Society. An Economic History of Britain 1100–1500.* Weidenfeld and Nicolson, London

Shiel, R S. 1991. Improving soil productivity in the pre-fertiliser era. In: Campbell B M S, Overton M (eds.). *Land, labour and Livestock, Historical Studies in European Agricultural Productivity.* Manchester University Press, Manchester

Titow J Z. 1972. *Winchester Yields. A Study in Medieval Agricultural Productivity.* Cambridge University Press, Cambridge

Cholera, 1832

Extracted from RJ Morris 1976 *Cholera, 1832: The Social Response to an Epidemic*, London (Croom Helm), 79–83.

Cholera killed some 32,000 people in Britain in 1831 and 1832. Of most of these people, no more was recorded than where and when they died. For some the local Board of Health Minute Book or a well-kept parish register contain a brief outline of the manner of their death and their state in life: 174 entries were carefully written into the records of the Oxford Board of Health.

> James Bristow, age 26, residence, Castle Gaol of Oxford, Criminal Prisoner in the Castle Gaol, seized 24 June at 10 p m., died 25 June at 4 p.m., buried in the Castle, his surgeon was Mr J.F. Wood.
>
> John Watts, age 42, he lodged at the Shoulder of Mutton in St Thomas's; his condition of life, a travelling mendicant drawn by four dogs, seized 30 June at 3 p. m., died 3 July at 11 a.m., buried in St Thomas's, his surgeon was Mr John Symonds.
>
> James Wright, age 35 of St Thomas's, a labourer, seized 6 July and died 8 July, buried in St Ebbe's, treated by Mr Dickeson.
>
> Adam Henderson Bowell, age 2¼, of Godfrey's Row, St Ebbe's, condition of life simply recorded as 'labourer', seized and died on the 6 July and buried in St Ebbe's.
>
> Elizabeth Bowell, age 11 months, again condition of life 'labourer', seized 7 July, died 7 July, buried St Ebbe's.

These short chronicles were followed by others, some children, some prisoners and mendicants on the fringes of society, most were labourers, craftsmen, or their wives.

The parish register of Leith in the County of Edinburgh was even more sparing in detail.

> John Jack, tidesman, age 60, buried 1st May at 5 a.m., died 29 April.
>
> Philadelphia Fortheringham, relict of tidesman, age 57, buried 2 May at 6 a.m., died on the 1st.

John Hercules, labourer, buried 12 May at 5 a.m., having died on the 10th.

These men and women were hurried to their graves at dawn by the anxious and fearful authorities of Leith.

The letters, returns and post-mortem reports of the correspondents of the Central Board of Health contain brief portraits of victims, where death and official attention has recorded the end of a life that otherwise would have attracted little notice. Most were wage-earners, labourers and craftsmen, like Rodenbury, 'the industrious shoemaker' of Sunderland who 'dined and supped on Pork, drank no fermented liquor, and went to bed well'. He awoke with terrifying vomiting and purging which 'filled several chamber pots' and was dead by afternoon. Others came from the fringes of society. They did not even have that claim on the national product which selling their labour might command. John Solomon, Providence Court, White's Yard, Rosemary Lane, a member of London's poor Jewish community, made his living picking coal and wood from the waterside until he died of cholera aged 50. In Newcastle, Ann Dennison died in December 1831; she 'has been debauched for some time and had an abortion a fortnight ago'. A prostitute from the Nungate was among the first to die in Haddington. She was a drunkard, blind and addicted to narcotics. Cholera also found many passive patient victims waiting in the poverty into which unemployment and casual labour had brought them. In late November, Dr Barry found two daughters in the cholera hospital at Sunderland. The mother and the other two children were sick at home, with no food, the one blanket given them two days before, and another child dead.

Not all victims came from the poor and working classes. Glasgow especially had been worried by its middle-class cases. At Rothesay, the first case was a 'respectable' person in 'comfortable circumstances' who lived by the Bridge, followed by the death of an old doctor, Dr Fyfe, but 'he was very intemperate and irregular in his habits'. The case of Mrs Haslewood, the wife of the Sunderland surgeon, showed the fortunes of a middle-class victim. She had attended the post-mortem of Rodenbury and Sproat on 1 November. She was, her husband reported, age 28 and in perfect health. She was seized at church with dreadful pains in the stomach, and carried home to a warm bed, where she was subjected to bleeding, opium and brandy followed by rhubarb and magnesia with beef tea and negus when the spasms ceased. Negus was a comforting drink of wine, warmed before the fire, and mixed with boiling water and lemon, with nutmeg and sugar to taste. Mrs Haslewood was then carefully nursed back to health. The rest of the family, including the baby, nine months old, remained well and sent their thanks to Dr Daun for his 'kindness and attention' in looking after Mrs Haslewood. The middle class was able to provide extra comfort and attention which scarcely concealed the pain of the disease or the haphazard, often savage nature, of the treatment offered.

There are few sources of objective information about the epidemic which indicate whether these sketches and portraits were typical of the 32,000 dead. The most complete records were made by the Central Board. Form 5, 'General Statistical Return' was sent out to local boards with each circular. The information on this form was collated by Sir William Pym at the end of the epidemic. He constructed a map which was deposited in the Royal Library at the wish of the King, though it no longer appears to be in that library. He also made a voluminous table or index, 'Cholera Returns in Great Britain', a copy of which is still in the Privy Council papers.

A few places did collect detailed statistics in a systematic manner. The initial question is a somewhat surprising one; was anyone in a real sense a victim of cholera? Did cholera cause extra deaths or just replace other, perhaps less painful, causes of death in the dangerous urban environments of 1832? At the time many claimed that cholera did not raise the death rate and observed that apart from cholera, 1832 was an exceptionally healthy period. The claim that cholera was a replacement cause of death rather than an extra cause of death is a difficult one to test because of the lack of firm national figures for cholera, and the lack of any overall figures at all for death rates. There was local evidence. Both Robert Cowan in Glasgow and James Stark in Edinburgh used the parish registers to provide information on the total deaths within the two cities, so that the figures are burial rates rather than true death rates. Cowan certainly included the burial of still-born children in his totals and these represent something like 2 per thousand in the burial rates given in Table 1. Stark's figures were consistently lower, suggesting that Edinburgh was the healthier city. This may have been true, but direct comparison between the cities is unwise on these figures, for Stark may well have excluded still-born burials and have been less thorough in his survey of the registers. Comparison between years within the same city is valid and shows clearly that cholera caused an increase in deaths and that there was no compensating fall in death rate after 1832. The rates rarely fell back to those of the 1820s and indeed in the typhus year of 1837 the death rate again approached that of 1832.

TABLE I: BURIAL RATES IN GLASGOW AND EDINBURGH, 1827–1837

		GLASGOW*	EDINBURGH*
Population 1831		202,420	139,123
Cholera Deaths 1832		3,174	1,159

YEAR	BURIALS	CRUDE BURIAL RATE	BURIALS	CRUDE BURIAL RATE
1827	5,136	28.5	3,347	25.9
1828	5,942	32.0	3,696	28.1
1829	5,452	28.5	3,164	23.6
1830	5,185	26.3	3,510	25.7
1831	6,547	32.3	3,664	26.3
1832	10,278	49.0	5,262	37.8
1833	6,632	30.6	4,312	30.9
1834	6,728	30.0	3,657	26.2
1835	7,849	34.0	3,543	25.4
1836	9,143	38.3	3,968	28.4
1837	10,886	44.3	5,009	35.8

* Data for Glasgow included the Gorbals and Barony areas.
Source: Robert Cowan, *Vital Statistics of Glasgow*, Glasgow, 1838, pp. 7 and 10; James Stark, *Inquiry into some points of the Sanitary State of Edinburgh*, Edinburgh, 1847, p.11.

Cholera not only added to deaths but also selected its victims from the age groups in a manner different from the normal causes of death. Cleland's careful statistical work provided the age structure of Glasgow's population in 1831, which the official census does not, and age-specific burial figures for 1830 and 1832, including overall totals and cholera figures. These figures have been converted into age-specific burial rates (Table 2). The pattern of death in a normal year had two characteristic features. There were massive casualties among children under five. The rate was even higher among the youngest of this group. Once past the age of five, life became relatively safer until the fifties age group, when deaths again rose above the average. The cholera pattern was different. Children were relatively safe, teenagers even safer. For adults the chance of death from cholera rose much more rapidly than the risk of death from other causes. Thus the 'extra' deaths which were caused by cholera were principally among the middle-aged. The bulk of the normal death toll consisted of young children. Whilst it would be wrong to underestimate the suffering and sadness left in the vast majority of families by child deaths, these deaths nevertheless did the minimum of social and economic damage to the family, if only because most families were organised to produce large numbers of children, and so ensure that some remained to reach adulthood. Cholera added to deaths among age groups for which the family had no such compensation. Many victims had families dependent on them for economic and emotional support. When they died, the widows and orphans were left as an extra charge on the Poor Law, and the children suffered all the disruption of a broken home, not by the breakdown of marriage, but by premature death.

TABLE 2: IMPACT OF CHOLERA ON THE POPULATION OF GLASGOW, 1832: AGE STRUCTURE

AGE IN YEARS	POPULATION 1831[a]	BURIALS 1830[b]	AGE-SPECIFIC BURIAL RATES PER 1000 1830[c]	CHOLERA BURIALS 1832[d]	AGE-SPECIFIC BURIAL RATES PER 1000 FROM CHOLERA IN 1832[e]
Under 5	30,277	2,000	66.06	130	4.29
5–10	25,707	253	9.84	106	4.12
10–20	41,956	276	6.57	132	3.14
20–30	38,185	334	8.74	358	9.37
30–40	26,419	313	11.84	529	20.02
40–50	18,014	348	19.31	639	35.47
50–60	11,648	352	30.21	556	47.73
60–70	6,920	339	48.98	444	64.16
Over 70	3,300	499	151.21	272	82.42
Total	202,426	5,185*	25.61	3,166	15.64

*(total includes 471 still-born)

Sources:
a. and b., J. Cleland, *Enumeration of the Inhabitants of the City of Glasgow*, Glasgow, 1832, p.11.
c. Calculated from a. and b. Hence liable to be underestimated.
d. J. Cleland and J. Carbindale, 'Conspectus of Cholera in Glasgow . . .', *E.M.S.J.*, vol. 39, 1833, pp. 500–6.
e. Calculated from a. and d., hence liable to be overestimated.

Malaria

Extracted from T Kjaergaard 1994 *The Danish Revolution,
1500–1800, an Ecohistorical Interpretation,* Cambridge
(Cambridge University Press), 182–5.

MALARIA

Malaria, which today is known only outside Europe, was one of the most
prominent diseases in the ecological system prevailing in Denmark prior to the
period of major changes. Malaria was common during the Middle Ages and the
Renaissance; Christiern Pedersen, in his book of medicine of 1533, describes in
detail daily, three-day, and four-day variants of the disease, and so does Henrik
Smith in his manual of medicine of 1577. In the latter work mention is also
made of a malaria epidemic in 1556, the earliest instance in Denmark about
which we have any information.[1]

In F. V. Mansa's account of the history of common diseases in Denmark
until the beginning of the eighteenth century, mention is made of malaria
epidemics in 1629, 1652, 1678, and 1680. In addition, several of the fever
epidemics placed by Mansa in the typhus class may well have been malaria,
because during the outbreak phase the symptoms of both diseases bear a certain
similarity, especially high fever and the shivers.[2] Malaria occurred all over
Denmark, though with a certain preponderance in low-lying regions, primarily
Lolland, which is why malaria is also sometimes referred to in Denmark as
'Lolland fever'.[3] Like plague, malaria was unable to resist the changes brought
about by the ecological revolution.

In order to understand this it is necessary to know the main characteristics
in the epidemiology of malaria.[4] The malaria parasite, *Plasmodium*, is introduced into human beings by stings from infected malaria mosquitoes of the
genus *Anopheles*, of which the species *A. atroparvus* is the most important in
Denmark and throughout most of Western and Central Europe – apart from
Italy. The sting of the malaria mosquito introduces the plasmodia into the
blood. After propagation in the liver the parasites return to the blood, whereupon they attack the red blood corpuscles and develop explosively in an asexual
series of propagation.

A remarkable characteristic of *Plasmodium* parasites is that, according to
the type in question, they develop in a regular cycle, as a rule lasting two or three

days. When a cycle is over, all the parasites simultaneously attack new red blood corpuscles instead of the old, destroyed ones, which are now abandoned. During an attack of this kind the number of red blood corpuscles in the body is violently decimated. The result is one of the periodic attacks of acute fever preceded by shivers that gave rise to the disease's former name, ague. When the invasion of the red blood corpuscles is over, the newly placed *Plasmodium* parasites leave the body in peace; the attack of fever ceases, reproduction of red blood corpuscles can recommence, and the patient feels well until the next attack comes.

If the patient does not die and the disease is not renewed by new stings, it will gradually burn itself out, because the malaria parasite's asexual propagation has a limited course. To conclude its life cycle the parasite has to return to the malaria mosquito. A number of the parasites develop into sexed forms (male and female gametocytes), which the malaria mosquito sucks up when it stings a malaria-infected person. Not until the plasmodia have been brought back to the malaria mosquito can sexual propagation take place, and new parasites be formed, in the malaria mosquito, which, through infecting human beings, can keep the disease going.

The weak link in the life cycle of the malaria parasite is its dependence upon the malaria mosquito, not only for it to be transferred to a human being but also, through renewed stings, for it to be brought back to the malaria mosquito. Observations made by the Danish zoologist C. Wesenberg-Lund and others have shown that certain malaria mosquitoes perform this role unwillingly. This applies, for example, precisely to *A. atroparvus*, the most wide-spread malaria mosquito in Denmark. *A. atroparvus* is zoophile and prefers to sting cattle and other domestic animals rather than human beings. The opportunities for its doing so increased during the last half of the eighteenth century, when the green revolution brought about a pronounced increase in the number of herds of domestic animals in Denmark. This proved fatal to the malaria parasite because cattle do not develop malaria, and the parasite's life cycle was therefore severed.[5]

The results of this decline in malaria gradually become visible. In 1776 Peder Rhode referred to malaria as still the most frequent disease on the islands of Lolland and Falster:

> Their [the inhabitants'] most common disease is fever (which both strangers to, and natives of these parts seldom escape), of all kinds, somewhat severe, but not dangerous and seldom lethal; the three-day kind usually keeps recurring for a year or two: I have fought with it for a year-and-a-half, and finally cured it with digestive powders and there-after prepared quinine.[6]

During the years 1815–24 malaria is referred to as having disappeared from the county of Maribo on the island of Lolland,[7] though it had not done so entirely. During the following years it flared up from time to time, and even in the 1860s there were still four to five thousand cases, a considerable number of them in Lolland. However, attacks became increasingly milder, and by the turn of the century malaria virtually was no longer part of the Danish disease pattern.[8]

There would appear to be no doubt that the green revolution, which decade by decade from the latter half of the eighteenth century increased the numbers of domestic animals in Denmark, was responsible for the withdrawal of malaria. Whenever animals were kept in stalls, as was the case wherever summer stall feeding was introduced, the effect was particularly beneficial, because zoophile malaria mosquitoes collect in stalls. Not until late in the nineteenth century, by which time the disease had long since been on the retreat, did medical treatment of malaria with quinine, and later, after the Second World War, with chloroquine, become common.[9]

The popular notion that malaria is expelled by drainage, which destroys the breeding grounds of the malaria mosquito, does not apply to Denmark, where the malaria mosquito is still to be found in large numbers, especially in cowhouses. As Wesenberg-Lund expressed it, 'there cannot be many cowstalls that do not have sufficient anopheline material with which to furnish the inhabitants of the farm with malaria'.[10] Water level control was a central phase in the green revolution, and therefore there was a connection between drainage operations and the disappearance of malaria, but in Denmark it was indirect.

NOTES

1 Vilhelm Møller-Christensen (1959) Feber. *Kulturhistorisk leksikon for nordisk middelalder*; Christiern Pedersen (1533) *Christiern Pedersen's Lægebog* (facsimile ed. with an introduction by Poul Hauberg, 1933), pp. 77r-78v; Henrick Smid (1577) *Lægebog*, I, pp. 162v-175v. Cf. Paul Horstmann (1986) Malariaens forsvinden fra Danmark. *Bibliotek for læger*, CLXXVIII , p.70.

2 F. V. Mansa (1873) *Pesten i Helsingør og Kiøbenhavn 1710 og 1711*, pp. 297, 384–5, 476, 478–9.

3 Poul Horstmann (1986) pp. 76–7.

4 The following is based on L. J. Bruce-Chwatt (1985) *Essential Malariology*, pp. 12–165 and passim.

5 L. J. Bruce-Chwatt and J. de Zulueta (1980) *The Rise and Fall of Malaria in Europe: A Historico-epidemiological Study*, p. 25; cf. p. 118; C. Wesenberg-Lund (1921) Undersøgelser over danske Malariamyg og dansk Malaria. *Nordisk hygieinisk tidsskrift*, II, pp. 237–9. Cf. Søren Mørch (1982) *Den ny Danmarkshistorie 1880–1960*, pp. 185–6 and Poul Horstmann (1986), pp. 86–7.

6 P. Rhode (1776–94) *Samlinger til de Danske Øers Laalands og Falsters Historie*, I, p. 12. Cf Christian B. Reventlow (1902–3) *En dansk Statsmands Hjem omkr. Aar 1800*, I, p. 89.

7 A.F. Bremer (1848) Om Koldfeber-Epidemierne i Danmark i Aarene 1825–34. *Det kongelige medicinske Selskabs Skrifter*, new series, 1, p. 129.

8 Paul Horstmann (1986), pp. 74–7, 80–2.

9 C. Wesenberg-Lund (1921). On the subject of medicine, especially the significance of quinine; C. Wesenberg-Lund (1921), p. 236; Svend Heinild (1979) *Sygdomsmønstrets ændring gennem 100 år*, p. 16 and 1989a; Jens Larsen (I) (1977) Myggestik. *Skalk*, no. 3., p. 26. Views differing in some respects from these are in Poul Horstmann (1986), pp. 89–92. On malaria's simultaneous withdrawal from England and the rest of northwest Europe: William McNeill (1977) *Plagues and Peoples*, pp. 246–7.

10 C. Wesenberg-Lund (1921), p. 236. Cf. Jens Larsen (I) (1977), pp. 25–6.

Critical Extracts

ARTICLE 22A:

From D Daiches 1964 *The Paradox of Scottish Culture,* Oxford (Oxford University Press), 27–8.

Ramsay was indeed a mixed and confused character . . . Isaac Bickerstaff and Gavin Douglas; a gentleman of the Augustan Age and an ardent Scottish patriot; an admirer of Pope and Gay and Matthew Prior and a devoted champion of the older Scottish makars and of the use of vernacular Scots by contemporary Scottish poets; a seeker after polish and good breeding and a vulgar little gossip whose schoolboy snigger spoils many of his poems and songs; a sentimental Jacobite and a prudent citizen who cannily absented himself from Edinburgh when Prince Charlie held court in Holyrood in 1745; a champion of Scottish folk-song and a wrecker of scores of such songs by turning them into stilted would-be neo-classic effusions – the dualism in Ramsay's life and character was deep-seated and corresponded to a dualism in the Scottish culture of his day. He could defend the coarsest and frankest language in poetry and yet dress up a Scottish song in intolerable false elegancies. At the same time he could demonstrate that he possessed the Horatian elegance of the English gentleman by rendering Horace's, 'Vides ut alta stet nive candidum' in vivid and homely Scots verse.[1]

NOTES

1 'Eighteenth-Century Vernacular Poetry', by David Daiches, in *Scottish Poetry: A Critical Survey*, edited by James Kinsley (London, 1955).

ARTICLE 22B

From H Ouston 1987 'Cultural Life from the Restoration to the Union', *in* Andrew Hook (ed), *The History of Scottish Literature II,* Aberdeen (Aberdeen University Press), 28–30.

In the 1690s Jacobite Virtuosi such as Pitcairne and Sibbald remained influential. Pitcairne's example inspired both printers and the members of Ramsay's Easy Club, and Sibbald maintained a wide correspondence even though nothing came of his Royal Society of Scotland, the list of whose potential members included few Whigs. In the 1690s the medical, legal and academic institutions of Scotland retained a Jacobite bias. However the Jacobite tradition was probably too conservative in intellectual terms to survive, even if it had retained a political power base. Its lasting influence was worked out through institutional organisation among the professions, and individual example and patronage. After the 1702 Act of Indemnity, though the years of severe Presbyterian reaction were over, Jacobite intellectual influence became fragmented. Though men such as the Virtuoso politician the Earl of Cromarty and David Gregory worked with the government, the greatest official intellectual innovation of the early eighteenth century, the reorganisation of Edinburgh University, was the work of the Whig Carstares. By the time of the Union, moreover, the terms of reference of the debate had changed from those of 1660–1700, the Episcopalian Sibbald for example being firmly Unionist and the nationalist Fletcher firmly Presbyterian.

The tensions and uncertainties over Scotland's future between 1688 and 1707 produced an unprecedented maturity of political life. A tradition of historiography or of memoirs or diaries had not existed previously, and political writing had been taken up with ecclesiastical issues, or their political implications . . . the standard of secular, public political argument was raised by the development around 1700 of parties, newspapers, clubs and oratory, all applied to issues relating to the Union.

Two leading writers in favour of the Union came from pre-Revolution Virtuoso backgrounds: William Seton of Pitmedden and the Earl of Cromarty, formerly Viscount Tarbat. But the outstanding political writer of the pre-Union period was its most famous opponent, Andrew Fletcher of Saltoun. His political discourses of 1698 discussed economic and social issues, and put forward his plan for national regeneration through a militia, which would teach moral and intellectual improvement to help protect Scottish liberty. These ideas can be compared to contemporary Presbyterian ambitions expressed in the societies for the reformation of manners, with which Defoe became involved on his visit to Scotland in 1705, in the Visitation of the Universities, and in the 1696 Education Act which, though of no immediate impact, was the first to suggest ways of financing the Reformation ideal of a school in every parish. Such patriotic intellectual ideals were very different from those of the Jacobite Virtuosi with their emphasis on aristocratic and professional cultural obligations.

Both Presbyterian and Jacobite however helped to provide Scotland with a cultural identity which allows George Davie to describe the Union as 'unity in politics combined with a diversity in what may be called social ethics', where there was a 'distinctive life of the country not in its religion alone but in the mutual interaction of religion, law and education.'[1] The Presbyterian church and education system were preserved in the Act for Securing the Protestant Religion, 1706. Articles XVIII and XIX of the Act of Union itself allowed for the Scottish law and courts to continue in most areas. The survival of these professions has been described as 'recognition of the sources of political power in Scotland',[2] but that power in fact had lain largely in the old parliament, which was incorporated. The distinctive identity which allowed the Scottish professions to survive the Union lay rather in their recently developed intellectual institutions and cultural role. Hence those areas of public life that were left untouched by the Union guaranteed the continued independence of Scottish culture. In the long term the Union meant increased prestige and authority for the Scottish professional classes, and in so far as these classes provided the social and cultural context out of which the Scottish Enlightenment emerged, they eventually allowed Scotland the kind of cultural 'union' of equals which Fletcher had wanted politically.

NOTES

1 G E Davie, *The Democratic Intellect* (Edinburgh, 1961) p xiv
2 P H Scott, *The Union of Scotland and England* (Edinburgh, 1979) p 53

ARTICLE 22C

From T Nairn 1977 *The Break-Up of Britain*, London (NLB), 139–40.

. . . Scottish civil society advanced much farther than had been imagined possible under its foreign monarchy and State. Its dominant class had sacrificed statehood for participation in the English and colonial 'common-market' of the day, trusting that this would aid the diffusion of Polite Society in their tenebrous land. In fact, society 'took off' beneath their feet, towards a revolutionary condition of industrialization. Within the larger economic area they had entered, they had created an autonomous sub-system – in effect, an epicentre now borne along upon the grander tide of English imperial expansion. They had entered its flow at a moment when, still in formation, it could tolerate the existence of such a sub-system. Hence they were neither crushed by it, nor compelled into nationalist reaction against it – the standard fates which, one can be certain, they would not have escaped if the Union had been delayed until the end of the 18th century.

As part of this advance, there occurred a significant florescence of Scottish national culture. In comparison with the theocratic gloom of the 17th century, this appeared strange even to some of its protagonists. In a very celebrated letter, David Hume asked: 'Is it not strange that, at a time when we have lost our Princes, our Parliaments, our independent Government, even the Presence of our chief Nobility, are unhappy, in our Accent & Pronunciation, speak a very corrupt Dialect of the Tongue which we make use of; is it not strange, I say, that, in these Circumstances, we shou'd really be the People most distinguished for Literature in Europe?'[1] The question has been posed and re-posed ever since. It has deeply vexed nationalists, in particular, that the most illustrious phase of our cultural history should have been so strikingly non-national*ist* – so detached from the People, so intellectual and so universalizing in its assumptions, so Olympian in its attitudes. This vexation is understandable, yet misplaced. The Edinburgh *philosophes* were neither traitors to their country – as that country then was, and as they perceived it – nor cosmopolitan poseurs. They simply belonged to a unique, pre-nationalist stage of socio-economic expansion. Concentrated in such a small area and time, in a land transported by so incredibly quickly out of Barbarity into Civility, they were the chief exemplars of the European Enlightenment's vision of Progress. That is, of a vision of development which was everywhere discredited and made impossible, after 1800.

NOTES

1 David Hume, letter to Gilbert Elliot, 1757, in J.Y.T. Greig (ed) *The Letters of David Hume* (1932), vol. I, p. 235. For the background to the letter, see E.C. Mossner's *The life of David Hume* (1954), ch 27, 'Scotland's Augustans'. Mossner maintains that Hume was 'certainly overstating the case for Scottish Literature', *ibid.*, p. 389, but is there any overstatement in saying that no other region of Europe comparable in population, size, and previous history was more 'distinguish'd for Literature' at this period? A contemporary list of the 'many Men of Genius this Country produces' is given in T.C. Smout's *A History of the Scottish People 1560–1830* (1969): 'Hume, Smith, Burns, Black, Watt, Telford, Robert Adam and Hutton in the first rank, Ferguson, Millar, Reid, Robertson, Allan Ramsay junior, Raeburn, William Adam, Rennie, Boswell and Hogg in the second, and a third rank crowded with talent . . .' (p. 470).

ARTICLE 22D

From K Simpson 1988 *The Protean Scot*, Aberdeen (Aberdeen University Press), 77–9.

The tension between individuality and authority which underlies so much of Scottish literature since 1707 gained force from the criteria of the *literati*. It is understandable that educated Scottish society should have been concerned to resolve as soon as possible the problems of cultural identity which it was experiencing, and which it had helped create, by becoming acceptable to English eyes in terms of polite literature. The intention of the members of the Select Society was 'by practice to improve themselves in reasoning and eloquence, and by the freedom of debate, to discover the most effectual methods of promoting the good of the country'.[1] In the belief that 'gentlemen educated in Scotland have long been sensible of the disadvantages under which they labour, from their imperfect knowledge of the ENGLISH tongue, and the impropriety with which they speak it',[2] the Select Society sought instruction in the proper reading and speaking of English. The man for the hour was Thomas Sheridan, father of the dramatist, and – a nice irony – an Irishman . . . Under the aegis of the Select Society, Sheridan gave lectures in Edinburgh in the summer of 1761 on Elocution and The English Tongue. All of this amounted, undeniably, to a manifestation of the practical spirit of the Scottish Enlightenment, a spirit which proved so beneficial in many other fields. The concern of the *literati* was entirely genuine, and they believed they were acting with the best interests of Scotland at heart. But in terms of imaginative literature the effect of their actions was to accelerate the disjunction from the older Scottish tradition.

It would be superfluous to labour the point already made in various studies of the period – that the desire for recognition as the equals of the English led the *literati* to neglect the Gaelic revival and the lowland vernacular tradition (and in particular the ballads, in which the embryonic Romantic spirit was soon to show an interest), and instead to enthuse over the spurious 'Celtic' literature. Suffice it to note that the programme of the *literati* lent strength to the division between popular and polite literature in Scotland. There has been a tendency among some writers on the period to overstress the contribution of the *literati* and to suggest that they were almost entirely responsible for this cultural dichotomy . . . it is [however] undeniable that the values of the *literati* did hasten a process of cultural polarisation that was already under way. And a further effect was to encourage an emphasis in Scottish education (which endures to this day) on the written rather than the spoken. Possibly it was dissatisfaction with the Scottish accent that led to the suppression of spoken activity in the Scottish classroom. The overall result was that individuality became subjugated to grammatical and rhetorical regularity.

Another important aspect of their cultural programme was the concern of the *literati* with the cultivation of taste. The concept of Taste came to occupy European thinkers of the eighteenth century as the effects of the growth of empiricism came to be felt. If one had to experience things for oneself by what standards was one's experience to be evaluated? Were such standards relative purely to the individual, or could any general criteria be identified? Such questions were not confined to Scotland, of course, but they were asked with a frequency and an urgency which resulted directly from the wish to match the English as writers and critics and the concomitant need for standards.

NOTES

1 *The Scots Magazine* XVII (March 1755), 126.
2 'Regulations' published by the Select Society for promoting the reading and speaking of the English language in Scotland', cited E C Mossner, *The Life of David Hume* (London, 1954), p. 372.

ARTICLE 22E

From C McGuirk 1987 'Scottish Hero, Scottish Victim: Myths of Robert Burns', *in* A Hook (ed), *History of Scottish Literature, Vol II*, Aberdeen (Aberdeen University Press), 236.

Ralph Waldo Emerson seemed to take note of Burns's eclectic achievement – and to point the way out of myth – in 1859, when he stressed the power, specifically, of his *language*: '[Burns's is] the only example in the history of a language made classic by the genius of a single man' (Low, p 435). This genius who brought 'Scotland' to the world at large is no merely local hero: his vision began at home, but carried 'home' into universal territory. Burns's 'Scotland' seems classic, coherent, and mythic to us precisely because he fashioned it out of diverse and classic literary elements, both traditionally Scottish and English. Like other eighteenth-century vernacular writers, Burns aligned himself with Scotland's continuing cultural difference by emphasizing it even in his vocabulary. But Robert Burns, unlike Robert Fergusson, his only real peer among eighteenth-century vernacular writers, chose dialect not only to assert the substantiality and validity of his Scottish world but also to disseminate it abroad: not so much to reflect Scotland as to evoke it. It was no naive farmer or helpless victim of ungovernable energies who managed this splendid and notably coherent achievement.

When Burns chose to blend English with Scottish dialect in his poems and songs, he was not employing a traditional language. Except for the continuing traditions of bawdry and comic elegy, Scots had died out as a literary language by the Union of 1707 – a casualty of the desertion of Edinburgh by James VI's and I's court and the repression of poetry and secular song by the Scottish church throughout the seventeenth century. All vernacular poetry in Burns's century was self-consciously crafted, and in deciding the appropriate ratio of Scots to English in every poem he wrote, Burns was making a self-conscious choice. If the marvelous blend in his language of real and ideal, scene-setting and scene-transfiguration, cooperated in the almost immediate foundation of myths, let us at least acknowledge that the myths did not exist before the *words* did. Burns's enterprise is not unparalleled (Ramsay, Fergusson, and many lesser eighteenth-century vernacular poets preceded him), but Burns is unparalleled in the broad success of his Scots/English mixture, which conveys vivid images of Scotland even to those who will never 'see' any Scotland but the poetic re-vision Burns renders in his burlesque or idealized landscapes.

Nonetheless, the notion persists that this distinctive synthesis in Burns's best work of dialect Scots, anglo-Scottish sentiment, and neoclassical English somehow make him a *poseur*, rather than an ironist or an artist. Perhaps it is a tribute to the vigour of Burns's projected and self-consciously synthesized 'views' of Scotland and the Scots that the closer scrutiny which dissipates the myth and reveals Burns's art disappoints us. We want him to be a camera, not a poet; we want his 'Scotland' to be real.

NOTES

Donald A Low (ed), *Robert Burns: The Critical Heritage* (London, 1974).

ARTICLE 22F

From A Noble 1985 'Urbane Silence: Scottish Writing and the Nineteenth-Century City', in G Gordon (ed), *Perspectives of the Scottish City,* Aberdeen (Aberdeen University Press), 78.

In enlightened Edinburgh there was a mixture of ancestral fear combined with contemporary condescension to the Highlander. It was assumed that the distinction between Highland and Lowland was a movement from barbarism to civilisation. Scott unthinkingly inherited this attitude. It combined with his fear of the fact that society might 'retrogade towards the brutal violence of primitive hostility'. In direct proportion to his fear of violence breaking out in his own society, Scott's fiction displays an increasing need to stress the terror of *regressive* violence. In *Waverley* the insurrectionary Highland anti-hero is finally, safely framed in a pleasingly nostalgic portrait. By the time of *Redgauntlet* the book pulses with a Gothic, diabolic clamour of Jacobite danger so that its menacing language is ludicrously contradicted by its plot when a Hanoverian *deus ex machina* steps in to resolve the near hysterical political terrors.

What lies behind such artistic confusion? Obsessed with the possibility of violent insurrection – an attitude based on a profoundly unreal analysis of the actual nature of Scottish society – Scott retreated from facing the elements tending toward violence in his own society to projecting violence backwards into the past and the Highlands. Thus instead of the complex analysis of the disturbing present as a product of history as we find in Scott's contemporary, Stendhal, we are given a kind of simplistic anthropology. The archetypal pattern of the Scott novel is of an immature hero who crosses a geographical boundary, the Highland line, to be brought face to face with real and not fantasy violence. Suitably chastened he happily retreats into marriage, inheritance and the allegedly safe creature comforts of the socially secure man of the new world. Fearing Jacobinism, Scott seized on Jacobitism as a safe surrogate enemy. The Highlander became a kind of ritual scapegoat. It was not, however, this kind of ancestral violence that really troubled Scott but the violence of harsh industrial and agricultural change.

ARTICLE 22G

From E Muir 1936 *Scott and Scotland,* London (Routledge), 144–6.

He was by instinct a Conservative who believed in the established order and tradition. But the phase which Scotland had reached in his time involved him in a divided allegiance. The established order was the Union, and possessing, as he did, 'a mind in a high degree concrete and practical', prepared 'to take arms against a proven abuse but not against a dubious theory,' he had no choice but to adhere to it; for it was rooted in history and sanctified by the past. But at the same time he saw this established order gradually destroying another established order, that of Scotland. That order was equally old, equally rooted in history and sanctified by the past, and moreover it was the order to which he was most intimately bound by birth, early memory and the compulsion of his imagination. From this inward conflict he never escaped. It is the underlying theme of his three greatest novels, *Old Mortality*, *The Heart of Midlothian*, and *Redgauntlet*; and it is deeply entangled with all his stories of Scottish life except the more purely contemporary and local ones such as *Guy Mannering*. We find it in his two romances about Mary Stuart; it recurs in *Waverley* and again in *Rob Roy*. In all these novels, directly or indirectly, Scott is working out his conflicting allegiances to Scotland and England. But as that conflict was a thing of the past, and its solution had already been reached in the established order of the Union, his treatment of it was inevitably a little romantic in the bad sense; the main figure, the hero, is never seriously involved in the calamities of his country; the actual theme may be a national disaster, but to him it becomes as harmless as an escapade: an excuse, at most, for a set of exciting adventures, crammed with fights and escapes.

ARTICLE 22H

From D Gifford 1988 'Myth, Parody and Dissociation: Scottish Fiction, 1814–1914', *in* D Gifford (ed), *History of Scottish Literature Vol III*, Aberdeen (Aberdeen University Press), 219.

In *Waverley* (1814), Scott took the first steps in fashioning an entirely new apparatus for the novel form which would allow him to express his unique vision of Scottish history. Scott's new use of history has been recognised; not so well recognised is the fact that he casts Edward Waverley's psychology in the mould of Harley's, as excessively imaginative, hyper-sensitive, disordered and self-indulgent. But where Harley was unbelievable other than as literary artefact, Waverley has to be a credible witness to the struggle for Scotland's soul. But Waverley is no mythic hero, rather the insipid pseudo-hero, rescued rather than rescuing. To this extent, his place is with the dreamers and failures of the . . . parodic tradition of Scottish fiction. The novel's importance for the mythic tradition is that it sets up the historical canvas of Scotland and places an anachronistic picaresque hero where later the mythic protagonist will stand. But *Waverley* also introduces a use of physical and landscape setting, together with first examples of that great, atmospheric symbolism which is so much the essence of the Scott-influenced novel from the Brontës to Melville. The eighteenth-century novel's pasteboard settings, coach journeys and inns, are transformed in *Waverley* to blue mountains and ravines which are symbolic barriers in Waverley's imagination as well as borders to the Highlands.

ARTICLE 221

From FR Hart 1978 *The Scottish Novel: From Smollett to Spark,* London (John Murray), 9–10. Copyright © the President and Fellows of Harvard College, reprinted by permission of Harvard University Press.

Scott's task came a generation later than Mackenzie's fiction, and Mackenzie found the form uncongenial. The question of why, in the 1770s, he did not become the first Scottish novelist in the mode of Scott, Galt, or Lockhart is actually two questions: Why did he not think to record Scottish manners? And why did he give up the novel to work in shorter narrative forms? The questions relate to Mackenzie himself, but also to the novel's late arrival in Scotland.

Ian Watt and others have associated the rise of the novel in England with early eighteenth-century socioeconomic individualism, with the new psychologism of John Locke and other empiricists, with the secularizing of spiritual autobiography, with the decorums of a newly affluent bourgeoisie and the providential optimisms of a new religious liberalism.[1] The novel in Scotland arose almost a century later in extremely different circumstances, the complex milieu of the late Enlightenment. This was a time of pioneering sociological thought, a seedtime of speculative interest in man's societal evolution not from a hypothetical contract but from primitive social impulses.[2] For some this distinctive sociological emphasis is a reassertion of the societal emphasis in Calvin. For the social historian T. C. Smout it proves the inapplicability to Scotland of the Weber-Tawney thesis that a close connection existed between Calvinism and the rise of economic individualism – a thesis crucial to recent theories of the English novel. In Scotland, says Smout, 'the ethic of the kirk-session, with its strong group discipline over moral behaviour fitted in . . . perfectly with the tradition of the guild and the burgh with their group discipline over civic and economic behaviour.'[3] Scotland's neo-Calvinism in this period stressed the communal over the individual.

The late Enlightenment was a time of of incredibly rapid socioeconomic change, 'Scotland,' notes Mitchison, 'packed into about thirty years . . . the economic growth that in England had spread itself over three centuries.'[4] Until Neilson's 'hot blast' of 1828, the change was predominantly agrarian – and this is of momentous import for the forming of Scottish traditions in the novel. It was in the countryside that the shock was felt, in the glens that the terrible Clearances occurred in the name of improvement and progress, exploiting and shattering ancient fidelities. But this was a time, too, of burgh reform, exceeding in importance for Scotland the later 1832 reform of a remote British parliament.

NOTES

1 Ian Watt, *The Rise of the Novel* (London: Chatto and Windus, 1957); G.A. Starr, *Defoe and Spiritual Autobiography* (Princeton: Princeton University Press, 1965); Kenneth MacLean, *John Locke and English Literature of the Eighteenth Century* (New Haven: Yale University Press, 1936).

2 Gladys Bryson, *Man and Society* (Princeton: Princeton University Press, 1945); Louis Schneider, ed., *The Scottish Moralists* (Chicago: Phoenix, 1967); 'The Athenian Age', in G.S. Pryde, *Scotland from 1603 to the Present Day* (London: Nelson, 1962).

3 T.C. Smout, *A History of the Scottish People 1560–1830* (New York: Scribner's, 1969), p. 95.

4 Rosalind Mitchison, *A History of Scotland* (London: Methuen, 1970), p. 345.

Education and the state in nineteenth-century Scotland

Extracted from R D Anderson 1983 in *Economic History Review* 36, 518–34.

... The conventional contrast between *laissez-faire* and state intervention is unhelpful when applied to education if it is taken to mean that the alternative to state intervention was the operation of market forces. Economic theory played practically no part in contemporary educational debates, which were notoriously dominated by questions of religion and Church-state relations. Whereas in England state intervention grew more or less continuously from nothing, in Scotland the parish schools already existed as the basis of a 'public' system and as a model for future development. In providing the parish schools Church and state were partners: churchmen saw it as the duty of a Christian state to provide for the intellectual as well as the spiritual welfare of the people, while from the secular point of view the parochial machinery was a convenient means (as with the poor law) for discharging a public obligation without resorting to a centralized bureaucracy. From the 1830s onwards, the nature of this partnership in the face of new educational needs was a controversial question, and one immensely complicated by the Disruption of 1843, which meant that the Church of Scotland could no longer speak for a majority of the nation ...

The parish schools were established by statute and financed by an assessment on land levied by the heritors, the principal landowners in each parish. Out of this the schoolmaster was provided with a schoolhouse and a fixed salary, though this formed only part of his total income, which was made up from the fees paid by parents. This permanent 'endowment' of the schoolmaster was seen as the strong point of the system. Its weak point was that normally each parish had only one statutory school, so that the legal provision was inadequate in the huge parishes of the Highlands and swamped by population growth in the industrializing areas. Moreover, the legislation did not apply at all to burghs, which had 'burgh schools' maintained by the town councils. In small towns these were very like parish schools, but in larger ones they acted as secondary schools for the middle classes, for whose education, therefore, Scotland had a tradition of public support. Occasionally town councils opened extra schools, or gave subsidies to private teachers, but they were not obliged to maintain more than one school, nor did they have rating powers for education. Public provision of elementary education in the towns was therefore impracticable, and it was there, and in lowland parishes which were becoming urbanized, that private adventure schools flourished, catering at different fee levels for different social classes.

In the countryside it seems to have been relatively uncommon for private schools to compete directly with the parish schools. Descriptive accounts throughout the early nineteenth century suggest that rural private schools were of two main types: small schools run by women, who took younger children or taught sewing to girls; and 'subscription' schools, where parents in the more distant parts of the parish clubbed together to pay a teacher's salary. The level of teaching was often modest, with the school opening only in the winter and employing a succession of young men passing through in search of a better post. Able private teachers certainly did exist in rural areas, but there was always a tendency to invest the parish school with more prestige and to regard it as an 'upper seminary' into which private schools might feed their more ambitious pupils.[1]

The efforts of the Church to supplement the parochial system were at first directed to the Highlands, where its defects were very marked and where poverty made private teaching unfruitful. Many schools were run by the Scottish Society for Propagating Christian Knowledge and by smaller philanthropic societies, and after 1824 the Church directly maintained a number of 'General Assembly' schools. Later, the General Assembly scheme was extended to the lowlands, but in the towns it was 'sessional schools' supported by individual congregations which became more significant. The sessional school movement started in 1813, but real expansion came only in the 1820s and 1830s. These schools, and others run by the churches, came to dominate the voluntary sector, but alongside them were to be found other types which should be distinguished from private adventure schools: endowed schools founded by bequest, charity schools supported by subscription, schools maintained by landowners, works and colliery schools, etc.

The sessional schools, and the very similar schools founded by the Free Church after 1843, aimed at reproducing the parish school model in urban conditions, and the ministers and philanthropic laymen who founded them were inspired by the traditional ideal of education as part of the Church's social mission, and by an analogy between the establishment or 'endowment' of religion and of education. These ideas were expressed with particular clarity by the Evangelical leader Thomas Chalmers, whose attempts to apply the parochial tradition of the Scottish Church to conditions in Glasgow forced him to reflect on what it stood for. In 1819 he published *Considerations on the system of parochial schools in Scotland, and on the advantage of establishing them in large towns.* Chalmers distinguished three ways of providing schools for the common people: the 'unendowed' system, where parents paid the full cost, rejected by him because it was unable to create 'a habit of general education'; free schools, equally undesirable because they stifled the spirit of initiative; and the 'medium system', combining endowment and fees, which had been devised by the Reformers and had produced such striking results in rural Scotland. Chalmers was interested in how the habit of education was created and sustained in the absence of legal compulsion, and he thought this depended on the existence of the schoolhouse, 'a marked and separate edifice, standing visibly out to the eye of the people', on the salary and secure tenure of the schoolmaster, and on the tie of 'locality' which bound the school to the life of the community over the generations.[2] Chalmers was evidently expressing widely held assumptions. His theory of the 'medium system' was incorporated almost verbatim into Sir John Sinclair's *Analysis of the Statistical Account of Scotland* (1826) and taken up and elaborated by Henry Cockburn in the *Edinburgh Review* in 1827.[3] It also appears in many writings by ministers, including the pamphlet *Scotland a Half-Educated Nation* (1834) by George Lewis. Lewis was joint secretary of the Glasgow Educational Society, which was devoted to promoting sessional schools on the lines recommended by Chalmers, and to campaigning for the extension of education under Church control; the Society also founded the Glasgow Normal Seminary for training teachers, since one of the features of the new kind of school was an emphasis on new methods and on the moral and intellectual qualities required by the teacher.

The Scottish view of 'endowment' saw the salary paid to the teacher as the vital point, using a subsidy to maintain quality while reducing fees. This sustained two central and interlinked features of the parish school tradition. First, schoolmasters were expected to be able to teach Latin and other higher subjects, so that they could meet local middle-class demands for university entry and help the occasional 'lad of parts' among the poor. The salary must therefore attract able men, preferably with a university training; the master should be well enough paid, added Cockburn, to be regarded as a 'professional person' and 'received with respect and kindness even in the houses of the gentry'.[4] Second, the schools were supposed to be open to all classes of the community, neither repelling the rich by reducing education to an elementary grind nor excluding the poor by the barrier of high fees. In practice, perhaps, social mixing was limited, but the ideal was prized, and it was emphasized by Chalmers when he opened sessional schools in his Glasgow parish.

From this point of view, the objection to private adventure schools was that they encouraged class division. A private schoolmaster with superior qualifications could charge high fees and build up a middle-class clientele, but the subsidy element in the parish schools and those modelled on them meant that 'a respectable independence cannot be made out of mere teaching, if it be confined chiefly to the teaching of the lower orders'.[5] Private adventure schools therefore tended to divide sharply between two types, and the effect of leaving education to the free market was 'to give to the rich the most enterprising, successful, and experienced teachers – and to leave to the poor, too generally, the sluggards and novices of the profession'.[6] Educational experts tended to condemn private adventure schools for their inferior quality, although, as West has pointed out, they had prejudices which led them to judge by criteria which were not purely educational.[7] Private schools alarmed those who saw education as a means of social control because they were not sufficiently under the eye of the public authorities, and because they did not offer the same guarantees for religious education as schools under church control. Kay-Shuttleworth, who was particularly inclined to think in this way, declared in 1853 that 'the condition of the great majority of the 'Adventure Schools' is an opprobrium to civilization'.[8] The clergy as a whole do not seem to have shared these prejudices, and in such sources for the years around 1840 as the *New Statistical Account*, or the annual reports on education by presbyteries published by the General Assembly from 1839, they revealed satisfaction, even complacency, with the general state of education. The private schools were seen as useful auxiliaries of the parish schools, and it was noted that most of them submitted voluntarily to ecclesiastical inspection. Only in the larger towns, especially those like Paisley or Dundee, where work in textile mills took children away from school early, was a note of alarm sounded, and action demanded. In the cities the sessional schools were expanding, and the clergy of Aberdeen in 1842 congratulated themselves on the extension of the 'parochial system', which had driven out the inferior adventure schools, and thought that 'the complete and speedy extinction of adventure schools for the lower orders might be hailed as a benefit to the cause of education'.[9]

In these years things seemed to be moving in the direction of an expanded national system, in which new schools under the auspices of the Church would be subsidized by the state. The Church, it is true, complained that the early state grants were for building rather than, as Scottish tradition demanded, for an endowment to support the schoolmaster, but in 1838 an Act providing parliamentary funds for extra schools in the Highlands accepted the endowment principle.[10] In 1843 the Disruption shattered these hopes of progress along traditional lines, and inaugurated a period of denominational rivalry. It became

impossible for the state to give any special favour to the schools of the
Established Church, which was now concerned only to hold on grimly to the
positions which it retained in Scottish life, including its control of the parish
schools . . .

Scottish public opinion was thus predisposed by the past achievements of the
parish schools to think in terms of public or 'national' solutions to educational
problems. The accepted view of recent history was that the parish schools had
worked reasonably well while Scotland was a rural country, but had broken
down under the stress of industrialization, and had never been effective in the
highlands. The areas of educational deficiency seemed to coincide with those
where the statutory provision was weakest, and the way to meet the deficiency,
therefore, was to extend the parochial or public system.

This view has been shard by most historians, including the author of the most
recent general survey of the question, T. C. Smout.[11] West, however, would
challenge it, arguing in particular that the statistics do not show the 'marked
contrast between the growing industrial towns and other areas' which the belief
that 'the industrial revolution was accompanied by educational failure and
decline' would require . . . .[12]

The first figures to show how pupils were distributed between different
types of school were produced by Brougham's Select Committee in 1818:[13]

	SCHOOLS	PUPILS
Parochial schools	942	54,161
Endowed schools	212	10,177
Dames schools	257	5,560
Ordinary day schools	2,222	106,627
Total day schools	3,633	176,525
Sunday schools	807	53,449

West's use of these figures is not very satisfactory. He gives in detail only
those for the parochial schools and for ordinary day schools, which he
rechristens 'private (unendowed) schools'. He then uses this categorization
to argue that 'in Scotland as a whole there were twice as many adventure
school pupils as parochial pupils', and that private schools were 'dominant'
in the rural lowlands; and since he does not cite comparable figures for later
years the reader is left to suppose that the situation remained similar in the
1860s.[14] In fact, however, the 'ordinary day schools' included other types of
schools besides private ones, notably those of the S.P.C.K. and other
societies in the Highlands; and since the 1818 figures pre-date the expansion of church schools they probably represent the peak period for private
education.

The educational census of 1851 provides us with a similar table which reflects the growth of the Church schools . . . The census described as 'public' all schools which received financial support from other sources than fees, and by this strict definition private schools had only 25 per cent of the pupils:[15]

	SCHOOLS	PUPILS
Parochial schools	937	63,987
Burgh schools	88	10,326
Others supported by taxation	14	1,118
Endowed schools	491	32,901
Run by religious bodies	1,385	93,211
Other public schools	434	30,899
Total public schools	3,349	232,442
Private schools	1,893	78,000
Total, all schools	5,242	310,442

In 1851, as in 1818, there were significant regional variations, which are shown in Table 1.

TABLE 1. *Regional Variations in Use of Private Schools, 1818 and 1851*

	pupils in unendowed schools as percentage of all day-school pupils, 1818	pupils in private schools as percentage of all day-school pupils, 1851
Highland & Northern counties		
Shetland & Orkney	63	17
Caithness	60	24
Sutherland	65	2
Ross & Cromarty	68	7
Inverness	75	9
Argyll	66	8
Bute	62	15
Lowland rural counties		
Nairn	45	25
Moray	49	19
Banff	60	30
Aberdeen	57	29
Kincardine	53	26
Perth	67	19
Kinross	45	28
East Lothian	49	18
Berwick	46	21

Selkirk	40	29
Roxburgh	38	21
Peebles	28	9
Dumfries	45	27
Kirkcudbright	31	9
Wigtown	55	27
Eastern industrial & semi-industrial counties		
Angus	60	29
Fife	63	27
Clackmannan	74	27
Stirling	72	26
West Lothian	50	23
Midlothian	69	23
Western industrial counties		
Dumbarton	64	35
Renfrew	80	36
Ayr	63	32
Lanark	79	33
SCOTLAND	64	25

Sources: *Digest of Parochial Returns made to the Select Committee on the Education of the Poor* (P.P. 1819, IX), Vol. III, Table following p. 1450; *Census of Great Britain, 1851. Religious Worship and Education. Scotland* (P.P. 1854, LIX), Table A.

Although the categories are not strictly comparable, it seems clear that private schools had suffered a relative, and probably an absolute, decline. The column for unendowed schools in 1818 puts together the dame school and ordinary day school categories, and the figures for the Highlands show the difference made by the inclusion of the society schools among the latter. In the rural lowlands, however, even this broad unendowed category accounted for fewer than half the pupils in the majority of counties. Table 1 . . . shows the exceptional position of the western counties centred on Glasgow: this was where private schools were most numerous, but also where the deficiences of education were most acute.

. . . The theoretical question of *laissez-faire* versus state intervention was not ignored in Scotland, but it was generally considered to have been settled in favour of the latter. In 1827 Chalmers published a book *On the Use and Abuse of Literary and Ecclesiastical Endowments* which argued that the principles of supply and demand could not be applied either to religion or to education, both of which needed to be publicly endowed. Generally an admirer of Adam Smith, Chalmers thought that he had made an egregious error in extending his doctrines to education, and regretted that through his influence opposition to endowments had assumed a 'philosophical aspect.'

Chalmers argued that intellectual and spiritual needs, unlike physical ones, do not create a spontaneous demand; supply must precede demand in order to stimulate it. 'It is not with the desire of knowledge, as it is with the desire of food. Generally speaking, the more ignorant a man is, the more satisfied he is to remain so ... There is no such appetite for knowledge as will secure a spontaneous and originating movement towards it, on the part of those who need to be instructed.' Government must therefore meet the people half way, and create the hunger for education. This was just what the parish schools had done, and without this 'aggression upon them from without' the people would not have broken out from their 'primeval ignorance'. It was therefore 'to a great national endowment that our national character is beholden' and that 'Scotland stands indebted for her well-taught and well-conditioned peasantry'. Chalmers admitted that there were many successful private schools, but argued that they owed their prosperity to the parish schools which had awakened the appetite for education in the first place, and he thought that the latter should continue to act as pilot institutions leading on to yet higher standards in the future.[16] With this argument, which soon became a standard one,[17] Chalmers clearly anticipated the justification of state intervention in terms of market failure which has been credited to J. S. Mill by West and, even more emphatically, by Mark Blaug.[18]

Adam Smith was prepared to see schools for the common people provided publicly, as in Scotland, but he was certainly hostile to endowment at a higher level, especially in the universities. Here again Chalmers took issue with him, and his book was especially concerned to justify state support for 'literature' (his word for culture) and for universities. Smith had stigmatized 'statutes of apprenticeship', i.e. educational requirements for entry to the professions; but according to Chalmers, such requirements (in particular, in Scotland, those imposed for entry to the ministry) were essential to the survival of higher subjects such as mathematics and philosophy, which 'can only flourish under the shade of endowments'. For higher learning, as for the rudiments, spontaneous demand was inadequate, and state-supported universities were needed to provide leisure and independence for scholars and to sustain 'an aristocracy of letters ... by which to qualify and to soften the vulgar aristocracy of mere rank and power'.[19] Chalmers' book was designed to influence the Royal Commission on university reform which was then sitting, and this duly reported that 'the principles applicable to trade' could not 'with propriety be extended to the education of the country'.[20] The Scottish universities were, and remained, state institutions whose professors lived, like the parish schoolmasters, on a combination of salary and fees.

If Chalmers derived his ideas from traditional clerical ways of thinking, other members of the Scottish intelligentsia based a belief in state action on political principles and continental examples. Some radicals, notably the phrenologist George Combe and his disciple James Simpson, argued for compulsory, secular education, and one influential educationalist connected with this group was James Pillans, successively rector of Edinburgh High School and a professor at Edinburgh University. But more moderate Edinburgh liberals, for example Henry Cockburn, John Leslie, or William Hamilton, also tended to look to a 'ministry of public instruction' to organize popular education, and argued that it was part of the state's duty, as in countries like France and Germany, to maintain the higher intellectual life of the nation and to 'promote the liberal education of the higher orders'.[21]

For whatever the strength of *laissez-faire* ideas within Britain, alternative continental models were always ready to hand. In the 1830s, the example of France was particularly important because of the *loi Guizot* of 1833, which laid the foundations of state primary education. The law's emphasis on local control and finance gave it features which recalled the Scottish system, but the actual model was Prussia, and the law was preceded by an influential report on German schools by the philosopher Victor Cousin. In 1833 the *Edinburgh Review* published articles on the Cousin report and Guizot's legislation by Pillans and Hamilton, both of whom linked admiration for continental progress with explicit refutation of *laissez-faire* doctrine, and aligned Scotland with the continental tradition. 'All that Scotland enjoys of popular education above the other kingdoms of the British Empire, she owes to the State', declared Hamilton, while Pillans thought that the application of *laissez-faire* to education 'may be ranked among the illegitimate offspring of the Free Trade System' and was now 'pretty generally regarded as a heresy scarcely worth refuting'.[22] Such views were not unknown in England, but they were on the radical margins of thought, whereas in Scotland they seem to have been the common property of the educated class . . .

NOTES

1 *The New Statistical Account of Scotland* (Edinburgh, 1845), III (Roxburghshire), p. 71 (Melrose).
2 Reprinted in *The Works of Thomas Chalmers* (Glasgow, n.d.), XII, pp. 193-219.
3 J. Sinclair, *Analysis of the Statistical Account of Scotland* (1826), Part 2, pp. 72-6; *Edinburgh Review*, XLVI (1827), pp. 108-13.
4 *Edin. Rev.*, XLVI, p. 118.
5 Ibid. p. 122.
6 *Hints Towards the Formation of a Normal Seminary in Glasgow* (n.d.), p. 6. For other examples of these arguments see [G.Lewis], *Scotland a Half-Educated Nation* (Glasgow, 1834), pp. 43, 51, 53; J. C. Colquhoun in *Hansard* (Commons), 3rd ser. XXIV, 17 June

1834, cols. 516-17; *New Statistical Account,* VI, pp. 914-22 (Presbytery of Glasgow); *Select Committee of House of Lords on Parochial Schoolmasters* (House of Lords Sessional Papers, 1845, XIX), QQ. 74, 183-5, 640.

7 E. G. West, *Education and the State. A Study in Political Economy* (London, 1965) and *Education and the Industrial Revolution* (London, 1995).

8 J. Kay Shuttleworth, *Public Education* (1853), p. 395

9 *Presbyterial and Parochial Reports on the State of Education in Scotland...1842* (Edinburgh, 1843), p. 134. Cf. pp. 27 (Paisley), 55, 121 ff. (Dundee); *Report on the Returns from Presbyteries Regarding the Examination of Schools in the Year 1840* (n.d.), p. 23 (Paisley); *Report on the Returns from Presbyteries on the State of Schools in the Year 1841* (n.d.), pp. 13-15, 44 (Airdrie), 71-2 (Dundee); *New Statistical Account,* VII (Renfrewshire), pp. 464-9 (Greenock).

10 D.G. Paz, *The Politics of Working-Class Education in Britain, 1830-50* (Manchester, 1980), pp. 36-41.

11 T. C. Smout, *A History of the Scottish People, 1560–1830* (paperback edn. 1972), pp. 421 ff.

12 West, *Education and the Industrial Revolution,* pp. 8, 63.

13 *Digest of Parochial Returns made to the Select Committee on the Education of the Poor* (P. P. 1819, ix), Vol. III, Table following p. 1450. The figures are not very reliable, as there were gaps and errors in the origional returns; e.g. for Ross & Cromarty the figures for parochial and endowed schools were transposed, showing one of the former instead of 31. Note also that in Scotland these figures (and later ones cited below) include middle-class as well as elementary schools.

14 West, *Education and the Industrial Revolution,* pp. 60, 64–5.

15 *Census of Great Britain, 1851. Religious Worship and Education. Scotland* (P.P. 1854, LIX), Table A (pupils in attendance).

16 Reprinted in T. Chalmers, *Church and College Establishments* (Edinburgh, 1848), pp. 36-42, 59.

17 For example *Scotland a Half-Educated Nation,* pp. 45-54; J. Wilson, *Popular Reflections on the Legislative Support of Parish Teachers and Parish Ministers* (Edinburgh, 1831), pp. 27-34.

18 E. G. West, *Education and the State. A Study in Political Economy* (1965), pp. 122-3; M. Blaug, 'The Economics of Education in English Classical Political Economy: A Re-Examination', in A. S. Skinner and T. Wilson, eds., *Essays on Adam Smith* (Oxford, 1975), pp. 582, 592. Blaug's treatment of Chalmers (p. 574) is inadequate, to say the least.

19 Chalmers, *Establishments,* pp. 23, 46-54, 64, 69, 85.

20 *Royal Commission of Inquiry into the Universities of Scotland. Report* (P.P. 1831, XII), p. 12.

21 W. Hamilton, *Discussions on Philosophy and Literature, Education and University Reform* (1852), p. 343 (written 1832).

22 Ibid. pp. 535-9; J. Pillans, *Contributions to the Cause of Education* (1856), p. 152.

The S.P.C.K and Highland schools in mid-eighteenth century

D J Withrington 1962 in *Scottish Historical Review* 41, 89–99.

'Even in 1758 there were no fewer than 175 Highland parishes still without a school or schoolmaster'. So wrote Henry Grey Graham sixty years ago,[1] and subsequent writers have given his statement the widest currency, using it, as he did, to highlight the continuing barbarity and ignorance of the Highlands despite the Act for Settling of Schools in 1696. Yet Graham's source on this point[2] – the Annual Report for 1758 of the Society in Scotland for Propagating Christian Knowledge – is rather differently phrased. There we read that 'No fewer than 175 parishes within the bounds of 39 presbyteries where the Society's schools are erected have no parochial schools.' The parishes in question, therefore, might not all be Highland (although this was very likely), because S.P.C.K. schools were to be found in such presbyteries as Langholm, Jedburgh, Brechin and Forfar. More important than that, however, the statement that 175 parishes in the country did not have *parochial* schools is not at all necessarily the same thing as saying that these parishes were *without schools or school-masters*. Everything, of course, depends on how the S.P.C.K. defined a parochial school and, unfortunately, the 1758 report gives no direct indication of the criterion employed; but a review of the data on which the estimate of 175 parishes without parochial schools was based – an enquiry carried out three years earlier – does help to determine what that criterion must have been.

On 15 November 1754 the standing business committee of the S.P.C.K. noted in its minutes that 'notwithstanding of the many letters wrote to presbyterys for having legall schools erected in their respective parishes, severall parishes have hitherto got no parochial schools settled in them' and resolved to find some remedy for this situation.[3] The problem was to discover in which parishes there were, and in which there were not, such legal schools. Accordingly, on 6 March 1755, the committee reported to the General Meeting of the Society that they, 'finding it necessary to know the situation of the severall parishes with respect to parochial schools, have ordered letters to be wrote to the severall presbyterys wherein the Societys schoolmasters are employed to know first the number of inhabitants above eight years of age in every parish; secondly, what of these parishes want parochiall schools; and thirdly, the names of the patrons of the severall parishes in their bounds and of the heritors of these parishes.'[4] The General Meeting endorsed this proposal, and on 20 March letters were sent by William Ross, clerk to the S.P.C.K., to the moderators of the presbyteries. A transcript of one of these letters, in the records of the presbytery of Alford,[5] shows, however, that the Committee asked for information additional to that outlined in the General Meeting minutes[6]: the moderators of presbyteries were to submit lists of parishes having no parochial schools, and individual ministers were to give an account of the length and breadth of their parishes, the total number of their inhabitants – 'including every individual old and young' – and the proportion of inhabitants who were papists .[7] Rather more than half of the replies from the parish ministers have survived and, from a reading of them, it is quickly apparent that there was considerable confusion over what was a 'parochial school'. Having been given no definition by the S.P.C.K., the ministers proceeded to define a 'parochial school' as they saw fit, and their answers may accordingly be classified in three groups.[8]

The largest group gave no indication of the criterion (or, more probably, the criteria) that had been used: seventy-two ministers reported simply that they had parochial schools, thirty-five that they had none, and all apparently showed no awareness that there could be any difference of opinion about what constituted a parochial school.

The other groups, either explicitly or by implication, expressed differing interpretations. 'I don't think there is one parochial school properly so called within the bounds of this presbytery,' wrote the minister of Walls, Shetland, 'that is, a school with a legal standing salary. But in my parish I have several little schools in different corners . . .'[9] It was not enough, however, to have a legal salary (or even a sum larger than 100 merks Scots) if that maintenance was divided among several schoolmasters. 'No parochial school properly so called, but there are five schools maintained by different heritors etc. and those at a much higher stent than what the law requires,' reported the reply from Kilcalmonell and Kilberry in Kintyre.[10] For the ministers in this group a parochial school was a single institution the master of which had a stipend of at least 100 merks Scots from the local heritors and tenants.

The reply from the clerk to the presbytery of Aberlour exemplifies the position adopted by the third group: 'I can assure the Society that every parish in this presbytery has a parochial school, though some of them are very poorly endowed, and few of them have the minimum of legal salary.'[11] The source of the maintenance paid to a public schoolmaster, not the level of that stipend, was the important thing. Thus the minister of Kilmorie in Arran, the situation of his parish not unlike that of Kilcalmonell and Kilberry, was able to tell the Society: 'I have 4 parochial schools situate at a convenient distance one from another.'[12] If the heritors provided a salary and the master was approved by the presbytery then, in the opinion of this group, that master, no matter how much or how little he was paid, taught a parochial school.

The two latter groupings are not marked by any obvious geographical, or indeed other, distinction; ministers even within the same presbytery showed diversity in interpretation of the term 'parochial school'. The dangers of reading into any one reply a meaning not intended by its writer were considerable. Auchterarder provides us with a good example here. One minister said of the schools in that presbytery: 'There are legal sallaries in all their parishes save Muckart, Glendevon and Monivaird where there are also schools kept and some sallaries although not legal.'[13] Yet in *his* return the minister of Glendevon reported, 'There is no parochial school in the parish,' leaving the reader to wonder whether he did have a school or schools, though without legal maintenance, or had no school at all.[14] The reply from Monivaird, unexpectedly, begins by stating that this parish provided a legal salary of 100 merks and then goes on: 'A large, rapid river Erne running very nigh thro' the midst obliges us to have two churches and two schoolmasters which makes us divide this sallarie and our Church dues betwixt them.'[15] When, one might ask, is a legal salary not a legal salary? With the case of Muckart, the task of judging what does and does not constitute a parochial school reaches a yet finer complexity. 'There has not been a parochial school here these dozen years and more', wrote the minister there. 'The last schoolmaster was deposed by our Synod for contumacy and having gone over to the Secession: he died not above a year ago. He taught and possest the school and schoolhouse as long as he lived. On his death I made a push for a schoolmaster in our way but was opposed by most of our heritors who are of the Seceding way, who, because I would not give my consent to their putting in a Seceding teacher into our school and schoolhouse, have just now built a schoolhouse to their man, who is now the only teacher, hard by the old schoolhouse.'[16] Whether the Muckart school was considered not to be parochial because the schoolmaster's stipend was less than legal or because the master, being a Seceder, was not approved by the minister or presbytery, cannot readily be judged.[17]

On the basis of the information sent in by presbyteries, a list of 175 parishes without parochial schools was drawn up by Dr Webster for the S.P.C.K.[18] It is hard to believe, however, that Webster would have accepted at face value the opinions of the moderators when it was clear that a single interpretation of the term 'parochial school' was not being employed. Unfortunately, this list of parishes has not been discovered in the records of the S.P.C.K. or of the General Assembly, and not all of the parish ministers' or the moderators' returns have survived. It is not possible, therefore, to be quite certain about the meaning of the Society's estimate of 175 parishes without parochial schools, but a summary of those parish ministers' replies which have survived gives a pointer to the criterion adopted by the S.P.C.K.

Just over 210 out of about 230 parishes in 23 presbyteries are covered, directly or indirectly, in the extant returns. 41 parishes gave no information at all about schools, supposing no doubt that this had been provided in the moderators' lists: our data therefore concerns only some 170 parishes. Of these 170, 72 were said to have, and 35 were said not to have, parochial schools, the constitution of these schools not being explained[19]: of the remainder, 28 certainly had schools whose masters received at least 100 merks a year, and 37 had schools none of whose masters, individually, had the minimum legal stipend. Considering only these 170 parishes, if we define a parochial school as one whose master was maintained at or above the legal minimum, there were 28 parishes which certainly, and as many as 100 parishes which possibly, had parochial schools: if we define a parochial school as one whose master was maintained by the heritors and tenants without reference to the level of his stipend, then at least 138 parishes, and probably more, had parochial schools. Conversely, by the former definition at least 72, and probably more, parishes were without parochial schools; by the latter definition, at most 34, and perhaps fewer, parishes were without parochial schools.

We may consider the 170 parishes, about which there is information, as an unbiased sample of all the parishes in the 39 presbyteries where the Society had schools, and we may assume, therefore, that the *proportion* of parishes without parochial schools (by the S.P.C.K. criterion) would be comparable both in our sample and in the total number of parishes in those 39 presbyteries.[20] The total number of parishes was 380; the number said to be without parochial schools was 175. The number of parishes in our sample is 170; the proportionate number of parishes, likely to have been classed by the Society as without parochial schools, is 79. A comparison of this expected figure and our estimates of 'at least 72' and 'at most 34' (noted in the preceding paragraph) indicates that the criterion for a parochial school employed by the S.P.C.K. must have been severe and that it was probably the existence of the minimum legal salary for one schoolmaster in the parish. The Society's declaration that 175 parishes were without parochial schools in 1758 almost certainly does not mean that these parishes were devoid of all means of education but rather that they did not pay those schoolmasters they had at least 100 merks per annum. Graham's version of the S.P.C.K. statement is untenable.[21] Some, at least, of the 175 'delinquent' parishes maintained schools.[22]

The phrasing in other contemporary documents brings further evidence that the S.P.C.K. employed this narrow definition of a parochial school. In 1758 the Society gave notice to the General Assembly of its intention to withdraw charity schools from parishes unprovided with parochial ones: as a result, the Assembly ordered presbyteries to have 'parochial schools, with legal salaries, erected in every parish, as the law directs'.[23] Two years later, the Hyndman-Dick report pointed out that the S.P.C.K. had 'established a rule to appoint no schools except in parishes where a schoolmaster with a legal salary is already settled', and consequently 'the greater part of the Highlands, being without legal schools, can receive no aid from this excellent institution'.[24]

The mistaken interpretation of such statements has led to the widespread belief that, throughout the Highlands, parsimonious heritors refused all opportunity of schooling to their parishioners' children. Without doubt there were heritors, more especially in areas where Catholicism was strong, who did nothing towards establishing public schools. Others, however, also stigmatised by the S.P.C.K. as 'backward' because they omitted to establish parochial schools, were certainly not avoiding their responsibilities. The Society appeared to pay no heed to the ways in which local effort was attempting to meet local need.

The minister of Inverchaolain in Argyll, for example, commented in 1755: 'There is no parochial school, nor would such a school if we had one, wheresoever it should be fixt, be of use to above a fifth of the parish but by boarding the children in the neighbourhood, an expense which the people are by no means able to bear, and hence it has come about that usually we have had five little schools kept about six months in the year, very trifling indeed as the numbers contributing to support them were but few and poor generally, and, after all, several detached mailings both upon the sea-side and behind the mountains had no benefit by any of these schools.'[25] The majority of the parishioners were scattered along a coastline fully 20 miles long, the remainder in inland glens separated by high mountains; provision for universal education – a principle basic to the conception in the First Book of Discipline and, through it, in the seventeenth-century education acts – was thought in Inverchaolain to be better made by several small schools than by one more strictly legal school.

In Skye and the Outer Hebrides attempts were made to overcome a difficulty long experienced in the remoter Highlands, [26] that of attracting 'sufficient' schoolmasters to teach schools there.[27] The prospect of a salary larger than that offered in less out-of-the-way parishes was found to be persuasive. By 1760 the parishes of Kilmuir, Snizort and Portree and those of Sleat and Strath had ceased to have separate schools: they had pooled their schoolmasters' salaries and provided common schools situated at some point convenient for most of the inhabitants in each parish.[28] The minister of South Uist in 1755 again asked for the S.P.C.K.'s opinion of a scheme drawn up by himself and the ministers of North Uist and Harris whereby 'one good school' in North Uist was to replace 'three trifling ones'.[29] When Hyndman and Dick visited the Isles in 1760, they reported uninformatively that there was a parochial school in North Uist but none in either Harris or South Uist.[30]

The case of the parish of Skipness and Saddale in Kintyre provides a still clearer illustration. A certain Lewis Drummond was employed by the Society in 1770 and 1771 to visit their charity schools and in both years reported on Skipness.[31] In 1770, he intimated that: 'Though a parochial school should take place, which I am informed would be the case were it not that the minister and heritors were of opinion that one parochial school would be of little conse-quence in such a long, narrow braik of country, the people pay double the sum they are obliged by law in order schools may be planted in different places in the parish.'[32] In 1771, his report was both brief and uninstructive – 'No parochial school.' In 1774 the S.P.C.K. announced once again that it would withdraw charity schools from parishes unprovided with parochial schools, it not being the purpose of the Society to relieve the heritors of their legal duty[33]; and the parish of Skipness and Saddale appeared in the attached list of parishes in which Society schools had been suppressed.

It was a strange conception of the dutifulness of heritors that considered acceptable the provision of one legally maintained school, and the consequent reduction in opportunity for schooling in a large and scattered parish, while the provision of several usefully-placed schools, costing twice as much to support, was deemed to be reprehensible. The insistent petitioning of the General Assembly by the S.P.C.K. (to have legal salaries provided in the parishes) was undoubtedly valuable in bringing pressure to bear on heritors to augment their schoolmasters' stipends to the legal minimum. Where there was only one public school in a parish, the emphasis on the payment of a legal salary was beneficial. But the insistence on having a legal salary provided in *every* parish – making this insistence thoroughly unconditional, and allowing for no mitigating circumstances – was ill-conceived and unfortunate.

The S.P.C.K. statement that in 1758 there were 175 parishes without parochial schools cannot be taken to mean that these parishes were all without schools and schoolmasters. Some areas seem not to have had many public schools, i.e. schools maintained by heritors and tenants – the extreme north-western Highlands and Shetland are among them – but even these areas had a few, and had, too, very small seasonal schools kept in the parishioners' houses at their own expense. There can be little doubt that only a limited number of parishes were without public schools in 1758 and that fewer still had no means of education at all. The Society's statement is an index of the ineffectiveness of the Act of 1696 only in the narrowest and most literal interpretation of that statute. There was much more schoolbuilding and schoolkeeping in eighteenth-century Scotland than has commonly been allowed.

NOTES

1 *Social Life of Scotland in the Eighteenth Century* (2nd ed., 1901), 422.
2 Graham does not in fact quote his source. The S.P.C.K. version of the statement is to be found also in *Annals of the General Assembly . . . from 1752 to 1766* (1840), p. 164.
3 S.P.C.K. records: Minutes of Committee (or Directors') Meetings, vol. 7. (All manuscript sources cited in this article, both for S.P.C.K. and Church of Scotland records, are held in the Scottish Record Office.)

   The Committee's concern was based on the conviction that they should refuse charity schools to parishes which had no parochial schools, its members believing that otherwise a charity school might be viewed as alternative, rather than supplementary, to a public school. For this reason, one presumes, requests by S.P.C.K. schoolmasters for permission to teach Latin had earlier been abruptly turned down (Minutes of Committee Meetings Vol. 1: 2 March 1713; Minutes of General Meetings Vol. 1: 12 March 1713; see also p. 97 note 4).
4 Minutes of General Meetings, Vol. 4.
5 Minutes: 30 April 1755.
6 The transcribed letter contained an incentive for ministers to comply quickly with the S.P.C.K.'s demands: 'If a distinct answer is not returned to these queries before the Assembly [25 May] no minister will have reason to be surprized if the Society's school in his parish be removed.'
7 One of the members of the Committee, and of the sub-committee which dealt with schools, was Dr Alexander Webster. There can be no doubt that he used the parish ministers' replies to this letter to collect data for his 'census' of 1755. The replies which have survived (and are now in the S.P.C.K. records in Register House) only seldom give the total number of inhabitants in a parish. Generally, a return was made of the number of parishioners on the minister's 'roll of examinables' (that is, those who could be examined on the catechism, being able to read, to remember, and apparently to understand it), and of the age at which he usually placed children on his roll. This age was most often seven, was at times six or eight, and might even be as late as ten years old.

   Webster apparently made an approximation of the total number of inhabitants in a parish from the number of examinables and the age at which the minister entered them on his list. From calculations scribbled on several of the returns it seems likely that he applied the following formula in such cases:

$$No.\ of\ examinables \times \frac{(30+n)}{31}$$

(where n is the year of age at which enrolment was made).

The minister of Boharm, for example, reported 700 examinable persons in his parish, these being entered at the age of 7 years. Using the formula, the total number of inhabitants was estimated as $\frac{700 \times 37}{31}$, i.e. 835 – which is the figure given in Webster's census. In a number of the cases where Webster's final figures have been checked, this formula did not produce the total quoted in the census of 1755: perhaps he obtained more accurate statistics where he could and applied his formula only where he could not avoid doing so. Occasionally, the census figure is quite obviously a bold estimate: the minister of Strathdon wrote that he had between 1,700 and 1,800 inhabitants of whom about 200 were papists; the entry for Strathdon in the census list records a total of 1,750 inhabitants, 190 of these being papists (S.P.C.K Records – Returns by Parish Ministers, 1755: Running No. 80: 1.5 and 2.4).

8 The writer's intention is not to make this classification definitive, but to indicate the more general divisions of opinion displayed in the returns. The difficulty of categorising the replies was often considerable, while it was sometimes altogether impossible to infer what a minister thought were the determinant features of a parochial school. The minister of Banchory Ternan, for example, merely pointed out that his school was 'not supported by the heritors as is usual in other places, but by money mortified for that purpose' (ibid., 80: 15.2).

9 Ibid., 80: 23.9.

10 Ibid., 80: 16.1.

11 Ibid., 80: 1.3a.

12 Ibid., 80: 16.6.

13 Ibid., 80: 3.10.

14 Ibid., 80: 3.11.

15 Ibid., 80: 3.7.

16 Ibid., 80: 3.9.

17 The Act of 1696 did not itself require the master's political and religious beliefs to be approved: it states only that a school should be settled and a schoolmaster appointed 'by advice of the heritors and minister of the parish'. Following the Revolution, however, every schoolmaster was obliged to sign an oath of allegiance to the monarchy and an act of submission to the presbyterian government of the church.

18 *Annals of the General Assembly*, p. 164; also Minutes of General Meetings of S.P.C.K, Vol. 5: 3 June 1773.

19 One of these 35 parishes was Cabrach, in Aberdeenshire, which did not have a schoolmaster between 1745 and 1758 (Minutes of Presbytery of Alford: 22 December 1757; 3 May 1758). Another was Cushney in the same presbytery, and a petition in 1757 noted that the schoolhouse there was in great disrepair (ibid., 27 April 1757). The lack of a parish school in 1755 did not mean that there had never been one.

20 Lack of bias may be presumed here because there is no evidence that the survival of a

particular return was anything but fortuitous; survival of the replies as the result of some prior classification related to our analysis is extremely unlikely.

21 Graham made the same assumption – that 'no legal school' meant no school at all – elsewhere in his book. 'Even up to 1735,' he writes (p. 421), 'in the Presbytery of Ayr – which is not even co-extensive with the county – there were twelve parishes in which was provided neither school nor legal means of maintaining one.' His source – A. Edgar: *Old Church Life in Scotland*, Second Series (1886) p. 75, which in turn quotes the presbytery records – states, however, that twelve parishes 'had no school provyded nor a sallary to a schoolmaster *according to law*'. They may well have had schools, though these were insufficient in terms of the 1696 Act. Graham's assertion that 'in the early part of the century a traveller must have journeyed through many parishes in Ayrshire . . . and found himself among an illiterate people who had never been to school and whose children had no school to go to' is very open to question.

22 Only the return from the island parish of Coll stated specifically that there was not only no parochial school but that there was no school of any kind.

23 *Annals of the General Assembly*, p. 165.

24 MS. Report (copy 1 in the Scottish Record Office) p. 88. Mr John Hyndman and Dr Robert Dick were commissioned by the Assembly to visit and report on catechists and missionaries employed under the Royal Bounty scheme. The S.P.C.K took the opportunity of enlisting them to report also on the Society's charity schools (*Annals of the General Assembly*, p. 196).

25 S.P.C.K., 80: 9.2.

26 A minute of 8 October 1707 in the records of the Synod of Ross states: 'In regard the want of schools in great measure proceeds from the scarcity of young men fit to teach, therefore the Synod recommends to the several presbyteries not to give recommendations to young men for burses at the profession until they pass some time in the bounds, after their graduation, as chaplains or schoolmasters: as also that they correspond with the Synods of Argyll and Moray to see if they can spare any young men fit for teaching schools.' This situation is to be compared with that in the Lowlands: in the 1690's several young men came before the presbytery of Linlithgow, were examined, approved and given testimonials of their good literature and fitness to teach grammar schools 'where in providence [they] may happen to have a call' or 'where [they] shall be trysted to be imployed' (Minutes of Presbytery of Linlithgow: 9 November 1693; 11 September 1696; 14 April 1697).

27 Most parishes sought, and expected to have, a graduate as schoolmaster, or at least a young man who had been at a college and was suitably versed in languages. In some replies to the S.P.C.K. enquiry in 1755 the lack of a classical school was regarded as rather discreditable. The minister of Maryton, Angus, for example, reported, 'we have one parochial school but the salary is but small and our schoolmaster teaches only English writing and arithmetic' (S.P.C.K., 80: 4.11).

28 Hyndman-Dick, pp. 51–52, 56–57.

29 S.P.C.K., 80: 19.2. It is difficult to judge what is meant by 'trifling' in the returns. On occasion it is used to describe a master's salary of 80 or 100 merks. We know that Kilmuir, Snizort and Portree contributed 100 merks each for their schoolmaster, and that in the

common school which had been established by the parishes of Bracadale and Duirinish, and which was vacant in 1760, the salary was 400 merks. (Hyndman-Dick, pp. 56–57.)

30 Hyndman-Dick, pp. 35–38. A letter from the moderator of the presbytery of Gairloch, in 1760, commenting on the circumstances obtaining in Wester Ross, notes: 'The necessaries of life are now so high that no man qualified for the teaching of youth can live by the salaries commonly granted by the Society, and the expense of education is such that they few of the people of better condition can afford to send their children to any great distance from themselves.' Yet the Society's salaries were very often larger than the 100 merk minimum for parochial schools. This letter goes on: 'We cannot but agree with the honest people in wishing that your plan of schools was different from what it is, as we are persuaded that one good school would moderately speaking be of greater use in the country than three of the present set of schools. As to the objection that your schools are intended for the benefit of the poorer sort, you cannot, sir, but be sensible that the schools which are best for the children of the richer sort are likewise best for the poor. And where a school is so bad that it is not worth the richer people's while to send their children to it, the poor will reap little benefit by it. Besides that, the example of the richer sort is necessary to bring the poorer to send their children to school . . . And this being the case, and the people [of Glenelg] willing to contribute so heartily towards the encouragement of a school-master, we presume the honourable Society will judge it reasonable to indulge them in a schoolmaster who can teach Latin or anything else they incline to their children. And as to the objection that you are not empowered by the constitution of your Society to have Latin, etc. taught in your schools, we humbly think, when you see from the above that the spirit and design of your constitution is fully answered, that it would be an injury to you to imagine you capable of giving up the spirit and design of your constitution for the letter of it' (James Robertson to William Ross, 27 March 1760: in MS. papers of William Ross, bundle 254).

31 S.P.C.K. records: Running No. 60.

32 Skipness was 22 miles long and 2 miles broad, and contained 1,160 inhabitants over 4 years of age.

33 *An Account of the Society in Scotland for Propagating Christian Knowledge from its Commencement in 1709* . . . (1774), p. 24. By the 1770's this was a well-worn theme. A minute of a General Meeting of the S.P.C.K. on 6 June 1717 details the following report from the Committee: 'The committee also showed that they, having had under considera-tion that in some places where the Societies schools are setled there are no parochial schools as law provides, whereby it falls out that the Societies schools serve only to ease the heritors and parochioners of the burden they are subject to by law, of maintaining a school in every paroch, which it was not the designe of the Society and contributers thereto . . .'